Contents

Contents

Shakespeare's
Mystery play

The opening of the Globe theatre 1599

Steve Sohmer

MANCHESTER UNIVERSITY PRESS

Manchester and New York

distributed exclusively in the USA by St. Martin's Press

Published by Manchester University Press
Oxford Road, Manchester M13 9NR, UK
and Room 400, 175 Fifth Avenue, New York, NY 10010, USA
http://www.man.ac.uk/mup

Distributed exclusively in the USA by
St. Martin's Press, Inc., 175 Fifth Avenue, New York,
NY 10010, USA

Distributed exclusively in Canada by
UBC Press, University of British Columbia, 6344 Memorial Road,
Vancouver, BC, Canada V6T 1Z2

British Library Cataloguing-in-Publication Data
A catalogue record for this book is available from the British Library

Library of Congress Cataloging-in-Publication Data applied for

ISBN 0 7190 5544 X *hardback*
       0 7190 5566 0 *paperback*

First published 1999

05 04 03 02 01 00 99   10 9 8 7 6 5 4 3 2 1

Typeset in Photina by Carnegie Publishing, Lancaster
Printed in Great Britain
by Bookcraft (Bath) Ltd, Midsomer Norton

1001605905

Foreword

Shakespeare knew that, as Lafeu puts it in *All's Well that Ends Well*, some 'philosophical persons . . . make modern and familiar things supernatural and causeless', causing us to make 'trifles of terrors, ensconcing ourselves into seeming knowledge when we should submit ourselves to an unknown fear' (2.3.2–6). The word 'modern' here means 'commonplace': Lafeu is commenting on the human tendency to seek refuge in reductive explanations for extraordinary phenomena, to hide from fear of the unknown by trying to explain it away on rational grounds. But Lafeu, like Hamlet – and, we may infer, Shakespeare – knows that 'there are more things in heaven and earth ... than are dreamt of in our philosophy'.

Many of Shakespeare's contemporaries, too, from Queen Elizabeth I downwards, felt sure that their lives were subject to extraterrestrial influence, and that they could find guidance in their everyday conduct by consulting the stars and making decisions on important or even trivial matters according to deductions or predictions derived from interpretation of astral significances. Simon Forman, who happens to be the only playgoer of the age to have left anything like detailed eyewitness accounts of Shakespeare's plays in performance, wrote a textbook of astrological medicine and was consulted professionally by many rich and powerful clients. Until well into the seventeenth century, almanacs sold in larger numbers than any other kind of secular book. Even members of the clergy practised astrology.

Shakespeare himself was, as always, aware of both sides of the question. In *King Lear* Edmond pooh-poohs his father, Gloucester's, belief that 'These late eclipses in the sun and moon portend no good to us' – but Edmond is the villain of the play. It is easy for modern readers, influenced by rationalist thought, to underestimate the extent to which Shakespeare was a creature of his own time, and so to read his plays with inadequate appreciation of the extent to which they reflect, and were shaped by, the intellectual climate of the age to which they belong. There is a sense in which his plays have become 'modern and familiar' to us, so appropriated into our own cultural expectations that we ignore, or are unaware of, the full range of resonances that they may have caused to sound in the ears of their first hearers. Considerations such as these should open our minds to arguments such as those advanced in this book, which has as its central thesis the hypothesis that Shakespeare and his colleagues consulted almanacs not, like Bottom and his fellows in *A Midsummer Night's Dream*, in order to discover whether the moon would shine on the night chosen to present their play before the Duke of Athens and his bride, but in order to select the most auspicious date for the opening of their new Globe theatre on Bankside in 1599. The chosen date, Dr Sohmer suggests, was 12 June – the date of the summer solstice according to the Julian calendar, coinciding exceptionally with a new Moon. The axis of the Globe, moreover, seems consciously to have been aimed at a point approximating to the rising point of the Sun on the date of the summer solstice. And these facts appear also to have swayed Shakespeare in his choice of subject matter for the first play to have been performed at the Globe.

In addition to their predilection for astrology, the Elizabethans unquestionably were far more familiar with the bible than is common today. Even uneducated citizens were accustomed to hearing it read at the church services that they were legally obliged to attend. Therefore, Dr Sohmer argues, they would have been sensitized both to recognize and to attach significance to biblical and liturgical allusions and parallels in plays performed in theatres that they attended by choice. In *Julius Caesar* he identifies numerous calendrical and temporal 'markers' – many of them relating to the highly topical controversy over the English adherence to the Julian rather than the Gregorian calendar – which link the play to June 1599 and which would have greatly enriched its texture to audiences experiencing it then. The bulk of this fascinating book is devoted to exploring these significances both in their own right and in relation to interpretation of the play.

In the process Dr Sohmer offers scholarly and rational challenges to many Shakespearian orthodoxies. He proposes that, far from being careless about the dates and times in his plays, Shakespeare is 'specific and precise' in his use of dates, and that 'coupled with Scriptural allusions, these dates can be clues to the subtext and meaning of a speech or scene, and may even be useful in dating the principal composition (or revision) of a play'. He sees Shakespeare as a dramatist who frequently wrote plays for initial performance on a specific date. So for example not only *Julius Caesar* but also *The Comedy of Errors, Twelfth Night* and *Hamlet* are discussed as 'occasional' plays – composed, that is, for initial performance on a deliberately chosen date and containing numerous textual pointers to this date which would have been recognized as significant by those present – though inevitably, of course, they would have dwindled in significance as time passed. He argues too that, rather than disappearing from the stage after the Star Chamber ban of 1589, plays about religious subjects 'sublimated to a new level of discourse'; so *Julius Caesar* meditates both explicitly on the emperor and implicitly on the great religious leader who bore the same initials. And Sohmer challenges the orthodox date of first composition of both *Twelfth Night* and *Hamlet*.

Dr Sohmer is exceptional in his capacity to bring to bear on Shakespeare areas of expertise – in biblical history, in liturgical history and practice, in classical literature, and in social and theatrical history – which are rarely conjoined in Shakespeare scholarship. He writes with clarity and a scholarly concern for evidence, but also with conviction and a deep sense of commitment to his beliefs. This is a book of challenging but rigorous originality which demands consideration from critics, scholars and editors both for its overall thesis and for its illuminating discussion of innumerable points of detail in the texts, especially *Julius Caesar*, that it discusses.

Stanley Wells
The Shakespeare Birthplace Trust
Stratford-upon-Avon
April 1998

Preface

The impetus for this research was the opening in 1997 of a new Globe theatre, the third of that name to occupy the Bankside south of London's River Thames. This seemed an apt occasion for revisiting two questions which centuries of scholarly inquiry had failed to resolve: first, the date on which Shakespeare's playhouse opened, a topic upon which commentators since Edmond Malone had speculated inconclusively; second, the identity of the play chosen from the repertory of the Lord Chamberlain's Men – or newly written – as the Globe's first presentation. I thought these two questions might be linked, and that addressing them in tandem might prove illuminating.

In the opening chapter I present evidence about the construction of early London playhouses which tends to narrow the window of the Globe's completion to the interval 3 June to 5 September 1599. I identify a tendency among seventeenth-century theatre companies to match plays to playing-dates, and suggest that William Shakespeare applied this rubric when he imagined his first play for the new theatre. After considering dates in the summer of 1599 which would have been recognized as significant or propitious by Elizabethans, I present data which draw attention to the summer solstice. On the basis of this information – and archaeological evidence about the groundplan of the Globe – I suggest that the summer solstice would have been a day of choice for the debut of the new theatre. Turning to the question of the play chosen or purpose-written for the Globe's premiere, I consider the claims of *Henry V* and *As You Like It* before taking up the late Arthur Humphreys's suggestion that *Julius Caesar* might have been 'one of the new theater's first productions, perhaps composed for its opening' (Humphreys, 1984, 1). By identifying previously unrecognized calendrical allusions in the text of *Julius Caesar*, I draw to the conclusion that Humphreys was correct.

Preface

Anyone who adores the theatrical stage may find this literary detective work intriguing. But the recovery of unrecognized links in *Julius Caesar* to the calendar for 1599 may have broader implications. Shakespeare's Roman tragedy has run through more editions, and more copies, than any play in any language. *Julius Caesar*'s bawdry-free, right-minded spectacle of murder-and-revenge has introduced generations of school children to Shakespeare. Unique in the canon, *Julius Caesar* has never been out of vogue. It has been continually recalled to the stage for four hundred years – a play for all times and all audiences. But, if the findings presented in this essay are valid, *Julius Caesar* is an occasional play. Its text is topical, and packed with allusions to an historical moment, its calendar and its liturgy. To be fully apprehended, this most familiar of all plays must be read anew against a new array of criteria. Indeed, if these findings are validated by scrutiny and debate, the ramifications for our understanding of Shakespeare's middle plays, and of the place of the first Bankside Globe in Elizabethan culture, may prove far-reaching.

Steve Sohmer
Lincoln College, Oxford,
and Bel Air, California
Matthias's Day 1998

Acknowledgements

To Dennis Kay above all. To Don McKenzie, who first encouraged my textual analyses. To John Pitcher, who recognized the importance of the relationship between 'Casca's almanac' and the Elizabethan calendar controversy. To Emrys Jones, who guided my early research. To Andrew Gurr, Gordon Kipling, Andy Kelly, Debra Shugar, Reg Foakes and Bill Carroll for encouragement and advice. To Mark Breitenberg, whose judgement and erudition helped shape this essay. To Tobie Pate, without whose patience and support this work could not have been undertaken. To Andrea, Brook, Alison, Mary Beth, Andrew and Kelly. And to Deidre, for ever, with love adoring. *Ave et salve.*

I

The building of the first Globe and the Elizabethan calendar controversy

1

Building Shakespeare's Globe

In 1821 the publication of the contract for the Fortune playhouse established the year of the first Globe's construction as 1599 (Malone, 1821, 3: 338–9). The date was further refined in 1871 when J. O. Halliwell-Phillipps published details of lawsuits arising from the demolition of James Burbage's old Theatre in Finsbury Fields. The carpenter-impresario had signed a twenty-one-year ground lease in 1576 with Giles Allen which permitted Burbage to 'take down the buildings he might erect' during his tenancy (Halliwell-Phillipps, 1887, 348). But Burbage died in February 1597 and the Theatre was closed, perhaps in April (Gurr, 1996, 283), but certainly after *The Isle of Dogs* scandal in July (Chambers, 1923, 2: 397). The 1576 lease expired and there is no evidence that the Theatre reopened.

While Cuthbert Burbage attempted to negotiate a new lease, the Chamberlain's Men rented and played at the Curtain (Gurr, 1996, 284). By winter 1598 Burbage apparently concluded that he could not effect satisfactory terms for a new lease. He engaged the builder Peter Street to dismantle and remove his playhouse structure as provided in the expired lease. Allen brought a suit alleging that on the night of 28 December 1598, Burbage, Peter Street and certain others did 'repayre unto the sayd Theater And then and there ... attempted to pull downe the sayd Theatre ...'.[1] Despite resistance by Allen's adherents, the kidnappers were successful and carted 'all the wood and timber therof unto the Banckside in the parishe of St. Marye Overyes, and there erected a newe playehowse with the sayd timber and woode' (Halliwell-Phillipps, 1887, 361). Allen subsequently brought a second action against Street for trespass and ground damage on 20 January 1599.[2] This suggests that the removal of the timbers was not completed until shortly before that date (Halliwell-Phillipps, 1887, 351).

In 1909 a series of remarkable documents concerning the Globe came

3

to light. In the German-language journal of English philology, *Anglia*, Dr Gustav Binz published excerpts from a traveller's account of a visit to England in 1599. Thomas Platter (b. 1574), a Swiss of the canton of Basle, had written

> *Den 21 Septembris nach dem Imbissessen, etwan umb zwey uhren, bin ich mitt meiner geselschaft über daz wasser gefahren, habin in dem streüwinen Dachhaus die Tragedy vom ersten Keyer Julio Caesare mit ohngefahr 15 personen sehen gar artlich agieren.*

> (Binz, 1989, 458)

> On September 21st after lunch, about two o'clock, I and my party crossed the water, and there in the house with the thatched roof witnessed an excellent performance of the tragedy of the first Emperor Julius Caesar with a cast of some fifteen people ...

> (Schanzer, 1956b, 466–7)

If Platter is describing a performance at the Globe of Shakespeare's *Julius Caesar*, this evidence marks 21 September 1599 as the latest date on which the theatre could have opened.

Then in October 1909, and again in April–May 1914, C. W. Wallace published documents which gave fresh insight into the company's removal to the Bankside. In connection with litigation brought in 1613 by Thomasina, widow of Globe sharer William Osteler, solicitors recapitulated the terms of the theatre's ground lease (Wallace, 1909, 2 October). The document was executed by landlord Nicholas Brend and 'Cutherbert Burbage and Richard Burbage, as half lessees, and William Shakespeare, John Hemynges, Augustine Phillipps, Thomas Pope, and William Kempe, as lessees of the other half' (Wallace, 1914, 30 April). The indenture was dated 21 February 1599, but included a retrospective right of occupancy to 25 December 1598. This suggests that the Chamberlain's Men had gone about relocating their playhouse with discretion and prudence. First, they privately reached conditional terms with the prospective new landlord prior to 25 December 1598. Only then did they attempt to dismantle the Theatre and remove its members to the new grounds south of the Bankside. And only after Peter Street's foray on 20 January 1599 and a further extraction of timbers did the sharers sign the new ground lease on 21 February.

The date of this lease perhaps sets a *terminus a quo* for the construction of the Globe. Wallace believed he could determine a *terminus ad quem* from documentary evidence of a *post mortem* inquisition on the estate of the lessor's father, Thomas Brend, held on 16 May 1599. This cited the deceased's interest in '*una Domo de novo edificata cum gardino eidem pertinenti ... in occupacione Willielmi Shakespeare et aliorum*' (Wallace, 1914, 1 May). Reviewing this body of newly discovered documents Wallace concluded:

> There has been much speculation as to when the Globe was completed, and certain plays have been variously dated upon hypothetical conclusions about it. [The Brend testament] is the only known record to declare a definite date. The Globe was ... finished before May 16, 1599.
>
> (Wallace, 1914, 1 May)

Early twentieth-century commentators, including the formidable T. W. Baldwin, accepted this date (1924, 451). But Baldwin's contemporary Joseph Quincy Adams was more circumspect, and believed that 'the words used [in the testament] seem hardly to warrant [Wallace's] conclusion' (1917, 249). Cooper's *Thesaurus*, the standard Latin–English glossary in Shakespeare's time, defines *in occupatione* broadly as 'holdyng or possessyng a place', and does not necessarily imply the conduct of commerce (*occupatione* PPppv). There is also a practical difficulty with the 16 May date. If the prudent Globe sharers did not begin construction until their ground lease was signed, the interval 21 February to 16 May was only twelve weeks. In 1923 Chambers speculated that construction of the Globe had required twenty-eight weeks (1923, 2: 415–34). He based this estimate on the contract for the Fortune theatre erected in 1600 by Peter Street for Philip Henslowe and Edward Alleyn (J. C. Adams, 1961, 404–7). The Fortune contract calls for the new theatre to mimic the Globe in many respects. Since Street bound himself to erect the Fortune in twenty-eight weeks, Chambers inferred that the builder required a comparable period (196 days) to erect the Globe. If construction of the new Globe began on 21 February and required 196 days, the theatre would have been completed by 5 September. This is compatible with Platter's memoir. However, other evidence suggests that Chambers's inference is not safe, and the Globe may have been erected in fewer than 196 days.

Although the design of the Fortune partially mimicked the Globe, the latter's construction differed radically in one time-intensive respect. The Globe was built from the existing, pre-cut timbers which were *in situ* on the Bankside when the lease was signed.[3] How much time these pre-cut timbers might have saved the Globe's constructors is not entirely a matter of conjecture. We know it required 136 days to cut, saw and deliver timber for the Fortune (Orrell, 1993, 127–44 and 1994, 15–17).[4] We also have a contract for another theatre built with *in-situ* pre-cut timbers: the Hope, erected in 1613 by Gilbert Katherens for Henslowe and Jacob Meade (J. C. Adams, 1961, 408–11). By the terms of the Hope contract dated 29 August, Katherens is first required to tear down an old bear-baiting house. Then he may utilize 'all the tymber benches, seates, slates, tyles, Brickes' from that structure, plus a quantity of pre-cut boards from a house which Henslowe had previously purchased and razed (J. C. Adams, 1961, 410). Katherens agreed to use these materials and to have the new playhouse ready 'bothe for players to playe in, and for the game of Beares and Bulls to be bayted' by 30 November – that is, 102 days after the contract date. If the time required for construction of the Globe was 102 days, and if construction commenced with the signing of the ground lease on 21 February, the Globe would have been substantially complete by Friday 3 June. This gives us a realistic window for the completion of the Globe, and a high probability that opening day fell between 3 June and 5 September 1599.

Certainly the Chamberlain's Men would have found it advantageous to open their new theatre early in the playing season. This would maximize the number of possible playing-dates. It would also have been desirable to open the new playhouse with a new play. Entries in the account book of impresario Philip Henslowe suggest that admission fees were doubled at the premiere performance of a new play. Henslowe's records may also support the inference that the Globe opened early in the interval 3 June to 5 September. The Globe had two established nearby rivals, the Rose (1587) and Swan (1595). We have fragmentary accounts of Henslowe's share of receipts from the Rose 'gallereys' for the period 1598–1600. A sharp drop in his takings occurred after 3 June 1599 (Greg, 1904, 2: 91, 48v). In prior years and in the spring of 1599 his weekly net (reckoned on Sundays) averages more than £10. However, after 3 June 1599 his earnings at the Rose drop precipitously. Of the succeeding 39 entries only three exceed £10.[5] This decline in Henslowe's weekly earnings could be due to any number of factors. But it is compatible with the arrival of a competitor. What is certain is that, by the time 1599 ended, Henslowe and Alleyn had decided to decamp from the Rose. In 1600 they followed their new Fortune to the Cripplegate district of north London, the sector of the city previously occupied by Burbage's Theatre.

Matching plays to playing-dates

Although Shakespeare's company performed on hundreds of occasions, we have only a few reliable performance dates during the playwright's lifetime. Intriguingly, on certain occasions the sharers seem to have consulted an almanac or church calendar when they selected a play for a performance date. We know that the company played *Henry VIII* – a play concerned with that monarch's break with the Church of Rome – on the feast of the pope, St Peter's Day, 29 June 1613. This ironic match of play and date suggests that spoofing old holy days may have been acceptable within limitation. We know that King James once encouraged the troupe to match a play to a date. On Shrove Sunday 1605 the company performed *The Merchant of Venice* for James. The company may have chosen the old play (1596) for this performance date because it contains episodes of Shrovetide masquing. Apparently the king responded to their choice. He commanded a reprise of the play two nights later on Shrove Tuesday (Kernan, 1995, 70).[6] The company also performed *Twelfth Night* at the Middle Temple on 2 February 1602 (Donno, 1992, 1). In this play 'Madonna' Olivia attempts to seduce a cross-dressed virgin, Viola–Cesario. There is a palpable irony here: 2 February is Candlemas, the Feast of the Purification of the original Madonna.

In *A Midsummer Night's Dream* Shakespeare spoofed a playwright who revises his text to suit a playing-date. As Peter Quince and the Mechanicals set about determining the characters required to perform his play, this dialogue ensues:

> *Snout.* Doth the moon shine that night we play our play?
> *Bottom.* A calendar, a calendar – look in the almanac,
> find out moonshine, find out moonshine.
> *Quince.* Yes, it doth shine that night.
>
> (3.1.48–51)

Robin Starveling is delegated for the part of Moon, and the play is rewritten to accommodate his presence (*MND* 5.1.239 and 252–4).

The prospect that the Lord Chamberlain's/King's Men matched plays to dates with conscious irony is also curiously consistent with Thomas Platter's report of a performance of *Julius Caesar* on 21 September 1599. But, before examining the possibility of a connection between Shakespeare's Roman tragedy and the date of the autumnal equinox, I want to assess the claims of two other plays thought to have been written *c.* 1599 which have been advanced as the Globe's first production. Andrew Gurr neatly summarized the candidacy of *Henry V*:

> The Chorus, with its emphatic display of modesty about the capacity of the playhouse 'cockpit' to show the 'vasty fields of France', has prompted a lot of speculation about the date of the play's first performance and which playhouse it was written for. If early in 1599, the Prologue's 'wooden O' must have been the Curtain, which Shakespeare's company used while they waited for the Globe to be built. If later in 1599, it could have been the new Globe. The Chorus is either being modest about an inferior old playhouse, built as long ago as 1577, or mock-modest about the grand new Globe playhouse.
>
> (Gurr, 1992, 6)

The suggestion that Shakespeare was being mock-modest about the new Globe has charm. But the stronger logic identifies the 'cockpit' as the old Curtain playhouse where the Chamberlain's Men performed between October 1597 and June 1599. An early date for *Henry V* is entailed also by the speech in which Chorus appears to analogize Henry's triumphal entry into London on 16 October 1416 with the anticipated return of a victorious Earl of Essex from Ireland:

> The mayor and all his brethren in best sort,
> Like to the senators of th'antique Rome,
> With the plebeians swarming at their heels,
> Go forth and fetch their conquering Caesar in –
> As, by a lower but by loving likelihood
> Were now the general of our gracious empress,
> (As in good time he may) from Ireland coming,
> Bringing rebellion broached on his sword,
> How many would the peaceful city quit
> To welcome him?
>
> (5.0.25–34)

Essex had been dispatched to the Irish wars on 27 March 1599. He returned in disarray on 28 September, and was placed under house arrest. If 'the general' referred to in these verses is Essex, Shakespeare's encomium would have been most appropriate at the time of the Earl's embarkation or soon thereafter. Within weeks of Essex's departure, reports of his frustration at the hands of the Irish rebels began filtering back to London. 'As early as June it had become evident that Essex could not possibly win a decisive victory' (Kay, 1992, 244). This information tends to suggest that *Henry V* was played between the reopening of the theatres after Easter (8 April 1599) and the end of May, which places the play at the Curtain.

Other matters concerning censorship and the Earl of Essex arose in the spring of 1599 which tend to suggest that Chorus's verses were composed early that year, and push the likely playing-dates of *Henry V* into the first weeks of April–May. In February 1599 Dr John Hayward published an account of the reign of Henry IV.[7] The book was dedicated to Essex. Its introduction implied that this history might provide a pattern 'both for private directions and the affayres of state' (A3r).[8] The Queen and her advisers imagined Hayward's description of the deposition of Richard II – coupled with his lavish praise of Essex – as a thinly veiled threat to the crown. Perhaps as a response, the notorious Order of the Bishops (March 1599) included an injunction that 'noe English historyes be printed excepte they bee allowed by some of her maiesties privie Counsell' (Patterson, 1984, 129). When Hayward attempted to publish a second edition of his book in April, all fifteen hundred copies were seized and burnt. On 11 July 1599 Hayward was interrogated before the Privy Council. The vitriolic Queen 'argued that Hayward was pretending to be the author in order to shield "some more mischievous" person, and that he should be racked so that he might disclose the truth' (*DNB on CD-ROM*). Hayward avoided execution only through the intercession of Bacon (Dutton, 1991, 121), and remained imprisoned until after Essex's execution in 1601.[9] Given the Hayward incident in February–March 1599, and the dismal news arriving from Ireland by June, it seems inconceivable that the Chamberlain's Men would have opened the Globe with a play containing (dangerous) verses comparing Essex to Henry V.

As You Like It, with its sylvan, bankside setting and expropriation of the Globe's putative motto 'All the world's a stage' (*Totus mundus agit histrionem*), has also been advanced as the new theatre's first presentation. This play has been dated variously to 1599 and 1600 (Wells and Taylor, 1987, 121; Latham, 1975, xxvi–xxvii) based on a 'blocking entry' in the Stationers' Register of 4 August 1600. The play may well have been written in 1599. But there are two perhaps insuperable obstacles to dating *As You Like It* as early as June of that year. First, it has long been thought that the part of Touchstone was written for Robert Armin, who appears to have joined Shakespeare's company in early 1600 (Fleay, 1886, 209; Baldwin, 1924, 454). More persuasive perhaps is the received gloss on Celia's remark that 'the little wit that fools have was silenced' (1.2.82–3), which is thought to be an allusion to the burning of satirical books on 1 June 1599 (Fleay, 1886, 208).[10] If this allusion is correctly identified, it suggests a later date for the principal composition or revision of *As You Like It*.

Turning to *Julius Caesar*, it may be that Thomas Platter witnessed a performance of Shakespeare's Roman tragedy at the Globe on 21 September 1599. Though obscure to moderns who reckon time by the Gregorian calendar, the irony of this match of play and date would have been apparent to any Elizabethan who had access to an almanac: 21 September was the 'official' date of the autumnal equinox. But, owing to a flaw in the prevailing English Julian calendar, this solar event had actually been observed in England on 13 September. In 1582 Pope Gregory XIII had reformed the calendar and restored the equinoxes to their traditional dates throughout the Catholic world. But Elizabeth had rejected Gregory's reform. By playing *Julius Caesar* on 21 September Julian – the vestigial, incorrect date of the equinox – the Lord Chamberlain's Men delivered a cheeky comment on Elizabeth's calendar. An English audience compelled to live and worship by the scientifically discredited Julian calendar could hardly have overlooked this irony.

If *Julius Caesar* was played on the wrong date of one equinox, an intriguing question arises: could the play have been performed on the official or actual date of the other three principal solar events of 1599? Certainly *Julius Caesar* could have been recalled to the stage for the winter solstice on 12/22 December. But it is unlikely that construction of the Globe was complete before the vernal equinox on 11/21 March; in any case, the theatres were closed for Lent. Andrew Gurr concluded that, even if the new Globe 'had a shorter building time because of its prefabricated timbers, it could hardly have opened much before midsummer' (Gurr, 1992, 6). Midsummer was the fourth principal solar event of 1599: the summer solstice, officially 24 June but observed in England on 12 June Julian.

There is intriguing circumstantial evidence that, like Peter Quince and company in *A Midsummer Night's Dream*, the Globe sharers consulted an almanac for June 1599 several months prior to opening their new Bankside playhouse. Working from Wenceslas Hollar's *Long View of London*, John Orrell deduced that the axis of the Globe was aimed at a point on the horizon roughly 48.7° north of east (1983, 152ff.). Recent archaeological excavations at the Globe site appear to confirm

Orrell's deduction (Blatherwick and Gurr, 1992). This point on the horizon approximates the rising point of the Sun on the summer solstice, its northernmost rising of the year. Since the Globe construction commenced during winter, the sharers and builder must have consulted an almanac or ephemerides to determine this azimuth of sunrise. Had they done so, they could not have failed to notice that a rare lunar–solar phenomenon was predicted for June 1599: a new Moon on the summer solstice.

As Figure 1 indicates, the last crescent of the waning Moon was visible on Sunday 10 June Julian. The first crescent of the waxing Moon appeared on 14 June Julian. The three intervening nights were moonless. The precise moment of new Moon occurred at 12.53 p.m. on 12 June Julian. We think of the solstice as the beginning of summer. But Elizabethans called Julius Caesar's old date for the solstice (24 June) 'Midsummer Day'. Since the Globe sharers had determined to aim the axis of their playhouse at the rising point of the Sun on 12 June 1599 Julian, they could hardly have been unaware of these solar and lunar events.

A new Moon on the summer solstice had important astrological connotations. New Moon was the proverbial time for moving to a new house, initiating new ventures and planting crops.[11] While it is difficult to assess the attitude of Shakespeare and his colleagues to astrology, the *fin de siècle* years of the sixteenth century were a time of heightened superstition – and actors were and are notoriously superstitious. Consulting with astrologers was the done thing among English people of means, and Keith Thomas writes, 'Scarcely any new venture was undertaken without an astrologer's pronouncement' (1971, 372). Henry VIII, Cardinal Wolsey, Protector Somerset, Burghley and Essex regularly consulted astrologers (with varying success). The Earl of Leicester had engaged John Dee to select the date of Queen Elizabeth's coronation (Thomas, 1971, 343). Because of the national penchant for astrology, English almanacs provided phases of the Moon and other celestial information. Printed ephemerides supplied positions of the Sun, Moon and known planets throughout the year. In Shakespeare's England only the Bible enjoyed larger press runs than the almanacs.[12] Had Shakespeare and his colleagues consulted an ephemerides, they would have discovered that an important conjunction occurred on 12 June 1599. Shakespeare was certainly familiar with the astrological significance of conjunction. In *2 Henry IV* young Hal observes Falstaff paddling with

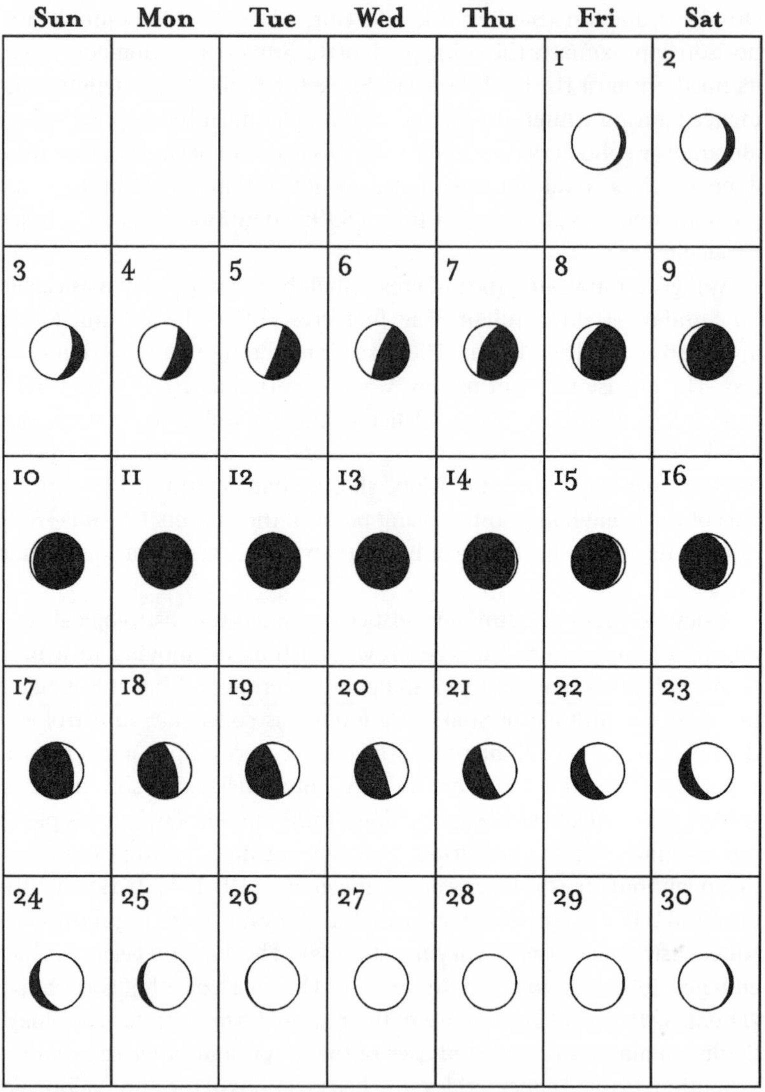

Sun	Mon	Tue	Wed	Thu	Fri	Sat
					I	2
3	4	5	6	7	8	9
10	II	12	13	14	15	16
17	18	19	20	21	22	23
24	25	26	27	28	29	30

Figure 1. Phases of the Moon during June 1599 (Julian)

Doll Tearsheet, and jokes about the unlikeliness of a conjunction between Saturn and Venus in the year, and refers Poins to the almanac
(*2H4* 2.4.265–6). An ephemerides would have revealed to the Globe
sharers that a conjunction of the Sun and Moon would occur on

12 June; at 5.02 p.m. the two bodies would be separated by only 2.665°.[13] This phenomenon is known as syzygy. As we like to say, 'The planets are lining up.' From the perspective of London, the Sun, Moon and Earth passed through syzygy at 5.02 p.m. local time on 12 June 1599 Julian.[14]

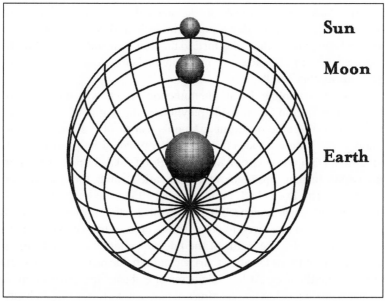

Figure 2. Syzygy at 1702 Universal Time, 12 June 1599 (Julian)

Had Shakespeare and company asked an Elizabethan astrologer to cast a chart for 12 June 1599, a number of other propitious auspices would have been apparent.[15] A conspicuous and favourable *stellium* (gathering) of five 'planets' (Sun, Moon, Mercury, Jupiter, Saturn) assembled in the constellation Gemini beginning at 3.40 p.m. Gemini rules during the period 21 May to 21 June. Of its twinned stars Castor and Pollux, the former favours intelligence, voyages and sudden success in legal and literary matters. The latter imparts an elusive, audacious character, with a fondness for gossip. On the afternoon of 12 June 1599 Mars set at 4.26 p.m. The Sun set at 8.21 p.m. After sunset Venus and Jupiter appeared brightly conjunct in the evening sky, a very opportune alignment. Jupiter is the 'lucky star', and Venus looks after beauty. In assessing this astrological data our modern scepticism is irrelevant. In

Shakespeare's time astrology 'was not a coterie doctrine, but an essential aspect of the intellectual framework in which men were educated' (Thomas, 1971, 338). The majority of Elizabethans believed that celestial events influenced earthly life for good or evil. Schoenbaum believed that Shakespeare was born on 23 April but not christened until 26 April because 'superstition intervened – people considered St. Mark's Day [25 April] unlucky. "Black Crosses" it was called; the crosses and altars were almost to Shakespeare's day hung with black, and (some reported) the spectral company of those destined to die that year stalked the churchyard' (1975, 25). Shakespeare may have taken a dose of superstition with his mother's milk.

There was another lunar phenomenon which was important to impresarios opening a riverside playhouse: the status of the Thames tides. Since the time of the new Moon's transit of the meridian was known, the Thames tides on 12 June 1599 could be predicted with precision. High tide occurred at London Bridge at 1.34 p.m. A fraction of a mile further upstream at Southwark strand, the tide crested c. 2 p.m.[16] The Rose (1587) and Swan (1595) were long established, and it is likely their audience's habits of transportation were, too. Many spectators – and most well-to-do patrons – crossed the Thames by boat (Gurr, 1987, 34). The status of the tide was a familiar consideration, and important to the fastidious. Arrival at high tide promised a pleasant stroll to the theatres. At low tide acres of evil-smelling Thames muck would lie uncovered. A tide cresting c. 2 p.m. was fortuitous for audience and impresarios alike.[17]

Until we unearth a playbill or eyewitness diary entry, we may never be able to say with certainty when the Globe opened, or identify the theatre's premiere production. But, as William Shakespeare contemplated the writing of his first Globe play in the winter of 1598–9, the summer solstice would have been in prospect as an appealing occasion for the new theatre's premiere. Documentary evidence of the construction of the Globe and other early London theatres suggests that this prospect was not unrealistic, and points to the interval 3 June to 5 September 1599 as the likely window for the theatre's debut. Opening early in the playing season was desirable, and a new play would have augmented the theatre's takings. A precipitous drop in Philip Henslowe's revenues at the nearby Rose is consistent with the arrival of a new competitor after 3 June. The orientation of the Globe ground-plan coupled with the summer solstice, a new Moon, and astrological auspices (and the tides) made 12 June a conspicuously attractive day for a Bankside theatre's debut. As to the identity of the first Globe play, there are formidable arguments against the claims of *Henry V* and *As You Like It*. But, as I will suggest in the following chapter, Julius Caesar was a hotly topical subject in 1599 – a particularly apt subject for the premiere play at a new theatre aimed at the rising point of the Sun on the summer solstice – a solstice which was officially 24 June, but which occurred on 12 June because Caesar's calendar was wrong.

Notes

1 The choice of 28 December for this foray may have been calculated. Innocents' Night was a regular playing-date for Shakespeare's company; we believe they performed *The Comedy of Errors* at Gray's Inn on 28 December 1594 (Foakes, 1962, 116–17). Perhaps the Chamberlain's Men believed that Giles Allen would not be vigilant on that night. They were wrong.

2 The feast of Sebastian and Fabian – a date remembered by Shakespeare in *Twelfth Night*. See Chapter 17.

3 This would account for the lease being retrospective to December 1598.

4 Construction of the Fortune commenced upon the signing of the contract on 8 January 1600. Payments for delivery of timbers to the construction site began on 20 March and continued through 21 May. In the interim, preparation of the site for the theatre went forward.

5 Henslowe makes no new entry until 6 October. The Admiral's Men are known to have travelled extensively during the latter half of 1599 (Gurr, 1996, 255).

6 *Merchant* also contains a master-leaving servant and an eloping daughter, both associated with leap years, which perhaps suggests that the play was first written, or extensively revised, in 1596.

7 Sir John Hayward, *The First Part of the Life and Raigne of King Henrie the IIII*, London: J. Wolfe.

8 'Among all sortes of humane writers, there is none that have done more profit, or deserved greater praise, then they who have committed to faithfull recordes of Histories, eyther the government of mighty states, or the lives and actes of famous men: for by describing the order and passages of these two, and what eventes hath followed what counsailes they have set foorth unto us, not onely precepts, but lively patternes, both for private directions and for affayres of state ...' (Hayward, A3r).

9 Scholars who believe that Elizabethan censorship was lax or *laissez-faire* at the close of the sixteenth century would do well to read Hayward's book and consider the treatment he received for it. Hayward is almost certainly innocent of any misdemeanour except poor judgement. He very nearly

suffered the rack, and might have lost his life. Coupled with the burning that June of satirical books by Nashe and others, 1599 was not a year in which any writer would wish to be thought controversial.

10 Included in the bonfire were works by satirist Thomas Nashe (1567–1601?), a small man numbered among the 'University Wits' ('little wit') whom Shakespeare may have memorialized as Moth (anagram of 'Thom') in *Love's Labour's Lost*.

11 For example: Gabriel Friend's *Prognostication for 1616*, etc. 'It is good to plant or graffe generally, the Moone increasing' (C2r). And, conversely: 'Doung Ground to prevent the growing of Weedes, the Moone decreasing' (C2v). The *OED* provides two citations, the first dating to AD 1200: 'Oðer [to think] newe mone betere ðan æld-mone in to newe huse te wænden.' *Vices & Virtues* 1200, 27. 'Believe the new moon better than an old moon to move into a new house.' Also: 'Sow Wheat and Rie about the New Moon.' Rider's *British Merlin*, October 1682.

12 The earliest extant almanac in English was produced by De Worde in 1498. The *STC* lists the imprints of more than two hundred printers who produced almanacs, plus another hundred anonymous publications. The most widely circulated printed document in England was the calendar, which appeared in Bibles, the prayer book, almanacs and ephemerides.

13 *Redshift2* astronomical modelling software © Maris Multimedia 1995.

14 Syzygy had both practical and metaphysical connotations. The conjunction is associated with the Gnostic concept of 'dualism', of good and evil, of God and the Devil, and of the dual human and divine natures of Christ. This line of inquiry may be relevant to a play about a man who became a god. As a practical matter, syzygy exaggerated the amplitude of the tides. Tides of heightened amplitude are known as 'spring' tides since they appear to 'spring up' and then recede at an unusually rapid pace.

15 I am indebted for this analysis to American astrologer Kramer Wetzel. A version of this argument appeared Sohmer, 1997.

16 According to an analysis prepared for the author in 1996 by Dr B. S. McCartney of the Proudman Oceanographic Laboratory (Merseyside).

17 In Chapter 6 I suggest that *Julius Caesar* contains an ironic reference to the tides of 12 June 1599.

2

Julius Caesar and the Elizabethan calendar controversy

No story so haunted William Shakespeare as the tale of honourable men who assassinated the greatest figure in secular history. Shakespeare had already begun to contemplate Caesar's fall when he wrote the first of his history plays, *2 Henry VI, c.* 1591. That play contains both Shakespeare's widely quoted allusion to Book 5 ¶14 of Caesar's *Commentarii* (4.7.59–63), and the playwright's all-but-ignored affirmation of Brutus's bastardy (4.1.136–40). For nearly a decade Shakespeare meditated the events of 44–42 BC. Allusions surface in *1–2–3 Henry VI*, *Richard II* and *III*, *Titus Andronicus*, *Love's Labour's Lost*, *The Merchant of Venice*, and of course *The Rape of Lucrece*, which marks the first appearance of Lucius Junius Brutus in the canon. During the period 1596–8 Shakespeare rehearsed several themes of *Julius Caesar* in *1–2 Henry IV* before taking up the murder on the Ides as his subject in 1599. And Caesar's fate (and legacy) was still vivid in the playwright's consciousness when he created *Antony and Cleopatra* in 1606 and *Cymbeline* in 1610. William Shakespeare was thirty-five years old when he wrote *The Tragedie of Julius Caesar*. The play is the fulcrum on which the dramatist's career turns. From *Julius Caesar* we look backward at *Titus, The Taming of the Shrew, Two Gentlemen of Verona, The Comedy of Errors, Richard II* and *III*, and the *Henry IV–V–VI* plays – work which is largely developmental, historiographical or pure entertainment.[1] Looking forward in the playwright's career, one finds the ruthless middle comedies, profound tragedies and, at a breathing distance, the romances. Before creating Caesar, Shakespeare created Falstaff; afterwards, he created Lear. Before creating Brutus, Shakespeare created Bolingbroke; afterwards, he created Hamlet. Before creating Cassius, Shakespeare created Beaufort; afterwards, he created Ulysses. And before creating Antony,

Shakespeare created Juliet; afterwards, he created Cleopatra. By 1599 Shakespeare had meditated the story of Julius Caesar for a decade. One might well ask: why did he choose this year to take up the old Roman as his subject?

Time is the subject of Shakespeare's story in *Julius Caesar*.[2] Only four plays in the canon contain more references to time.[3] Although Gaius Julius Caesar (100–44 BC) is best remembered by our age for his conquests, Elizabethans knew him as the *Pontifex Maximus* of Rome and the founder of their calendar. Caesar had imposed a new calendar by decree on 1 January 45 BC. His formulation corrected a faulty Roman Republican calendar (reformed 153 BC) which was lunar-based and only 355 days long. When a calendar is too short or too long, the dates of the equinoxes and solstices vary from year to year, the seasons drift from their proper months, and holy feasts from their seasons. Plutarch described the confusion which confronted Caesar in 48 BC:

> For the Romanes using then the auncient computacion of the yeare, had not only such incertainty and alteracion of the moneth and times, that the sacrifices and yearly feasts came by litle and litle to seasons contrary for the purpose they were ordained: but also in the revolution of the sunne (which is called Annus Solaris) no other nation agreed with them.
>
> (North, 1579, 791)

Caesar's reformed calendar was designed by the Alexandrian mathematician Sosigenes, who calculated the length of the year as 365.25 days.[4] To account for the odd 0.25 day, a 'bissextile' day was intercalated following 24 February every fourth year. Having determined the form for his new calendar, Caesar moved to set it afoot. He added a total of ninety days to 46 BC, making it the so-called 'long year' of 445 days. Caesar's reform created a seemingly permanent correspondence between the four principal solar events and particular dates (Table 1). The Vernal equinox was the Roman *Hilaria*, from which our 'April Fools' Day' tradition may have descended. It was also the feast of Cybele, mother of Jove.[5] Early Christianity was a wonderfully eclectic religion, and first-century Christians adopted Caesar's dates of the principal solar events to commemorate the (lost) dates of the conception and nativity of the founders of their religion (Table 2).

Table 1 *Caesar's dates for the equinoxes and solstices*

Vernal equinox	24/25 March
Summer solstice	23/24 June
Autumnal equinox	23/24 September
Winter solstice	24/25 December

Table 2 *Caesar's dates adopted as Christian holy days*

Vernal equinox	24/25 March	Annunciation to Mary
Summer solstice	23/24 June	Birth of St John Baptist
Autumnal equinox	23/24 September	Annunciation to Zacharias
Winter solstice	24/25 December	Birth of Jesus Christ

But Sosigenes had erred. He overestimated the length of the solar tropical year, which is actually 365.2422 days. His error of 11 minutes and 14 seconds was undetectable in a Roman's lifespan, but accumulated to a full day every 128 years. By the time of the Council of Nicaea in AD 325, this error had accumulated to three days, and the vernal equinox had regressed from 24 to 21 March. This confounded the dating of Easter, which depends on identifying the Paschal Moon. When the Council's mathematicians failed to solve the conundrum, the Nicaean fathers formulated a new rule: they declared 21 March the 'official' date of the vernal equinox.[6] Easter would be observed throughout the Church on the Sunday after the first full Moon following.[7]

The Nicaean decree conformed the observance of Easter. But it did nothing to correct the inherent slippage in Caesar's calendar. By the time the Venerable Bede correctly estimated Sosigenes' error in AD 730, the actual date of the vernal equinox had advanced to 18 March. This continuing regression led to the bizarre medieval practice of designating one Sunday *Pascha verum* (true Easter) and another *Pascha usitatum* (observed Easter). Understandably, this provoked controversy within the Church. In an effort to remedy the problem, in 1472 Pope Sixtus IV engaged the German mathematician Johann Müller to reform the calendar. But the issue was factious and explosive. Müller died – some thought by poison – and plans for reform were abandoned. Almost a hundred years later, Pius V summoned mathematicians to Rome to study the problem. He died before they submitted their recommendations. It fell to Pius's successor, Gregory XIII, to complete the work and promulgate a new calendar in Shakespeare's time.

The Papal Bull which Gregory signed on 24 February 1582 clashed with a number of English traditions. Gregory ordered the start of the civil year set at 1 January. This contradicted the English practice of dating the new year from 25 March, the date of the Annunciation and start of the 'Year of Grace'. Gregory restored the equinoxes by advancing his calendar ten days; the day after 4 October 1582 was declared 15 October. This left the English Julian calendar ten days behind. Gregory also decreed that only centennial years divisible by 400 would be leap years. This would leave England another day behind after 1700. Gregory's bull cast Elizabeth on the horns of a dilemma. The three consecrated documents of her English Church were the Bible, the Book of Common Prayer and that invisible finger turning the pages of both, the Julian calendar (Hassel, 1979, 7). Elizabethan Bibles and Books of Common Prayer included a calendar in their first pages (Hassel, 1979, 8). These were often printed with the red ink reserved for the words of Christ because the calendar was believed to be *revelatory*. Its orderly succession of lunar and solar-based holy days 'revealed a profound logic of resonances and connections. The meaning of these may escape the modern mind but their ancient significance was perfectly familiar' to Elizabethans (Laroque, 1993, 202). 'In the liturgy and in the celebrations which were its central movements people found the key to the meaning and purpose of their lives' (Duffy, 1992, 11).[8] We think of our modern secular calendar as fiscal, academic or simply chronological. But the Elizabethan calendar *was* the Church calendar.

Not one to be left ten days behind the whole world, Elizabeth determined to impose an English reform. She urged Archbishop Edward Grindal to approve a new calendar without delay.[9] But Grindal refused. Reforming the calendar would require a revision of the Book of Common Prayer, which could be moved only by Parliament, certainly not by the Antichrist Bishop of Rome. Grindal's price for accepting reform was an ecumenical review by the English Church 'in concert with our brethren overseas'. That was a price Elizabeth could not and would not pay. Allowing Grindal to confer with an international convocation would effectively repeal the Act of Appeals (Collinson, 1979, 270–1). Out-flanked, Elizabeth determined to persevere with Caesar's old calendar. With her decision England became a national anachronism.

But the question of English calendar reform did not, and could not, die. The inexorable creep of the equinoxes made the calendar controversy and, oddly enough, Julius Caesar himself grist for the pulp publishers of England.[10] Writers of popular almanacs hastened to supply explanations of the calendar controversy, and to stir the pot for an English reform. In these ubiquitous pocketbooks the English could read a surprisingly detailed history of Julius Caesar and his faulty calendar. To cite one example among many, in his almanac for 1584 John Harvey recalled how the ancient Romans 'a long tyme to have laboured, and paynefully travayled in searchyng out the direct course and true space of the yeere' (Harvey, Biir). Perhaps with a glance at Sir Thomas North's recent (1579) edition of *Plutarch's Lives*, Harvey explains how Numa Pompilius revised the primitive calendar of Romulus and began the evolution of the lunar-based Roman Republican calendar. Harvey records how Caesar recruited Sosigenes to devise a new solar-based calendar, which 'this most puissaunt Captayne, and learned Astronomicall Emperour' imposed 'in the .45. yeere before the happy byrth of our Saviour CHRIST' (Harvey, Biir). Harvey then explains Sosigenes' error, and closes his literate and scholarly treatise by inviting readers to 'have recourse to Suetonius ... to the fyrst booke of Macrobius *Saturnalia*, or to an Epistle of S. Iherome directed *ad Eustochium* ... which are all copious in this argument' (Harvey, Biiiv). This bibliographical reference suggests a popular appetite for information about the roots of the calendar controversy.

A more explicit appeal for English calendar reform appears in the 1587 almanac of William Farmer, whose narrative approaches *apologia* for the Gregorian formulation. This undertone is unmistakable in Farmer's discussion of the variations between the *Pascha verum* and the *Pascha usitatum*. He provides a table which demonstrates that the dates of the true and observed Easters fell on the same Sunday in only fifteen of the preceding thirty-two years. Of the remaining seventeen years, eight varied by one week, five by four weeks and four by five weeks. Farmer felt that a reform of the English calendar was indispensable and overdue. Equally apparent is his circumspection, and deference to his theological and astronomical superiors:

> Thus have I after rude and simple maner, made manifest the chiefe causes of this late Alteration [the Gregorian calendar]: but whether there be any necessitie that we should do lyke or not, I referre that to the judgement of the reverent Divines, and learned Astronomers, who are sufficiently able to determine that cause: The one, in respect of conscience, the other in respect of the communitie of Computation.
>
> (W. Farmer, 1587, C2r)

In the face of Elizabeth's rejection of Gregory's calendar, reform was not an issue upon which *any* writer would wish to appear outspoken. But the fact that popular almanacs continued to rehearse the history of the rival calendars year after year suggests that the subject was deliberated over time by a broad spectrum of the literate population. Most intriguing with regard to our interest in Shakespeare's *Julius Caesar*, the ubiquitous almanacs promulgated the story of Caesar's calendar and Sosigenes' error among lettered Elizabethans.

Then in 1598 a phenomenon occurred which brought the English calendar controversy to a head. That year saw the most extreme variation (five weeks) between the Protestant and Catholic Easters. In 1599 a pamphleteer described widespread confusion and frustration:

> In the yeare of our Lord 1598 lately by past, according to the decree of the Nicene Councell, and late Kalendar, set out by [the Italian mathematician] Lilius, Easter day, fell upon the twelft daie of March, in the olde Kalendare and Almancks, whereby we yet reckon in England and Scotland: And Whit Sunday upon the last daye of Aprill: And Fastings even, upon the twenty foure of Ianuary: Whereas after the vulgare maner and count, Easter daie was celebrate that yeare, the sixteenth daie of Aprill, Whit Sunday, the fourth of Iune: And Fastings even, the last of February. Yee see the distance betweene the one calculation and the other, is more then the space of a Moneth: what errour it may growe to by the proces of time, it is easie by this example to perceive.
>
> (Pont, 1599, 61)

The publication of this pamphlet is precisely contemporary with Shakespeare's *Julius Caesar*. Both documents pinpoint the historical moment when the English calendar controversy reached its zenith, a moment of perplexing uncertainty when 'the most basic category by which men order their experience [time] seemed subject to arbitrary political manipulation' (Burkhardt, 1968, 6). Stubbornly celebrating Easter on the wrong day – when everyone *knew* it was the wrong day – had turned the English Protestant Easter services of 1598 into a theatre of the absurd. Imagine yourself a devout Christian in an English church on 16 April 1598, reciting 'Christ is risen', hearing the Gospel's tale of his haunting whisper to Magdalene, all the while knowing that the true Easter had passed, ignored, on 12 March. Gregory's newfangled calendar may have been Catholic, but it was correct. To an English Christian, being compelled to worship by Caesar's calendar – a calendar repudiated by the whole world – was not merely absurd; it was degrading, humiliating, scandalous, mortifying. It was tyranny. Those who wonder why Shakespeare chose 1599 to write his play about the man who imposed the Julian calendar perhaps need seek no further.

We have now rehearsed as much of the root and cause of the Elizabethan calendar controversy as the average lettered Londoner might have known in 1599. Even so, it is difficult for a twentieth-century mind to grasp the oppressive day-to-day experience of living and worshipping by a scientifically discredited Julian calendar. In the winter of 1598–9 the English holy year had dissolved in a series of jangling discordances. On 21 December 1598 Elizabethan Protestants observed the Feast of St Thomas. But they knew that the rest of Europe and their Catholic recusant neighbours had already celebrated Christmas, St Stephen's Day and Holy Innocents, and were preparing to see in the New Year that very night. By the time Elizabethans were ready to welcome 1 January 1598, the Twelve Days of Christmas were long gone for their Catholic friends who were already dating their correspondence 1599. As Elizabethans prepared *billets-doux* on the Eve of St Valentine 1598, Catholic Europe was celebrating Shrove Tuesday 1599. And while Elizabethans were exchanging Valentine greetings the rest of the world was gravely observing Ash Wednesday and the onset of Lent. Even Julius Caesar's anniversaries were muddled: on the English Ides of March 1598 the Catholic world was observing the Annunciation to the Blessed Virgin Mary 1599. Worse, the Elizabethan date of the Annunciation fell on the Catholic Palm Sunday. Worst of all, the true Easter, 11 April 1599 Gregorian, fell on the date the English observed April Fools' Day. This was the historical moment in which Shakespeare wrote and staged his play about the Man-God who had imposed the Julian calendar.

Notes

1 The striking exception is *The Merchant of Venice*.
2 Although C. F. E. Spurgeon fails to discern a pattern of imagery in *Julius Caesar*, Marvin Spevack sensed that a 'dominant concern in the play is time' (Spurgeon, 1968, 346; Spevack, 1988, 19ff.).
3 Based on a count of the following vocabulary: time(s)(ly), hour(s)(ly), minute(s), day(s), month(s)(ly), year(s), (to)night(s)(ly), weeks(s)(ly), (to)morrow, morn(ing), afternoon, evening, holiday(s), feast, clock,

sundial, season(s). The plays which exceed *Julius Caesar* are *Richard III*, *Romeo and Juliet*, *1 Henry IV*, and *Hamlet*.

4 Cleopatra may have introduced the two men during the couple's halcyon days in Alexandria.

5 Cybele's rites engrossed the period 15–25 March. The 24 March was the 'Day of Blood', and centred on animal sacrifice. The rites concluded on 25 March with the ritual bathing of a statue of Cybele (Hornblower and Spawforth, 1996, 416).

6 Early Christians of Asia Minor and Judea (many of them converted Jews) routinely observed the feast of Christ's resurrection, Easter Day, on the Jewish Passover (14 Nisan). But, as Christianity spread west to Europe and engrossed gentile communities unfamiliar with the Passover ritual and complex Jewish calendar (lunar-based and eleven days short), a system for dating Easter by the Julian calendar emerged in the Western Church. These Christianized pagans 'kept their *Easter* upon the *Sunday* following the *Jewish Passover*, partly the more to honour the day, and partly to distinguish between *Jews* and *Christians*. These latter pleaded themselves the *Apostolical* Tradition' (Anonymous, 1710, 86–7). This practice made the determination of Easter dependent on the date of the Passover, which was itself reckoned by the Paschal Moon, i.e. the first full moon after the vernal equinox.

7 Fixing the vernal equinox on 21 March effectively dissevered the summer solstice from Midsummer Day. In fact, there could be *three* Midsummer Days: the day on which the solstice was observed; the 'official' date of the solstice, 21/22 June; and Caesar's old Midsummer Day, 23/24 June.

8 Cf. Hutton, 1994, 5–48.

9 Their correspondence is extant: British Library, MS. Add 32092, fols 26–33.

10 Not all Shakespeare's contemporaries were content to suffer Elizabeth's autocracy in silence. An entry in the *Journals of the House of Lords* records that a bill to reform the calendar came up for two readings in 1584/5: 'Item 1a *vice* lecta est Billa, An Act giving Her Majesty Authority to alter and new make a Calendar, according to the Calendar used in other Countries.' The bill was quashed.

3

Calendrical markers
in *Julius Caesar*

In prior chapters I have suggested that William Shakespeare conceived and wrote *The Tragedie of Julius Caesar* to serve as the premiere presentation of the new Bankside Globe on the summer solstice 1599. I have suggested that the playwright wrote at the height of the English Julian calendar controversy, and in response to that controversy. In this chapter I will extend this inquiry to the text of *Julius Caesar* by suggesting that the play contains a number of calendrical 'markers' which were recognizable to members of Shakespeare's first audiences. What I shall call 'markers' are instances where Shakespeare has borrowed from a passage of Scripture linked via the liturgical calendar to a readily identifiable date or holy day. (See Appendix 11.)

It is hardly an innovation to suggest that Shakespeare borrowed from Scripture. In his notes to the edition of 1785, George Steevens detects St Paul's Epistles to the Corinthians behind Sebastian's epithet for Feste, 'foolish Greek' (Johnson and Steevens, 1788, 9: 76).[1] Since taboos relaxed in the late nineteenth century, scholars have produced a shelf of commentaries on Shakespeare's exploitation of the Bible.[2] It is also common knowledge that the liturgical calendar links passages of Scripture to specific dates or holy days. Most moderns would have no trouble connecting Gabriel's salutation – 'Hail, thou that art highly favoured, the Lord is with thee: blessed art thou among women' (Luke 1:28) – with the Feast of the Annunciation, 25 March. Many of us could probably link John 2 – the changing of water into wine at Cana – with Epiphany, 6 January. On the other hand, few moderns would link John 2 with the Ides of March – even though the Book of Common Prayer has, for centuries, prescribed this reading for morning prayer on 15 March. Some links between Scripture and dates remain luminous in our minds – 'And when the days of her purification according to the law of Moses were accomplished' (Luke 2:22) – surely calls to mind the Feast of the Purification, 2 February. But other connections which were vivid for Elizabethans – for example, the link between the Books of Samuel and Lent – exist dimly, if at all, in the modern mind. It will not be a controversial statement to say that, generally, Elizabethans knew their Bible better than we do. But I wish to push beyond that commonplace to suggest that Shakespeare played on his audience's biblical knowledge as a mode of discoursing upon forbidden or dangerous subjects. I will suggest that Shakespeare's borrowings from Scripture are methodical and systematized; that they are connected with specific dates and/or holy days in the liturgical calendar; that members of his audience could recognize these borrowings and identify the relevant holy days and dates; and that Shakespeare expected the 'wiser sort' among his auditors to perceive these verses of Scripture and their related holy days or dates as a gloss on his play's text – or *vice versa*.

The calendrical markers in *Julius Caesar* are of two kinds: *textual* and *temporal*. When a marker is textual, the associated Scripture and holy day provide a gloss on the speech or scene where that marker is placed – or *vice versa*. Scholars may find these glosses useful for interpreting the play. When a marker is temporal, it identifies an historical date. Scholars may find these dates useful for identifying the year of principal composition of the play, or the date of a performance. Let me cite one example of a textual marker, and one of a temporal marker, in familiar passages of *Julius Caesar*.

A textual marker: wine-tasting on the Ides of March

In *Julius Caesar* 2.2 Shakespeare creates an ahistorical gathering of conspirators at Caesar's house on the morning of the Ides of March. As the group prepares to depart for the Capitol Caesar says, 'Good Friends go in, and taste some wine with me / And we (like Friends) will straight way go together' (1125–6). This is odd. A moment ago Caesar asked, 'What is't a Clocke?' and Brutus answered, '*Caesar*, 'tis strucken eight' (1110–11). It seems too early for drinking.[3] Doubly so to readers of Suetonius – including Shakespeare – who knew that the historian had praised Caesar for abstemiousness: 'That he was a most sparie drinker of wine, his very enemies would never denie' (Holland, 1606, 22). Further, Shakespeare certainly knew that only Decius

Brutus had come to Caesar's house on that fateful morning in 44 BC (North, 1579, 793).[4] Why has Shakespeare created an ahistorical and improbable circumstance of the conspirators and their victim tasting wine together?

Scholars have pondered the off-stage spectacle of Caesar tasting wine with those who betrayed him – a tableau so reminiscent of the Last Supper (Shaheen, 1987, 87). But there is another and more pertinent instance in the New Testament when Christ tasted wine with his disciples – including Peter, who denied him, and Judas, who betrayed him. The moment is recorded only in the Gospel of John and begins, 'And the third day there was a marriage in Cana ... and both Jesus was called, and his disciples' (John 2:1–2). At the marriage feast at Cana Jesus turned water into wine. In John's Gospel this first miracle seems to mark the beginning of the end for Jesus. Abruptly, he tells his mother, 'Mine hour is not yet come' (John 2:4). But within days he has journeyed to Jerusalem, driven the money-lenders from the Temple, and attracted the attention – and deadly envy – of the Pharisees. John's tale of Cana contains a wine-tasting: 'Now when the governor of the feast had tasted the water that was made wine ... [he] called out to the bridegroom, And said unto him, All men at the beginning set for the good wine ... but thou hast kept backe the good wine until now' (John 2:9–10). Turning water into wine may appear to us a rather minor miracle from a God who could raise the dead. But John's narrative of Cana had extra-ordinary importance during the Reformation. The gloss in the Rheims New Testament cites this miracle to support the Catholic view of the real presence of the body of Christ in the Eucharist: 'He that seeth water turned into Wine, nedeth not dispute or doubt how Christ changed bread into his body' (Rheims, 220). In the Elizabethan liturgy John 2 was the reading for the morning of the Ides of March. Intriguingly, John 2 also contains Jesus's prophecy that he will be raised from the dead on the third day: 'Destroy this temple, and in three days I will raise it up ... he spake of the temple of his body' (John 2:19–21). Shakespeare will move the murder of Cinna to the night of the Ides so that Caesar's ghost appears to Brutus on the third day after his death.[5]

Recovering this calendrical marker which connects John 2 with Shakespeare's portrait of events on the morning of the Ides of March raises a crucial question. If John 2 underlies Shakespeare's wine-tasting – and if 'the wiser sort' in his audience could recognize this connection – are we to infer Shakespeare was consciously drawing a parallel between Caesar and Jesus Christ? This is a difficult question to answer with confidence. When the playwright settled on the well-known, meticulously documented story of the assassination and deification of Julius Caesar as a subject for a play, he could have certainly recognized that the subject lent itself particularly well to the grafting of passages of Scripture. Although the Bible has been largely dehistoricized in our time, Christians of Shakespeare's age received the Bible as both the Word of God *and* literal history. Elizabethans believed that Christianity was the true religion because the events described in the Bible actually happened. Readers opening a typical Bible – for example, the Geneva 1560 – encountered a map of the holy land 'conteining the places mencioned in the foure Evangelistes' (AA. i). These holy places were identified by longitude and latitude on the reverse of this page. The translators' 'Argument' which precedes the Gospel according to St Matthew begins 'In this historie written by Matthewe, Marke, Luke and Iohn . . .'. It goes on to define the word 'Gospel' as history: 'And therefore under this worde [Gospel] is conteined the whole Newe testament: but communely we use this name for the historie, which the foure Evangelists write.' [6] For Elizabethans the Bible *was* history – and Reformation Christians tended to read all history, including Roman history, as progressive revelation.[7] Plutarch (b. AD 46) was an almost exact contemporary of the authors of the New Testament, and his *Lives* engrossed the history of the time of Christ and his first proselytes. In North's Plutarch, Shakespeare and lettered Elizabethans would have encountered a series of uncanny parallels between the lives of Julius Caesar and Jesus Christ. Plutarch recorded that a man with the initials JC had lived at the time of the first Caesars. He was an exalted religious figure (North, 1579, 766), renowned for his piety, beloved of the poor, mistrusted by the elite (791). Certain Romans dressed him in a purple robe (975). One offered him a crown (976). Adherents hailed him by the title of king (791). One closest in his love betrayed him (793). Omens and portents surrounded his last days (797). He was martyred, but rose and was seen to walk the earth (797). Some declared him god. He reformed the calendar (738).

It may seem inconceivable that Shakespeare would dare to draw parallels between his Caesar and Christ which were detectable by members of his audience. But the playwright had already parodied the Crucifixion in his portrayal of the death of York in *3 Henry VI* 1.3.[8] Shakespeare's principal source for that play was Hall. But he followed Holinshed's account of York's destruction:

> Some write that the duke was taken alive, and in derision caused to stand
> upon a molehill, on whose head they put a garland in steed of a crowne,
> which they had fashioned and made of sedges or bulrushes; and having
> so crowned him with that garland, they kneeled downe afore him (as the
> Jewes did unto Christ) in scorne, saieng to him; Haile king without rule,
> haile king without heritage, haile duke and prince without people or
> possessions.

(Holinshed, 1587, 659.1.63)

According to Holinshed, York's murderers performed an overt parody
of the mortification of Christ. Shakespeare alters the perspective from
the killers to York himself, but preserves Holinshed's Christ-image in
Margaret's 'stage direction':

> Come make him [York] stand upon this molehill here,
> That wrought at mountains with outstretched arms
> Yet parted but the shadow with his hand.

(1.3.68–70)

York's 'outstretched arms' are iconographic for Christ on the cross. The
phrase 'wrought at mountains' is an allusion to the power of faith in
Mark 11:23. The parting of a 'shadow' remembers the rending of the
temple veil at Christ's death (Matthew 27:51, Mark 15:38, Luke 23:45).
If Shakespeare was engaged with such manifest (and daring) devices at
this early stage of his career (1591–2), his skill at managing biblical
parodies may have matured by 1599. Over a decade as playwright and
player, Shakespeare's appreciation of his audience's cognitive abilities
(and the limits of their tolerance) would have sophisticated. A remarkable example of the playwright's skill at parody of holy day ritual
appears in *Julius Caesar* 1.1. The series of devices reveals the deft hand
of an experienced practitioner. It also displays the playwright's confidence in his audience's ability to recognize, remember and synthesize
fragments of information. At line 68 the impious plebeians have departed, 'tounge-tyed in their guiltinesse' and the two Tribunes are alone
onstage. Flavius appoints a course of action:

> Go you downe that way towards the Capitoll,
> This way will I: Disrobe the Images,
> If you do finde them deckt with Ceremonies.
>
> *Mur.* May we do so?
> You know it is the Feast of Lupercall.

> *Fla.* It is no matter, let no Images
> Be hung with Caesars Trophees:
>
> (71–7)

Unable to assail Caesar or discourage his adherents, the Tribunes resolve to vent their indignation on the emblems of Caesar. But what are these 'Trophees' of Caesar? In his *Life of Caesar* Plutarch records 'there were set up images of *Caesar* in the city with Diadeames upon their heades, like kinges' (North, 1579, 792). But in his *Antony* Plutarch mentions only one 'crown', a laurel wreath which Caesar refused and which 'was afterwards put upon the head of one of *Caesars* statues or images, the which one of the Tribunes pluckt of' (North, 1579, 976). Shakespeare has altered his source in Plutarch and invented multiple 'images' or statues of Caesar which are not crowned with diadems but hung with 'Trophees'. When Casca describes the crime for which the Tribunes have been punished, Shakespeare slyly reveals that these Trophees are 'Scarffes'. Casca says, '*Murrellus* and *Flavius*, for pulling Scarffes off *Caesars* Images, are put to silence' (390–1). Auditors who followed this trail of details could deduce that Caesar's images are hung with his trophies *and* that these trophies are scarves. It did not require any great leap of imagination to supply the colour of the scarves: *purple*. From Plutarch Shakespeare was aware that Caesar was entitled to wear a purple robe in perpetuity. At line 1100 Shakespeare's Caesar calls out as he prepares to leave for the Capitol on the Ides of March: 'Give me my Robe, for I will go.' The colour of the scarves which Murrellus and Flavius pulled off Caesar's trophies was purple, the colour of triumph, the colour of the robe Caesar was privileged to wear as *triumphator*. Flavius specifically calls for Caesar's images to be *disrobed* (72), strengthening the connection between scarves and robe. Prior to the Reformation, statues draped in purple scarves were a familiar sight to English churchgoers during Passiontide. Images of the saints – and the Cross – were robed in purple on Palm Sunday and uncovered on Good Friday, the day of Christ's martyrdom. This unveiling ceremony, known as Creeping to the Cross, climaxed with the disrobing of the crucifix. We can visualize the ritual. The parishioners and clergy kneel. Three times they chant the *Venite adoremus*. Only then does the principal celebrant – barefoot – bend to kiss the sacred Cross. That is, the congregation watches as he 'bootless' kneels.[9] Brutus will kneel 'bootless' before Caesar on the morning of his martyrdom: 'Doth not Brutus bootlesse kneel?' (1285).[10] This is a parody of the Catholic Good Friday ritual of Creeping to the Cross. Elizabethans believed that Christ was crucified on Good Friday 25 March AD 33.[11] By the Protestant calendar this was 15 March, the Ides of March, the date of Caesar's wine-tasting, the date of his martyrdom.

A cautionary word may be useful before leaving John 2, the Ides of March and the wine-tasting at Caesar's house. Where we moderns perceive a relationship between a sixteenth-century text and verses of the Bible, we are conditioned to read the later text as informed by the earlier. That is, if we suspect a connection between John 2 and Caesar's wine-tasting, our training disposes us to adopt the perspective that the playwright is exploiting John 2 to comment on the play's text. That line of reasoning might lead us to speculate that Shakespeare is mining John 2 to invest his Caesar with qualities associated with Christ: for example, like Christ, Caesar is about to become a (sympathetic) sacrificial victim. But this mode of interpretation is mere usage, a habit. If the two literary documents indeed have a relationship, it is equally logical to read Shakespeare's wine-tasting as a commentary on John's. Reasoning this way we might speculate along the line that, like Caesar, Christ was a mortal man who claimed divine antecedents. I will suggest in later chapters that Shakespeare is exploiting Scripture not metaphorically but anamnetically, and that several passage of *Julius Caesar* comment on the New Testament.

A temporal marker: the Cynicke Poet and the feast of Barnabas

Whereas a textual marker identifies a passage of Scripture and a holy day which may serve as a gloss on the play text (or *vice versa*), a *temporal* marker exploits a passage of Scripture which is linked via the liturgical calendar to an historical date. An instance of a temporal marker in *Julius Caesar* occurs in 4.2. Brutus and Cassius are engaged in a rambling argument about tactics, money and love. As their wrangle climaxes, a 'Poet' barges into Brutus's tent, and a scene begins which scholars have long found inscrutable:

> *Poet.* Let me go in to see the Generals,
> There is some grudge betweene 'em, 'tis not meete
> They be alone.
> *Lucil.* You shall not come to them.
> *Poet.* Nothing but death shall stay me.

Cas. How now? What's the matter?
Poet. For shame you Generals; what do you meane?
       Love, and be Friends, as two such men should bee,
       For I have seene more yeeres I'me sure then yee.
Cas. Ha, ha, how wildely doth this Cynicke rime?
Bru. Get you hence sirra: Sawcy fellow, hence.
Cas. Beare with him Brutus, 'tis his fashion.
Bru. Ile know his humor, when he knowes his time:
       What should the Warres do with the these Jigging Fooles?
       Companion, hence.
Cas. Away, away be gone.   *Exit Poet*

                                                    (2109–24)

Shakespeare found this anecdote in Plutarch, who describes how one
Marcus Phaonius

> despite of the doorekeepers, came into the chamber, and with a certaine
> scoffing & mocking gesture which he counterfeated of purpose, he re-
> hearsed the verses which old Nestor sayd in Homer:
>
> > *My Lords, I pray you harken both to mee,*
> > *For I have seene moe yeares than suchye three.*
>
> Cassius fel a laughing at him: but Brutus thrust him out of the chamber,
> & calle him a dogge, and counterfeate Cynick.

                                                    (North, 1597, 1071)

One can see that Shakespeare made a number of alterations to
Plutarch's incident. Shakespeare's stage direction designates Phaonius
as 'a Poet'. Cassius rather than Brutus identifies the man as a Cynicke.[12]
This is problematic. A Globe audience could *hear* that the interloper was
a rhymester. But how does Cassius recognize the man as a Cynicke?
And how could Cassius's epithet make sense to an audience most of
whom had not read Plutarch? To deepen the mystery, Shakespeare
rewrites Phaonius's verses. Plutarch's man quotes Homer: 'My Lords, I
pray you harken both to mee, / For I have seene moe yeares than suchye
three.' Shakespeare alters his source here, too. His Cynicke commands,
'Love, and be Friends.' This is doubly puzzling; Shakespeare certainly
knew that a cynic 'disbelieves in the sincerity or goodness of human
actions' (*OED* cynic a. and n. 2).

   If it wasn't an aural clue which identified the intruder as a Cynicke
to Shakespeare's Cassius and the Globe audience, perhaps the clue was

visual. Elizabethans familiar with classical literature would have known that the Cynickes were itinerant evangelicals who preached contempt for worldly goods, including apparel.[13] There is a formidable mass of scholarship detailing the similarities between the Cynickes and early Christians who were taught: 'Take no thought for your life, what ye shall eat: neither for your bodie, what ye shall put on' (Luke 12:22).[14] Like the Cynickes, early Christian evangelicals dressed simply, wandered and preached, 'living off what others provided, inveighing against wealth, reprimanding hypocrisy, and expecting trouble for their pains' (Downing, 1992, 2).

Shakespeare's device can be understood by relating the Poet's doggerel verses to the holy days of June 1599. St Barnabas's Day was observed on 11 June. In the Book of Common Prayer the Gospel reading for that day was John 15:12–17: 'This is my commandement, that ye love one another, as I have loved you … Ye are my friends, if ye do whatsoever I commande you … These things commande I you, that ye love one another' (John 15:12, 14, 17). This passage is a cornerstone of Christian doctrine. Christ gave his disciples many tenets. He taught with many parables. But he gave the world only one commandment. Strictly speaking, 'Love, and be Friends' is not *a* commandment; it is *the* commandment. When Shakespeare's Poet barges in commanding, 'Love, and be Friends', the playwright is not rewriting Plutarch and Homer. He is rewriting Jesus Christ.[15] If Shakespeare wrote *Julius Caesar* for performance at the Globe on 12 June 1599, he must have been aware that the entrance of the Cynicke – and his doggerel of John 15 – would electrify auditors who had heard these verses preached on the previous day.

Notes

1 Steevens asks, 'Can our author have alluded to St. Paul's epistle to the Romans [*sic*], ch. i. v(erse). 23 – "to the Greeks foolishness?"' In fact, the citation should be 1 Corinthians 1:23, which the Geneva records as: 'But wee preach Christ crucified: unto the Jewes, even a stumbling blocke, and unto the Grecians, foolishnesse.'

2 See the bibliography: Noble, 1935; Shaheen, 1987 and 1993; Milward, 1973; and others.

3 A scruple the Elizabethans apparently shared. Cf. *Twelfth Night* 5.1.195–9, where the Doctor who is drunk at eight in the morning is a 'passy measures panym'.

4 'Plutarch's Caesar ... is temperate in both food and drink, and it is this moderation, this consistency ... which distinguished him [from Plutarch's Alexander]. Caesar's request that the conspirators have a glass [*sic*] of wine with him strikes a tone of moderation like that of a Last Supper, the eve of a betrayal' (Homan, 1975, 206). At least one commentator has noted a possible connection between this scene and Christ's Last Supper, which is perhaps why Shakespeare chose not to stage Caesar and his assassins actually drinking together. But there is another connection to an important event in the founding of Christianity which may also be glanced at here. Christ's Last Supper was an evening meal. The scene at Caesar's house takes place in the morning. It is early for drinking. Brutus has just announced, '*Caesar*, 'tis strucken eight.' During the first Baptism of the Spirit at the Pentecost, the descent of the Holy Ghost caused the Apostles to lapse into glossolalia, speaking in tongues, a phenomenon not uncommon in the New Testament (1 Corinthians 14:1ff.), and still practised among Pentecostal Christians. The onlooking Judeans, hearing the Apostles speaking in tongues, assumed the men were drunk with 'new wine' (Acts 2:13). St Peter responded: 'Yee men of Judea, and ye that inhabite Hierusalem, be this knownen unto you, and hearken unto my words. For these [the Apostles] are not drunken, as yee suppose, since it is but the third houre of the day' (Acts 2:14–15). The Geneva gloss to 'third houre of the day' explains, 'After the sunne rising, which may be about seven or eight of the clockè with us.'

5 A full discussion of the calendar of Caesar's death and the appearance of his ghost is found in Chapter 13 below.

6 A few lines later, the same text characterizes the apostles as 'writers of this historie' (AA. ii).

7 Shakespeare certainly exploited a Renaissance commonplace when he characterized Augustus's *Pax Romana* as the 'time of universal peace' (*A&C* 4.6.4) which was the *sine qua non* of the coming of Christ in the prophecy of Isaiah (39:8–40:3).

8 'Parody' is employed throughout this essay absent its modern sense of ridicule. The sixteenth-century 'Parody Mass' borrowed pre-existing pieces of music (motets, chansons, madrigals) and substituted sacred words for their secular lyrics.

9 'What these details imply is a practice like the one condemned in the Elizabethan homily *Against perill of idolatries, and superfluous decking of churches* ... The corollary to this is that Caesar-worship is something akin to Roman Catholic worship' (Kaula, 1981, 198–9).

10 Shakespeare plays on the same pun in *1 Henry IV* (3.1.63–6).

11 According to the widely read *Golden Legend* of Jacobus de Voragine, Christ was crucified on 25 March (Ryan, 1993, 119).

12 Mark Hunter accounted for Shakespeare's invention this way: 'North's doggerel rendering doubtless suggested to Shakespeare the idea of making

[Phaonius] not only a counterfeit Cynic, but a miserable rhymster' (Furness, 1913, 215n).

13 Like Stoicism, Epicurianism and Academic Scepticism, the Cynic philosophy (founded by Antisthenes *c.* 445–365 BC) was an established school at the time of Caesar and Christ.

14 All Scripture citations from The New Testament, tr. L. Tomson, (London: Barker 1599). Citations of *Julius Caesar* follow the text and lineation of Hinman's edition of *The First Folio of Shakespeare* (1968). The text of The Tragedie of *Julius Caesar* occupies folios 109–30.

15 To underscore his mischief, Shakespeare may have injected another cue. When Brutus grows angry at the Poet, Cassius chides: 'Beare with him *Brutus*, 'tis his fashion.' Brutus grumbles, 'Ile know his humor, when he knowes his time: / What should the Warres do with these Jigging Fooles?' (2120–3). Modern editors interpret 'Jigging' as 'alluding to the light, rapid, jerky dance called a jig' (Humphreys, 1984, 202n). This has no basis in the play text and cannot be correct. By the mid-seventeeth century 'jig' signified doggerel versions of the Psalms (*OED* jig n.3.). Is this the sense of 'jig' Brutus employs to scorn the Poet's doggerel version of the Gospel for St Barnabas's Day? And should this not be the *OED*'s first occurrence of the usage?

4

Temporal markers to mid-June 1599 in *Julius Caesar*

I have suggested that temporal markers can be useful in dating a play's principal composition or its occasional performance. In addition to St Barnabas's Day, temporal markers in the text of *Julius Caesar* may refer to other holy days in Midsummer 1599. A glance into any of the dual Julian–Gregorian almanacs reveals a rich series of holy day discordances during the second week of June. Monday was both 11 June Julian and 21 June Gregorian. On this day English Protestants observed the Feast of St Barnabas. Tuesday 12/22 June was the solstice. On this day Catholics observed the Feast of St Alban.[1] Wednesday 13/23 June was the Protestant Feast of Saint Antony of Padua. That evening Catholics observed the Vigil of the Nativity of John Baptist. Temporal markers to Julian dates would be more accessible to Shakespeare's auditors. Above I examined the marker for St Barnabas's Day. I will begin this chapter by identifying the temporal marker for St Antony's Day in *Julius Caesar*.

13/23 June: St Antony's Day in the Foro Romano

Elizabethan almanacs routinely identified the days of the month by their Roman designations of *Calends*, *Nones*, and *Ides*. A glance into an almanac for June 1599 would have revealed that the 13th was the Ides of June. Had the opening of the Globe been planned for 12 June 1599, 13 June would have been the theatre's second day. Caesar dies on an Ides during the second day of dramatic time in Shakespeare's play. June 13 was also the date of the (suppressed) Feast of St Antony of Padua, canonized a year after his death in 1232 (D. H. Farmer, 1992, 27). A gifted debater and preacher, St Antony attracted crowds of as many as thirty thousand 'and spoke in the market-places instead of the churches'. Shakespeare rewrites Plutarch so that his Antony regales a throng from a 'Pulpit' (1291) in a 'Market place' (1323) on the Ides:

> Judgement! thou art fled to brutish Beasts,
> And Men have lost their Reason. Beare with me,
> My heart is in the Coffin there with Caesar,
> And I must pawse, till it come back to me.
>
> (1641–4)

'Brutish Beasts' conjures an image of preaching to animals.[2] St Antony was renowned for preaching to beasts. He once persuaded a horse to venerate the New Testament. Shakespeare's Antony calls Caesar's will 'this Testament' (1667). His plebeians cry to hear 'The Will, the Testament' (1691). Antony claims he found Caesar's will 'in his Closset' (1666). St Antony was frequently invoked as a finder of lost articles. Miraculously, St Antony's tongue survived intact after thirty years' burial; Shakespeare's Antony vows to 'put a Tongue / In every Wound of *Caesar*' (1765–6). The date of 13 June and St Antony's reputation for preaching fire and brimstone apparently drew Shakespeare to Chapter 13 of the apocalyptic Book of Revelation. His Antony repeatedly borrows from Revelation 13. Even his famous 'lend me your eares' may be a cue to Revelation 13:9: 'If any man have an eare, let him heare.' Shakespeare knew that Mark Antony's funeral oration ruined the Republic and led to the creation of the Roman Empire. Elizabethans believed that the author of Revelation had described these very events and warned Christians against their consequences in the mystical verses of Revelation 13. The lengthy Geneva gloss draws a parallel between the enmity of the Roman Empire towards the early Church, and the malice of the popish establishment toward the English Reformed Church (Ppp4r). Protestant theologians of Shakespeare's day routinely associated the Antichrist and the Pope with the Caesars,

> especially in the several Elizabethan commentaries on Revelation, which regarded Caesar as the founder of the universal empire later inherited by the popes. In his worldly power and magnificence and in his claim to supreme authority as pontifex maximus ... Caesar and not St. Peter was actually the first pope.
>
> (Kaula, 1981, 202)[3]

This may be why Revelation 13 was alive in Shakespeare's mind. Mark Antony had laid the foundation of the Roman Empire with his funeral oration over the body of Caesar forty-four years before the birth of Christ.[4]

There is another temporal marker to 13/23 June which occurs in Antony's soliloquy in 3.1 and explains Shakespeare's curious choice of Ate as the companion for Caesar's revenging spirit. After the assassins have left the Capitol to publish the news of Caesar's death Antony proclaims, 'Over thy wounds, now do I Prophesie' (1487). First, he raises the spectre of a terrible civil war: 'Domesticke Fury, and fierce Civill strife, / Shall cumber all the parts of Italy' (1491–2). Then Antony conjures a series of bizarre supernatural images. He predicts that

> *Caesars* Spirit ranging for Revenge,
> With Ate by his side, come hot from Hell,
> Shall in these Confines, with a Monarkes voyce,
> Cry havocke, and let slip the Dogges of Warre,
> That this foule deede, shall smell above the earth
> With Carrion men, groaning for Buriall.
>
> (1498–503)

Shakespeare's choice of Ate as Caesar's companion has never been satisfactorily explained. But now that we recognize the connection between the text of *Julius Caesar* and the liturgical calendar, it is possible to resolve both these cruces.[5] Ate destroyed her victims by blinding them to the difference between right and wrong, and between 'advantageous and disadvantageous courses of action' (Howatson, 1989, 69). At Sardis and Philippi, Shakespeare contrives for Antony's prophecy to be *literally* fulfilled. Brutus complains of 'the weaknesse of mine eyes' (2290). Cassius despairs, 'My sight was ever thicke' (2501). And Pindarus's vision is faulty when he describes Titinius's capture (2512). Shakespeare's choice of Ate may depend on the curse in Psalm 69: 'Let their eyes be blinded that they see not' (69:24). Psalm 69 was the prescribed reading at evening prayer on St Antony's Day, 13 June.

Like the saint from Padua, Shakespeare's Antony preaches in a marketplace. What he says turns the tide of opinion against Brutus and the assassins. Given the pivotal importance of Antony's funeral oration, it may be useful to say a word about Shakespeare's perspective on this character. Shakespeare marks his Antony as the fulcrum of his play in an intriguing way. The Folio text runs 2730 lines. Line 1366 exactly begins the second half of the play. It reads simply, '*Enter Antony.*' Although the lineation of Shakespeare's texts is subject to endless debate, Antony's entrance is either the precise midpoint of the text of *Julius Caesar* or so close to the precise midpoint that its placement is unlikely to be happenstance.[6] Shakespeare knew his Spenser and his Chaucer. Both his masters produced numerical cues to a character's dramatic function. From his sources Shakespeare knew that Antony was chief priest of the *Lupercii*, and later became *Flamen dialis* of the shrines to *Divus Julius.*[7] This explains a puzzling detail in Brutus's greeting to Antony when he arrives at the Capitol after the assassination of Caesar:

> To you, our Swords have leaden points *Marke Antony*:
> Our Armes in strength of malice, and our Hearts
> Of Brothers temper, do receive you in,
> With all kinde love, good thoughts and reverence.
>
> (1394–7)

The conspicuous trisyllable which completes this speech, 'reverence', could mean 'respect felt or shown towards a person on account of his or her position or relationship; deference' (*OED* n. 1. a).[8] But the majority of appearances of 'reverence' in the Shakespeare canon signify 'veneration for some thing, place, or person regarded as having a sacred character' (*OED* n. 1. b). Why, one wonders, would Brutus address Antony with 'veneration for a person having a sacred character'? And why would this salutation have seemed appropriate to an Elizabethan audience? The answer may depend on Antony's wardrobe. We know the playwright was somewhat particular about what his Antony wore; at line 84 a stage direction describes '*Antony for the Course'.*[9] From his sources Shakespeare knew that Antony was entitled to wear the toga with a purple stripe of a priest. Being an augur, Antony would have carried the curved wand (*lituus*), similar to the crosier staff of a bishop or abbot. An Antony coming to the Capitol to meet Caesar's killers – and fearing for his own life – might well have attired himself with all possible dignity. Priestly vestments would have been particularly appropriate for Antony speaking in the order of Caesar's funeral. Indeed, Shakespeare's company possessed priestly robes; they are worn by Canterbury and Ely in *Henry V*. Of all the principal men in *Julius Caesar*, only one is never associated with a sword or dagger: Antony. Like St Antony, his weapons are the testament (3.2) and the pen (4.1). But Shakespeare – and his canny Julius Caesar – also knew Mark Antony for a liar. The diagnostic exchange between the characters occurs on the Lupercal. Caesar observes, 'Yond *Cassius* has a leane and hungry looke, / He thinkes too much: such men are dangerous' (296–7). Antony replies, 'Feare him not *Caesar*, he's not dangerous, / He is a Noble Roman, and well given' (298–9). Antony's remark seems innocent, and Caesar appears to accept it at face value. But as the pair turn to leave the stage, Caesar instructs Antony to 'Come on my right hand, for this eare is deafe, / And tell me *truly*, what thou think'st of him' (315–16, emphasis mine). Caesar's conviction that Antony is a liar and chameleon is underscored by his habit of referring to Antony variously as 'Antonio' (91), 'Antony' (306), and 'Mark Antony' (1046).[10] While Cassius recognizes Antony as a 'shrewd contriver', Brutus underestimates his adversary to his despair. Shakespeare contrives for his audience to underestimate Antony, too. Our first impression is that, like Casca, Antony is another of Caesar's fawning sycophants.[11] When the dictator says, 'Forget not in your speed / To touch *Calphurnia*', Antony's response is grandiloquent flattery: 'I shall remember, When *Caesar* sayes, Do this; it is perform'd' (99).[12] Granville-Barker recognized that 'Shakespeare keeps Antony in ambush throughout the first part of the play. Up to the time when he faces the triumphant conspirators he speaks just thirty-three words' (Granville-Barker, 1946, 2.368 23).[13]

Shakespeare was interested in Antony as a liar, and as a writer. The playwright knew that, like St Luke, Antony wrote to a correspondent named Theophilus. While we may never know the identity of the Theophilus to whom Luke addressed his Gospel and his Acts of the Apostles, Antony's Theophilus was governor at Corinth. In *Antony and Cleopatra* Shakespeare's Antony tells his friends to sail for Corinth and promises, 'You shall / Have letters from me to some friends that will / Sweep your way for you' (3.11.15–17).[14] Shakespeare rewrote Plutarch to make his Antony the 'author' of each of the principal actions in *Julius Caesar*. Although Plutarch recorded that Caesar's dismissal of Murellus and Flavius from office had galvanized the opposition to Caesar,[15] in Shakespeare's play Antony's offer of the coronet to Caesar sets the assassination afoot.[16] Antony also authors the counter-action of the play. Once Caesar is dead, Brutus and the conspirators see only Caesar's 'body' (1571). But Antony envisions the power which Caesar's death has unleashed: '*Caesars* Spirit ranging for Revenge', etc. (1498–1503). After observing the effect of Caesar's bloody corpse on Octavius's servant (1511–14), Antony concocts the oration and the spectacle of

Caesar's stigmata, and 'puts a Tongue / In every Wound of *Caesar* that should move / The stones of Rome, to rise and Mutiny'. By fomenting insurrection Antony authors the death of the poet Cinna, and the civil war. Antony is also the first to give Octavius his new name. Addressing Octavius's servant Antony says, 'You serve Octavius *Caesar*, do you not?' (1505). Shakespeare's decision to put this name in Antony's mouth contradicts the sources. The historical Antony bitterly resented Octavius's famous name – '*et te, o puer, qui omnia nomini debes*' – 'and you, o boy, who owe everything to your famous name'.[17] Shakespeare's Antony is *literally* author of the 'black proscriptions' (4.2); his hand holds the pen which pricks the names of the doomed: 'He shall not live; looke, with a spot I dam him' (1860). In the same scene Antony dictates the agenda for the war against the assassins: 'Brutus and Cassius Are levying Powers; We must straight make head', etc. (1887–93).[18] Before the play ends, Antony takes the leading authorial role in the 'rewrite' of Caesar's assassination (see Chapter 14). He also delivers the final encomium over the body of Brutus, authoring his enemy's epitaph.

Throughout his play Shakespeare contrives to make priest-liar-writer Antony the author of the fall of the Roman Republic and the establishment of the Empire of the Caesars. At line 1339 Caesar lies dead and his assassins are preparing to depart the Capitol when their way is barred by the arrival of Antony's servant. The man claims to quote his master verbatim when he declares:

> *Brutus* is Noble, Wise, Valiant, and Honest;
> *Caesar* was Mighty, Bold, Royall, and Loving:
> *Say, I love Brutus*, and I honour him;
> *Say, I fear'd Caesar*, honour'd him, and lov'd him.
>
> (1344–7)

Antony's use of 'loving/love/lov'd' is calculated, and insistent. Antony offers Brutus love and honour. But he regarded Caesar with fear, honour and love. These are the three duties due to God enumerated in the order prescribed in Deuteronomy: 'And now, Israel, what doth the LORD thy God require of thee, but to feare the LORD thy God, to walke in all his wayes, and to love him …' (Deuteronomy 10:12).[19] Antony's servant's speech climaxes with a figure which readers of Roman history would have recognized as a prodigious lie:

> If *Brutus* will vouchsafe, that *Antony*

> May safely come to him, and be resolv'd
> How *Caesar* hath deserv'd to lye in death,
> *Mark Antony*, shall not love *Caesar* dead
> So well as *Brutus* living; but will follow
> The Fortunes and Affayres of Noble *Brutus*,
> Thorough the hazards of this untrod State,
> With all true Faith.
>
> (1349–55)

The expression 'all true Faith' is an instance of Shakespeare tuning the ears of his audience to theological innuendoes. (See fuller discussion of this device below.) A torrent of these allusions appear in Antony's funeral oration. As Antony begins his address in the marketplace his first statement is a bold-faced lie: 'I come to bury *Caesar*, not to praise him' (1611).[20] The Globe audience had only just heard Brutus instruct Antony to 'speake all good you can devise of *Caesar*' (1472). In fact, Antony's intention is to praise Caesar to the ruination of his assassins. His next statement presents an extraordinary idea:

> The evill that men do, lives after them,
> The good is oft enterred with their bones,
> So let it be with *Caesar*.
>
> (1612–14)

What is the evil Caesar did which lives after him? We are about to discover it is Caesar's 'Testament'.

> Let but the Commons heare this Testament:
> (Which pardon me) I do not meane to reade,
> And they would go and kisse dead *Caesars* wounds,
> And dip their Napkins in his Sacred Blood;
> Yea, begge a haire of him for Memory,
> And dying, mention it within their Willes,
> Bequeathing it as a rich Legacie
> Unto their issue.
>
> (1667–74)

Nowadays the distinction between 'will' and 'testament' has been lost. But it was lively under English common law in Shakespeare's time, and the playwright palters with it.[21] 'Testament' had a theological ring to Elizabethan ears as it does to ours.[22] God's first testament was the Covenant of Life 'made with Adam for himself and his posterity upon condition of obedience' (*OED* covenant n.8.a). The 'New Testament' was God's Covenant of Grace with that Second Adam, Christ, and his elect. Antony predicts that the hearing of Caesar's 'Testament' will incite the kissing of stigmata. He declares Caesar's blood 'Sacred'. The treasuring and passing down of a 'haire of him' echoes the practice of conserving the relics of saints. Auditors would remember that Decius had promised Caesar that his blood would be coveted 'For Tinctures, Staines, Reliques, and Cognisance' (1081–2). In Elizabethan parlance 'Tinctures' and 'Staines' were bits of cloth dipped into blood – as sympathizers were wont to dip rags into the blood of martyrs quartered at Tyburn (Harsnett, 1603, 83). 'Cognizance' was the 'colours' which religionists would wear as the sign of their profession (Wills, 1995, 100). The concordance of 'Testament' with 'Sacred Blood' in Antony's oration recalls the moment when Christ gave his Apostles his new testament/covenant. Elizabethans believed that St Luke's Gospel and his version of the Last Supper was the earliest and most authoritative record of the occasion: 'Likewise also after supper he tooke the cup, saying, This cup is that new Testament in my blood, which is shed for you. Yet behold, the hand of him that betrayeth me, is with me at the table' (Luke 22:20–1). The audience knew that Caesar had tasted wine with those who betrayed him on the morning before his assassination. Antony now characterizes the contents of Caesar's new testament:

> Have patience gentle Friends, I must not read it.
> It is not meete you know how *Caesar* lov'd you:
> You are not Wood, you are not Stones, but men.
>
> (1677–9)

Caesar's testament is a profession of love for the people, as is Christ's. Antony bluntly contradicts Murellus's castigation of the plebeians, 'You Blockes, you stones, you worse then senselesse things' (42). This image is borrowed from St Luke's portrait of Christ's triumphal entry into Jerusalem on Palm Sunday.[23] Shakespeare's plebeians cry out. They chant, 'The Will, the Testament', (1691). But, as Antony prepares to read the document, his technique suddenly shifts from rhetoric to spectacle.

> You will compell me then to read the Will:
> Then make a Ring about the Corpes of *Caesar*,
> And let me shew you him that made the Will:
> Shall I descend? And will you give me leave?

All.   Come downe.
2.   Descend.
3.   You shall have leave.
4.   A Ring, stand round.
1.   Stand from the Hearse, stand from the Body.
2.   Roome for *Antony*, most Noble *Antony*.
Ant.   Nay presse not so upon me, stand farre off.
All.   Stand backe: roome, beare backe.

(1694–705)

Antony's descent from the pulpit to the stage, the formation of the ring and the repetitious calls for playing room are recognizable devices from the old Mystery plays (Purvis, 1957, 153; Rose, 1962, 431, 458). Antony begins his street spectacle by exhibiting Caesar's 'mantle':

> You all do know this Mantle, I remember
> The first time ever *Caesar* put it on,
> 'Twas on a Summers Evening in his Tent,
> That day he overcame the Nervii.

(1707–10)

Antony's image of a quiet respite after battle is vivid and affecting – and a lie. Readers of Plutarch knew that the decisive battle against the Nervii was fought not in the summer but during the winter of 58–57 BC (North, 1579, 773). Nor could Antony have been present in Caesar's tent. Antony did not join Caesar's army until at least three years after this battle. From this point Antony's lies become increasingly transparent.

> Looke, in this place ran *Cassius* Dagger through:
> See what a rent the envious *Caska* made:
> Through this, the wel-beloved *Brutus* stabb'd,
> And as he pluck'd his cursed Steele away:
> Marke how the blood of *Caesar* followed it,
> As rushing out of doores, to be resolv'd
> If *Brutus* so unkindely knock'd, or no:
> For *Brutus*, as you know, was *Caesars* Angel.
> Judge, O you Gods, how deerely *Caesar* lov'd him:
> This was the most unkindest cut of all.
> For when the Noble *Caesar* saw him stab,
> Ingratitude, more strong then Traitors armes,
> Quite vanquish'd him: then burst his Mighty heart,
> And in his Mantle, muffling up his face,

Even at the Base of *Pompeyes* Statue
(Which all the while ran blood) great *Caesar* fell.
(1711–26)

The Globe audience knew that Antony was outside the Senate house
during Caesar's murder. Antony could not know which holes in Caesar's
cloak Cassius, Casca or Brutus made. Nor could he have witnessed
Caesar 'muffling up his face'. Antony now characterizes Caesar's murder with a startling theological allusion: 'O what a fall was there, my
Countrymen? / Then I, and you, and all of us fell downe' (1727–8).
The moment all fell was Adam's fall in Genesis 3. Hearing this, the
plebeians begin to weep. Antony exclaims: 'Kinde Soules, what weepe
you, when you but behold / Our *Caesars* Vesture wounded?' (1732–3).
Suddenly, the plebeians are 'Soules' and Caesar's 'mantle' has become
his 'Vesture'. There is a famous story of Romans dandling a dead man's
'vesture' in the Gospel of St Matthew: 'And when they had crucified
him, they parted his garments, and did cast lots, that it might be fulfilled,
which was spoken by the Prophet, They parted my garments among
them, and upon my vesture did cast lots' (Matthew 27:35).[24] Elizabethans believed that this lottery took place on 25 March AD 33, the
Ides of March in their vestigial Julian calendar.

12/22 June: the summer solstice, and the feast of St Alban

While the Julian dates of the Feasts of Sts Barnabas and Antony would
be more accessible to an Elizabethan audience, there are, as we have
seen, three other notable occasions in the interval 11–13 June: the
summer solstice, the feast of Saint Alban, and the Vigil of the Nativity
of St John Baptist. If Shakespeare was consciously placing temporal
markers in the text of *Julius Caesar* with an eye to a premiere on the
summer solstice, we ought to expect the text to contain markers for
these three important events. In fact, it does. With the opening line of
Julius Caesar Shakespeare signals that the calendar is on his agenda. As
a procession of merry plebeians crosses the stage, Tribune Flavius challenges them: 'Hence: home, you idle Creatures, get you home: / Is this
a Holiday?' (5–6). One can see the irony, the humour and the magic if
these words were written to be spoken from the Globe stage on 12 June
1599. Queen Elizabeth's official Midsummer Day – 24 June – would not
arrive for almost two weeks. But adherents of Caesar and his calendar

would have turned out – both on-stage and in the audience – paying homage to the true summer solstice. London's Midsummer's festival was a day of picnics, games, bonfires and revels. On Midsummer Night the watch would be augmented by bands of beery citizens marching the boundaries with torches (Hutton, 1994, 39).[25] The torch-bearing vigilantes who catechize and kill Cinna the Poet in *Julius Caesar* 3.3 would have been instantly recognizable to a Globe audience.

Flavius condemns the Roman revellers as 'idle Creatures'. 'Idle' was indistinguishable from its homonym, 'idol' – that is, 'pagan, idolatrous' (*OED* idol n. 1). The epithet is equally appropriate to the on-stage mob and to a playhouse audience living by Caesar's calendar. Molly Mahood recognizes that when Shakespeare employs 'clownish quibbles such as those in the opening scene of *Julius Caesar* they tune up the audience's responsiveness to words' (Mahood, 1988, 28). Although the Elizabethans' pronunciation of 'holiday' was indistinguishable from 'holy day', the Folio text discriminates between them. Flavius demands, 'Is this a Holiday?' (6), an apt question on the suppressed holy day of the English protomartyr St Alban. Thirty lines later 'Holiday' becomes 'Holy-day' as the Cobbler declares, 'But indeede Sir, we make Holy-day to see *Caesar*, and to rejoyce in his Triumph' (36–7). Twenty lines later Murellus falls captive to the Cobbler's idiom when he blusters, 'And do you now cull out a Holyday?' (56).[26] Although it is commonplace to dismiss these variations as compositional accidents, that practice is not safe. The text of *Julius Caesar* is the most error-free of all Folio plays.[27] It is possible that the copy for the Folio discriminated between 'Holiday' and 'Holy Day'. Shakespeare's Cobbler is arguing that, yes, men can make a holiday. Their calendar controversy had made it irritatingly clear to Elizabethans that this was so. But Murellus is scandalized:

> O you hard hearts, you cruell men of Rome,
> Knew you not *Pompey* ...?
>
> ...
>
> And when you saw his Chariot but appeare,
> Have you not made an Universall shout,
> That Tyber trembled underneath her bankes
>
> ...
>
> And do you now cull out a Holyday?
> [For one who] comes in Triumph over *Pompeyes* blood?
> Be gone,
> Runne to your houses, fall upon your knees,

Pray to the Gods to intermit the plague
That needs must light on this Ingratitude.

(43–62)

Murellus's hard hearts, God, plagues, chariots and trembling waters call to mind the Book of Exodus (M. Rose, 1992, 257). Shakespeare gleaned these unmistakable cue-words from Exodus chapters 4–14, verses which include Moses' imposition of a new calendar: 'And the LORD spake unto Moses and Aaron in the land of Egypt, saying, This month shall be unto you the beginning of months: it shall be the first month of the year to you' (Exodus 12:1–2). Elizabethans knew that Moses was a calendar-giver. Thanks to the English calendar controversy and the almanacs, they knew that Julius Caesar had imposed a calendar. Jesus Christ had proclaimed to the stunned ears of the Nazareth congregation that he had come to alter the calendar:

> The Spirit of the Lord is upon me, because he hath anointed me to preach the gospel to the poor; he hath sent me to heal the brokenhearted, to preach deliverance to the captives, and recovering of sight to the blind, to set at liberty them that are bruised,
>   To preach the acceptable year of the Lord.

This is Luke 4:16–19, the prescribed Gospel reading for 20 June 1599 Julian. English recusant Catholics would have read it on 10 June Julian. These words of Christ explain why calendar reform was a theological issue with colossal consequences. To follow Christ one *must* follow his calendar. But in 1599 which calendar was his? Was it Elizabeth's discredited Julian? Or was it Gregory's mathematical marvel? Then again, wasn't Christ's calendar the vast clockwork of the cosmos which caused the Sun to rise on the solstice at the aiming point of the axis of the Globe regardless of any human calendar?

From the liturgical calendar Shakespeare could have divined that Elizabethans who observed morning prayer on the 12th day of June would have found the assassination of Julius Caesar an apt subject for the premiere of a new play at a new theatre that afternoon. Sacrifice and bloodletting were associated with the founding of important edifices; Elizabethans believed that the mortar for the walls of the city of London had been mixed with blood. Lettered Elizabethans knew this association predated the Christian era; the cornerstones of the Roman Capitol were founded upon skulls. In Mark 12:10 Jesus glances at this tradition in the parable of the vineyard, predicting that his martyrdom will provide the foundation for a church: 'The stone which the builders refuse is made the head of the corner.' The liturgical calendar prescribed Mark 12 as the New Testament reading for the second lesson during morning prayer on 12 June. This chapter also contains Christ's famous reference to a Caesar when the Pharisees ask

> Is it lawfull to give tribute to Cesar, or not? Should we give it, or should we not give it? But he knew their hypocrisie, and said unto them, Why tempt yee me? Bring me a penie, that I may see it. So they brought it, and hee said unto them, Whose is this image and superscription? And they said unto him, Cesars. Then Jesus answered, and said unto them, Give to Cesar the things that are Cesars, and to God, those that are Gods.
>
> (Mark 12:14–17)

As he crafted his text of *Julius Caesar*, Shakespeare could have imagined that many Londoners who heard or read Mark 12 on the morning of 12 June would cross to the Bankside in the afternoon to render their pennies to Caesar.

But there is an irony in Flavius's challenge: 'Is this a Holiday?' which would have been particularly sharp for recusant Catholics on 12 June 1599. The 12/22 June was the (suppressed) feast of St Alban (fl. AD 300), England's first Christian martyr. The protomartyr's holy day had been struck from the calendar during the Henrican reforms. But Alban's history was in circulation, in Geoffrey of Monmouth's *Historia Regum Britanniae*, in Bede's *Ecclesiastical History*, and in John Lydgate's elaborately embroidered *Life of Saint Alban and Saint Amphibal* (1534).[28] It was Bede who inserted the date 22 June and the place of Alban's martyrdom into an already well-developed legend. Linking the martyrdom of the earliest English saint with 22 June awakened unmistakable resonances. Owing to the regression of the solstices against the flawed Julian calendar, the summer solstice fell on 22 June at the time of Alban's martyrdom. This links Alban with John Baptist, another protomartyr. Julius Caesar also figures prominently in the Alban back story, both in Lydgate's poem and in his sources.[29]

13/23 June: the Vigil of the Nativity of St John Baptist

Early Christians adopted Julius Caesar's date for the summer solstice as the Nativity of John Baptist.[30] The feast celebrated the birth of the son promised by the Angel Gabriel to Zacharias in Luke 1:5–25. John was

Christ's cousin, and his precursor. Because of the ten-day disparity between the rival Julian and Gregorian calendars, in 1599 the Vigil of the Nativity of St John Baptist fell on 13 June Julian. Shakespeare commemorated this holy day with the most expansive and carefully constructed of his temporal markers in *Julius Caesar*. The playwright infused into his Lupercal more than a dozen ahistorical details, all of them drawn from passages of Scripture which the prevailing liturgical calendar prescribed for reading on the Vigil of the Nativity of John Baptist.

North's *Plutarch* is universally acknowledged as Shakespeare's principal source for *Julius Caesar*. As James Siemon has observed, 'nowhere is the debt of Shakespearean drama to historical sources more pronounced ... Character, incident, imagery, even entire speeches are taken, sometimes verbatim, from North's Plutarch and incorporated into the play' (Siemon, 1985, 115). However, a substantial number of details in Shakespeare's portrait of the events on the Lupercal have no basis in Plutarch or in any of the conjectural sources.[31] For example, Tribune Flavius castigates the plebeians:

> And do you now put on your best attyre?
> And do you now cull out a Holyday?
> And do you now strew Flowers in his way,
> That comes in Triumph over *Pompeyes* blood?
>
> (55–8)

Shakespeare is conflating the Lupercal of 44 BC with Caesar's triumph in the autumn of 45 BC celebrating his victory over Pompey's sons at Munda (on 17 March). The conflation of these two occasions is Shakespeare's invention. He also invents Caesar's instruction to Antony:

> *Caes.* Forget not in your speed Antonio,
> To touch *Calphurnia*: for our Elders say.
> The Barren touched in this holy chace,
> Shake off their sterrile curse.
> *Ant.* I shall remember,
> When *Caesar* sayes, Do this; it is perform'd.
> *Caes.* Set on, and leave no Ceremony out.
>
> (94–100)

Shakespeare found a description of the running of the young men on the Lupercal in Plutarch, including the striking of women with the *februa* to cure infertility.[32] From Plutarch and Ovid, Shakespeare would have known that Antony ran the 'course' on the Lupercal because Caesar had appointed him Master Priest of the new college of Julian Lupercii created in Caesar's honour in 44 BC (Frazer, 1989, 391).[33] But Caesar's pietistic language ('holy chace … leave no Ceremony out') is the playwright's invention. In Suetonius Shakespeare would have found a hint of Caesar's longing for a male heir, and his decision to adopt Gaius Octavius, the son of his niece, Atia, by a wealthy equestrian *arriviste* (Holland, 1606, 34).[34] But Caesar's preoccupation with his posterity on the Lupercal is Shakespeare's invention, as is Caesar's characterization of Calpurnia's barrenness as a 'sterrile curse'. There is also a noteworthy ambivalence in Caesar's prefatory phrase 'our Elders say' which suggests that Caesar does not believe in the cure but does not wish to appear impious. Caesar's scepticism about a supernatural cure for Calpurnia's infertility is a Shakespearian invention – as is Caesar's famous encounter with a supernatural being:

> *Sooth. Caesar.*
> *Caes.* Ha? Who calles?
> *Cask.* Bid every noyse be still: peace yet againe.
> *Caes.* Who is it in the presse, that calles on me?
>   I heare a Tongue shriller then all the Musicke
>   Cry, *Caesar*: Speake, *Caesar* is turn'd to heare.
> *Sooth.* Beware the Ides of March.
> *Caes.* What man is that?
> *Brut.* A Sooth-sayer bids you beware the Ides of March.
> *Caes.* Set him before me, let me see his face.
> *Cassi.* Fellow, come from the throng, look upon *Caesar*.
> *Caes.* What sayst thou to me now? Speak once againe:
> *Sooth.* Beware the Ides of March.
> *Caes.* He is a Dreamer, let us leave him: Passe.

> (101–14)

Plutarch reported that the Soothsayer

> had geven *Caesar* warning long time affore, to take heede of the day of the Ides of Marche, for on that day he shoulde be in great daunger. That day being come, *Caesar* going unto the Senate house, and speaking merily to the Soothsayer, tolde him, the Ides of Marche be come: so be they, softly aunswered the Soothsayer, but yet are they not past.

> (North, 1579, 793)

Shakespeare invents a meeting between Caesar and the Soothsayer on the Lupercal, and then employs the final passage of Plutarch's anecdote almost verbatim at the opening of Act 3. After Caesar pronounces the Soothsayer 'a Dreamer', all exit except Cassius and Brutus, and the great scene of subornation begins:

> *Cassi.* Will you go see the order of the course?
> *Brut.* Not I.
> *Cassi.* I pray you do.
>
> (116–18)

Although Plutarch provides a vivid description of Antony offering a crown to Caesar, Shakespeare moves this action off-stage and instead presents an invented dialogue between Cassius and Brutus. (See discussion of their conference in Chapter 10 below.) While they confer, three great shouts are heard. When Casca re-enters, the pair question him about the noise. Casca's report closely follows Plutarch: Antony made multiple offers of a crown to Caesar and the plebeians cheered each time Caesar rejected it (North, 1579, 792).[35] But Casca's report varies from Plutarch on essential points. Plutarch reports only two offers of a crown; Shakespeare invents a third. Plutarch's Antony offered Caesar a 'Diadeame'. Shakespeare invents a 'coronet': 'I sawe *Marke Antony* offer him a Crowne, yet 'twas not a Crowne neyther, 'twas one of these Coronets'. (339–41). According to Casca, Caesar does not immediately depart after rejecting the coronet three times; instead, Shakespeare invents a seizure. His Casca describes how

> the rabblement howted, and clapp'd their chopt hands, and threw uppe their sweatie Night-cappes, and uttered such a deale of stinking breath, because *Caesar* refus'd the Crowne, that it had (almost) choaked *Caesar*: for hee swoonded, and fell downe at it.
>
> (347–52)

Caesar's swoon on the Lupercal is Shakespeare's invention.[36] Casca's report quickens Cassius:

> *Cassi.* But soft I pray you: what, did *Caesar* swound?
> *Cask.* He fell downe in the Market-place, and foam'd at mouth, and was speechlesse.
>
> (355–7)

Caesar's chronic 'falling sickness', epilepsy, is reported by Plutarch.[37]

But the seizure on the Lupercal and Caesar's specific symptoms – Caesar 'foam'd at mouth' and was 'speechlesse' – are Shakespeare's inventions. Casca reports that when Caesar came to himself he said

> If hee had done, or said any thing amisse, he desir'd their Worships to thinke it was his infirmitie. Three or foure Wenches where I stood, cryed, Alasse good Soule, and forgave him with all their hearts: But there is no heed to be taken of them; if *Caesar* had stab'd their Mothers, they would have done no lesse.
>
> (374–8)

The worshipful 'wenches' and their sympathy for Caesar are Shakespeare's invention. On hearing this, Cassius asks if Cicero was present. Casca reports he was, and that Cicero passed a remark in Greek – another of Shakespeare's inventions. (See Appendix 7.)

Having rewritten Plutarch's narrative of the off-stage crowning scene, Shakespeare now provides proof that Casca's report is to be accepted within the dramatic framework of the play. When Caesar and his train re-enter, their demeanour has changed. Brutus observes

> The angry spot doth glow on *Caesars* brow,
> And all the rest, looke like a chidden Traine;
> *Calphurnia*'s Cheeke is pale, and *Cicero*
> Lookes with such Ferret, and such fiery eyes
> As we have seene him in the Capitoll
> Being crost in Conference, by some Senators.
>
> (285–90)

This tableau of Caesar and his distressed entourage is Shakespeare's invention. Finally, as Caesar leaves the stage Shakespeare injects a memorable touch of human frailty into the great man. His Caesar confides to Antony: 'Come on my right hand, for this eare is deafe, / And tell me truely, what thou think'st of him [Cassius]' (315–16). Caesar's deafness is Shakespeare's invention, too.

Let me abstract the events on the Lupercal as Shakespeare presents them:

> During a once-in-a-lifetime moment of personal distinction, an elderly priest wearing a purple robe encounters a supernatural being. Though the priest's wife has long been barren, the seer predicts the birth of a son. Out of sight, the priest is offered a coronet. He suffers a seizure which leaves him speechless. The episode evokes sympathy among the

bystanders, and a commentary in Greek. We learn that the priest is partially deaf.

With the exception of Caesar's purple robe, Shakespeare's portrait of the events on the Lupercal depends on a series of details which have no precedent in Plutarch, or in any of the conjectural sources of the play:

1 the conflation of Caesar's triumph with a religious festival
2 Caesar's instructions to Calpurnia to stand in Antony's way
3 Caesar's pious language ('holy chace ... leave no Ceremony out')
4 the reference to the childlessness of Caesar and Calpurnia
5 Caesar calls Calpurnia's barrenness a 'sterrile curse'
6 Caesar's scepticism towards a supernatural cure for sterility
7 Caesar's meeting with the Soothsayer on the Lupercal
8 the 'off-stage' crown scene, which Plutarch describes 'on-stage'
9 the third offer of the crown
10 the coronet
11 Caesar's swoon, and
12 the symptom – 'foam'd at mouth' – which accompanies it
13 Caesar's speechlessness
14 the 'wenches' who cried 'Alasse good Soule'
15 the presence of an observer who comments in Greek
16 the signs of distress on Caesar and his train as they re-enter
17 Caesar's deafness in his left ear

Although these details have long been ascribed to Shakespeare's invention, I will try to demonstrate that each is drawn from the Gospel reading prescribed for the Vigil of St John Baptist: St Luke's report of the annunciation of the birth of John to Zacharias.[38] The text in the Geneva Bible runs:

5 In the time of Herode King of Iudea, there was a certeine Priest named Zacharias, of the course of Abia: & his wife was of the daughters of Aaron, and her name was Elisabet.
6 Bothe were iust before God, and walked in all the commandements and ordinance of the Lord, without reprofe.
7 And they had no childe, because that Elisabet was barren: and both were well stricken in age.
8 And it came to passe, as he executed the Priests office before God, as his course came in order.
9 According to the custome of the Priests office, his lot was to burne

incense, when he went into the Temple of the Lord.

10 And the whole multitude of the people were without in prayer, while the incense was burning.

11 Then appeared unto him an Angel of the Lord, standing at the right side of the Altar of incense.

12 And when Zacharias saw him, he was troubled, and feare fell upon him.

13 But the Angel sayd unto him, Feare not, Zacharias: for thy prayer is heard, and thy wife Elisabet shall beare the a sonne, and thou shalt call his name John.

14 And thou shalt have joy and gladnesse, and many shall rejoyce at his birth.

15 For hee shall be great in the sight of the Lord, and shall neither drinke wine, nor strong drinke: and he shalbe filled with the holy Ghost, even from his mothers wombe.

16 And many of the children of Israel shall he turn to their Lord God.

17 For he shall goe before him in the spirit and power of Elias, to turne the hearts of the fathers to the children, and the disobedience to the wisdome of the just men, to make ready a people prepared for the Lord.

18 Then Zacharias said unto the angel, Whereby shall I know this? for I am an olde man, and my wife is of a great age.

19 And the Angell answered, and sayd unto him, I am Gabriel that stand in the presence of God, and am sent to speak unto thee, and to shew thee these good tidings.

20 And behold, thou shalt be dumme, and not be able to speake, until the day that these things be done, because thou beleevest not my wordes, which shalbe fulfilled in their season.

21 Now the people waited for Zacharias, and marveiled that he taried so long in the Temple.

22 And when hee came out, hee could not speake unto them: then they perceived that hee had seene a vision in the Temple: for hee made signes unto them, and remained dumme.

23 And when it came to passe, when the daies of his office were fulfilled, that he departed to his owne house.

24 And after those dayes, his wife Elisabet conceived, and hid her selfe five moneths, saying,

25 Thus hath the Lord dealt with me, in the daies wherein he looked on me, to take from mee my rebuke among men.

(Luke 1:5–25)

Both Caesar and Zacharias were priests who lived in the Herodian age and were married to a barren wife. Caesar's epithet for Calpurnia's barrenness, 'sterrile curse',[39] parallels Elisabeth's view of her infertility as a 'rebuke'. To emphasize Caesar's priestly status, Shakespeare puts oddly pietistic language into his mouth: 'holy chace ... leave no Ceremony out' – hardly the diction we would expect from a dictator celebrating his triumph over the sons of Pompey at the battle of Munda in 45 BC. On the Lupercal and in the scenes at Caesar's house on the morning of the Ides, Shakespeare emphasizes the priestly dimension of Caesar, who had been *Pontifex Maximus* of Rome for twenty years. Like Caesar and Calpurnia, Zacharias and Elisabeth are 'well stricken in age' (Luke 1:7). Caesar (b. 100 BC) was fifty-six at the time of his murder. Though the date of Calpurnia's birth is lost, she married Caesar in 59 BC, and had been his wife fifteen years.[40] By combining the Lupercal of 44 BC with the celebration of Caesar's triumph in 45 BC, Shakespeare conflated a religious festival with the apogee of Caesar's career. Luke's Zacharias is also at the apogee of his career as he enters the Temple to burn incense.[41] Since the number of Jewish priests at that time was *c.* eight thousand (Jeremias, 1969, 200), 'the privilege of offering incense before the Lord could normally be expected only once or twice in a lifetime' (Nolland, 1989, 27).[42] Although Plutarch describes Antony's offer of a crown to Caesar 'on-stage', one of Shakespeare's inventions is to relocate Antony's offer of the crown 'off-stage.' In Luke 1:10 Zacharias goes 'off-stage' when he enters the Temple's altar of incense.[43] Luke's narrative shifts to the point-of-view of the congregation: 'And the whole multitude of the people were without in prayer, while the incense was burning' (Luke 1:10). Shakespeare may be winking at the worshippers outside the Temple when Casca reports Caesar addressed the plebeians as 'their Worships' (374).

Both Caesar and Zacharias encounter a supernatural being. Luke begins his report, 'Then appeared unto him an Angel of the Lord standing at the right side of the altar of incense' (Luke 1:11). Luke's description of the Angel standing 'on the right side of the altar' concords with the layout of the communion table in Elizabethan churches. (Figure 3).[44] The 'right side' of the altar corresponds to the north side of English churches of Shakespeare's day. The Gospel was preached from this side, which was considered most favourable or honourable. The Angel's appearance at the right of the altar 'would convey to Zacharias that the angel's visit to him was not ominous' (Fitzmyer, 1985, 325). Luke writes, 'And when Zacharias sawe him [the Angel], he was troubled, and feare fell upon him' (Luke 1:12). In most biblical confrontations

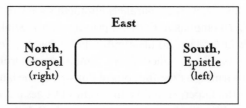

Figure 3. Orientation of communion table in English churches

with divine incarnations, humans kneel or prostrate themselves at the moment of recognition.[45] Luke reports only that 'Feare fell' upon Zacharias because the old priest was already lying prostrate.[46] Zacharias's prostration concords with Shakespeare's invention of Caesar's swoon. The Angel prophesies that Zacharias will have a son. 'But the Angel said unto him, Feare not, Zacharias: for thy prayer is heard, and thy wife Elisabet shal beare thee a sonne, and thou shalt call his name Iohn' (Luke 1:13). There is an ironic parallel between the Angel's good news and the Soothsayer's warning to Caesar. By the terms of Caesar's will, upon his death Octavius would become his son and heir. Shakespeare had good cause to recognize a connection between the sons of Caesar and Zacharias. The birthday of Octavius was 23 September, Christianity's traditional date of the conception of John Baptist.

Another parallel between Caesar and Zacharias arises from their response to the supernatural being. Zacharias expresses scepticism: 'Then Zacharias said unto the Angel, Whereby shal I knowe this? for I am an olde man, and my wife is of a great age' (Luke 1:18). Shakespeare's Caesar is sceptical towards the Soothsayer's warning: 'He is a Dreamer, let us leave him: Passe' (114). Commentators have read Caesar's remark as a blunt dismissal of the Soothsayer.[47] This is not safe. In a play marked by uncanny, prophetic dreams, Caesar's epithet – 'Dreamer' – demands scrutiny.[48] Every other appearance of the word in Shakespeare is associated with a preternatural vision which proves true. For example, although King John dismisses Peter of Pomfret as a 'dreamer' (4.1.153), his prophecy proves true 'That ere the next Ascension Day at noon, / Your highness should deliver up your crown' (4.1.147–52).[49] In the dream- and prophecy-ridden environment of *Julius Caesar*, Caesar's judgement that the Soothsayer is a 'Dreamer' conveys not disdain but misgiving.

In response to Zacharias's scepticism, the Angel reveals his identity.

He identifies himself as Gabriel, reprimands Zacharias for doubting his holy word, and punishes him: 'And behold, thou shalt be domme ...' This concords with Casca's report that Caesar fell down and was 'speechlesse'. Luke's narrative then shifts to the point of view of the people outside the temple. Like Zacharias's emerging from the temple, Shakespeare's Caesar re-enters with his train. Like the Jews awaiting Zacharias, Brutus perceives 'signs' that an extraordinary event has passed: Calpurnia looks 'pale'; Cicero's eyes are red; all the rest appear 'chidden' – reprimanded, as Zacharias is reprimanded by Gabriel (Luke 1:19–20). Brutus perceives 'the angry spot doth glow on *Caesars* brow'. This detail has no basis in Plutarch, and scholars have not been able to explain it. But 'angry spot' could describe a condition of blotchy redness of the skin known as *naevus flammeus*, the flaming spot – 'A hypertrophied state of the blood-vessels of the skin, forming spots or elevations of a red or purplish colour' (*OED*). Among the superstitious, the *naevus* has been called 'mother's kiss' or 'angel's kiss'. One biblical commentary nearly contemporary with *Julius Caesar* associates the condition with contact with the Holy Spirit: 'The Image of God ... perhaps in them [who] hath more naeves and blemishes' (*OED*).[50] Shakespeare's Caesar also exhibited another symptom associated with supernatural contact; according to Casca, he 'foam'd at mouth'. In Shakespeare's time, Caesar's chronic epilepsy was called '*morbus sacra*' – the sacred disease – because its cause was believed to be the visitation of a divine or supernatural spirit. Luke reports Christ healing a boy who foamed at the mouth.[51] In Luke's narrative the Jews waited impatiently for Zacharias and 'marveiled that he taried so long' (1:21). The Jews could not disperse to their homes until the priest emerged and delivered a closing blessing. When the old priest finally emerges, he cannot speak. But the Jews' impatience is transformed to sympathy when they recognize he has seen a vision (Luke 1:22). Their sympathy parallels Casca's report that 'Three or foure Wenches cryed, Alasse good Soule, and forgave him with all their hearts' (374–6).

Shakespeare's source in Plutarch recorded that Antony offered the crown to Caesar twice. But the playwright invents a third offer, which concords with Luke's (4:1–13) version of the temptation of Christ by the devil.[52] Shakespeare also substitutes a 'coronet' for the 'crowne' or 'Daideame' which Plutarch describes: 'yet 'twas not a Crowne neyther, 'twas one of these Coronets' (339–41).[53] There is an important distinction between Plutarch's 'crown' and Shakespeare's 'coronet'. A crown is a 'cincture or covering for the head, made of or adorned with precious metals and jewels, worn by a monarch as a mark or symbol of sovereignty' (*OED* crown n.2.a). In Shakespeare's time 'coronet' also signified 'a chaplet or garland of flowers for the head' particularly formed of 'a whorl of small flowers as in Labiates'(*OED* coronet n.2.b). These 'labiates' are a class of undershrubs which include the so-called 'dead' nettles known for their thorns. By inventing a 'coronet' Shakespeare conjures an image of the soon-to-be-martyred priest wearing a purple robe being offered a coronet of nettles. *Now* we can understand why Shakespeare moved this tableau off-stage. In his funeral oration Antony will describe his coronet as 'a Kingly Crowne' (1633). At Philippi Octavius will chide Brutus, 'Witnesse the hole you made in Caesars heart, / Crying long live, Haile Caesar' (2362–3). These reminiscences complete Shakespeare's iteration of the Gospel accounts of the mocking of Christ: Romans dressing him in a purple robe, placing a coronet of thorns upon his head, and mocked him with the cry, 'Hail, King of the Jews' (Matthew 27:29; Mark 15:18).

Shakespeare's portrait of Caesar on the Lupercal contains one more memorable invention: Caesar's deafness. This detail has no basis in Plutarch or any of the conjectural sources. Scholars have concluded that Shakespeare invented this detail to emphasize the human frailty of Caesar.[54] But Caesar's deafness has a precedent in Luke so conspicuous that Shakespeare could not have overlooked it. When Elisabeth's child is born, the godfathers determine to name the boy 'Zacharias, after the name of his father' (Luke 1:59). Mindful of the Angel's instructions, Elisabeth insists the child be named John. The godfathers refuse, arguing from Jewish tradition which requires newborns to be named for deceased ancestors: 'There is none of thy kindred that is named with this name' (Luke 1:61). In frustration, the godfathers 'Then made signes to his father [Zacharias], how he would have him called' (Luke 1:62). The making of signs to Zacharias indicates that the old priest is *deaf* as well as dumb. The word which Luke used to describe Zacharias as he emerged from the Temple was the Greek *kophos* – meaning, 'blunt or dull'. In the New Testament *kophos* is used 'in a figurative sense as both deaf and dumb' (Fitzmyer, 1985, 329), and 'more often the latter' (Nolland, 1989, 33). Zacharias's deafness provided Shakespeare's cue to create a Caesar who is deaf in one ear. If valid, this inference creates a problem in logic. According to Luke, Zacharias's hearing is not restored until *after* the birth of his son. If Shakespeare followed Luke to the letter, his

Caesar would remain deaf until after the 'birth' of his son Octavius – that is, until after Caesar's death. Shakespeare's solution to this dilemma is to make his Caesar deaf in his left ear only. Although this notion may seem frivolous, there is precedent for it in the Gospel. According to Luke, Gabriel stood at the right of the altar as Zacharias lay prostrate before him. We may, therefore, infer the blocking in Figure 4. Gabriel's deafening voice was directed towards Zacharias's left ear. Caesar is deaf in his left ear.[55]

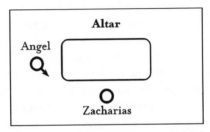

Figure 4. Zacharias encounters Gabriel

In sum, Shakespeare infused the events on the Lupercal with seventeeen invented details, all of which can be traced to the Gospel of Luke 1:5–25. Luke's text runs only to twenty-one verses and 531 words. This is intensive, methodical borrowing.

Julius Caesar is not the first work in which Shakespeare parodied the Gospel of Luke. T. W. Baldwin recognized borrowings in *The Rape of Lucrece*.[56] Shakespeare chose to fuse his Lupercal with Luke's tale of the nativity of John Baptist because Zacharias's encounter with Gabriel was the prescribed Gospel for 23 June. In 1599 the Gregorian 23 June fell on 13 June Julian. But in addition to this elaborate marker for the Vigil of St John Baptist, Shakespeare also embedded an unmistakable temporal marker for John Baptist's feast day, 24 June. Early in his funeral oration Antony characterizes his relationship with the dead Caesar, declaring, 'He was my Friend, faithful, and just to me' (1622). Although this phrase sounds homely and mild to secular modern ears, the first Epistle of John proclaims, 'If we acknowledge our sinnes, he is faithfull and just, to forgive us our sinnes, and to cleanse us from all unrighteousnesse' (1 John 1:9). This passage of Scripture lay at the heart of Elizabethans' hope for salvation. The Geneva gloss cites these words emphatically as the *sine qua non*: 'So then our salvation hangeth upon the free promise of God, who because he is faithful and just, will performe that which he hath promised' (1560, sig. Ooo3v). The liturgy prescribed this passage of 1 John 1 for St John Baptist's Day, 14/24 June 1599.

Gregory's reform and the compression of time in Julius Caesar

The proximate cause of the discordances between the Protestant and Catholic holy days in the summer of 1599 was Pope Gregory's decision to excise ten days from the calendar for October 1582. In the Gregorian calendar for that year the night of 4 October became the eve of 15 October. In performance, one of the curiosities of *Julius Caesar* is that the night of the Lupercal appears to become the eve of the Ides of March. Commentators have noted how Shakespeare manipulates dialogue and action in 1.3 so that two nights which fell four weeks apart (14/15 February – 14/15 March) coalesce into one.[57] Scholars have long recognized that Shakespeare attached importance to this compression of time: 'Indeed, if Shakespeare had omitted all reference to the holiday [Lupercal], he could have begun the play with Cassius' approach to Brutus, and avoided the conflation of a month's time' (Liebler, 1988, 175). Of course, the compression of time is not unusual in Shakespeare's plays. Only *The Tempest* strictly observes the unities. *The Comedy of Errors* compresses eight hours, *Hamlet* digests months, *Macbeth* sixteen years, and whole generations are engrossed in the three plays of *Henry VI*. In each of these works Shakespeare effortlessly (and seamlessly) compresses large spans of historical time into concentrated dramatic time. What is unusual in *Julius Caesar* is that Shakespeare contrives to make his audience *keenly aware* of the compression of time by injecting a series of reminders that the night of the Lupercal and the eve of the Ides of March are merging into one night. On the Lupercal Brutus tells Cassius that he would not be further moved towards rebellion (265–6). On the eve of the Ides – a month later – Brutus asserts that he has not slept since Cassius moved him (682–3). When Cassius apologizes for arriving so late, Brutus reiterates that he has been awake all night (715). On the Lupercal Cassius declares he will see Brutus that night (610–12). On the eve of the Ides Cassius visits Brutus before dawn (713). On the Lupercal Cassius says he will throw letters in at Brutus's window (422–3). On the eve of the Ides Cassius instructs Cinna to throw a letter in at Brutus's window (591–2), and Lucius discovers such a letter (653–4).

As if these were not sufficient to draw attention to his compression of time, Shakespeare adds another tier of precedents and succedents. On the Lupercal Cassius asks Casca to sup with him (393). Casca declines saying he has a prior engagement (394). On the eve of the Ides Shakespeare mischievously reminds his audience of Casca's prior engagement when Cicero asks Casca if he has brought Caesar home (433). Although Cassius and Casca had agreed on the Lupercal to dine on the morrow (395–8), on the eve of the Ides they apparently have not done so. The effect of this relentless series of precedents and succedents is to leave the indelible impression that the morning of the Ides follows the unruly night of the Lupercal without interval. No one has been able to say why Shakespeare created this effect. But Pope Gregory's calendar reform achieved the same effect when he declared the night of 4 October the eve of 15 October 1582.

Calendar, liturgy, audience

Suggesting this new perspective on Shakespeare's *Julius Caesar* and the troubled Julian liturgical calendar implies that Elizabethans were more alert to temporal symbolism than we are. There are compelling reasons to believe this is so. Though enforcement may have been desultory, compulsory church attendance was legally required of all Elizabethans.

> Absence from church on Sundays or holy days was punishable by a fine of 12 pence for each offense, the sum to be levied by the churchwardens for the use of the poor of the parish. The later Elizabethan Acts against Recusants and Puritans contained even stiffer penalties, including imprisonment and in extreme cases, death.
>
> (Davies, 1970, 220)

William Shakespeare's own father was fined for non-attendance (Kay, 1992, 37). The effect of this legislation was to ensure that 'most of Shakespeare's contemporaries, if not all of them, were exposed week after week, holy day after holy day, to the liturgical formulations of their universal prayer book' (Hassel, 1979, 7). In 1559 the Act of Uniformity (1 Elizabeth I, c. 2) had standardized the calendar, the prayer book and the order of liturgical readings. The Act provided that ministers of the established Church 'shall from and after the feast of the nativity of St. John Baptist next coming (24 June 1559), be bound to say and use the Matins, Evensong, celebration of the Lord's Supper, and administration of each of the sacraments, and all their common and open prayer, in such order and form' as prescribed in the Book of Common Prayer. In 1571 the text and order of the homilies was standardized. Even the noting of the Psalter was ultimately conformed.[58] Hassel has shrewdly characterized these documents as the 'dominant cultural force' in Elizabethan society (1979, 8). Elizabeth's calendar was more widely disseminated than even her Bible. Together, the Bible, Book of Common Prayer and the Julian liturgical calendar shaped the Elizabethans' conception of time.

The Elizabethans' experience of the Bible was also different from our own. Although every English church was required to own a Bible and maintain it available for reading, the individual's access to written Scripture was limited – and a majority of Elizabethans were probably illiterate. The population's principal contact with the Bible was *aural* – via the calendarized readings which, along with the Eucharist, comprised the foci of the sacred service. The distinction between *reading* the Bible and *hearing* the Bible should not be minimized. Not only the medium but the message was different. A printed Bible offers us a chronological narrative history. But the aural liturgy 'is not sequential, not narrative or historical in focus, but thematic' (King, 1998, 30). The readings prescribed by the liturgical calendar were 'arranged in a recurrent, interwoven pattern of significances which vicariously measured the passage of time' (King, 1998, 31). Beginning each year in Advent, the Church calendar and its cadence of liturgical readings recapitulated events surrounding the conception, life and death, and resurrection of Jesus Christ. Through endless repetition, passages of Scripture became inseparably linked with particular holy days. As noted, some links – particularly those to recurring solar holy days – were more obvious than others. For example, St Luke's narrative of the annunciation to Zacharias and the birth of John (Luke 1:5–41) was inextricably bound up with 24 June, the official Midsummer Day, the feast of the saint's nativity. Other links – particularly those between passages of Scripture and lunar 'movable' holy days – will be obscure to secular moderns, but were vivid to Elizabethans. For example: the reading of the Books of Samuel was prescribed to begin with the evening lesson on 29 March. This was the earliest possible date for the Octave of Easter. Each year the reading of Samuel continued to 24 April, the latest possible date for the Vigil of Easter. Though the connection is obscure to secular moderns, Elizabethan churchgoers had reason to perceive an intimate association between the Books of Samuel and the coming of Easter.

A third reason why Shakespeare's first audiences were more alert to temporal symbolism was that exploitation of the calendar as a literary device was an established element of contemporary aesthetics. Poets and playwrights before Shakespeare had routinely exploited the calendar as a structural device. To cite one example, Edmund Spenser's *Shepheardes Calendar* (1579) comprises twelve eclogues which follow the months of the year, and his *Epithalamion* (1595) digests the twenty-four hours of Midsummer Day. Shakespeare was certainly aware of this literary convention, and recent scholarship by François Laroque, Richard Wilson and David Wiles has begun to reveal how Shakespeare exploited it. Laroque suggests that, by connecting scenes with recognizable holy days, Shakespeare infused his plays with religious and cultural overtones which are dim to modern ears but resounded loudly for Elizabethans. When Nurse in *Romeo and Juliet* 'refers to the Lammastide festival [1 August] to work out Juliet's age, the Elizabethan public would, as it counted back nine months, immediately arrive at the implied festival of Hallowe'en as the likely date of Juliet's conception' (Laroque, 1993, 205). Elizabethans had many reasons to be more alert than we are to what Laroque calls 'temporal symbolism' in Shakespeare's texts. Generally, they knew their Bible better than we do, attended church more regularly – and their primary experience of Scripture was aural, thematic and intimately tied to the calendar. Furthermore, Shakespeare was following an enormously famous archetype – the Mystery plays – when he exploited the linkage between Scripture and the liturgical calendar in *Julius Caesar*. But his debt to this archetype had not been recognized until 1998.

Notes

1 By adjusting the calendar ten days to the radix of the Council of Nicaea instead of the thirteen days necessary to re-establish Caesar's original calendar, in 1582 Pope Gregory effectively moved Midsummer Day (the summer solstice) from 24 June to 21 June.

2 Amplified perhaps by the homonyms of 'Beare' (bear) and 'Pause' (paws).

3 See Marlorate, 1573, fol. 113v: 'For truely the Bishop of Rome matcheth the royall power … of Julius Caesar, boasting himselfe to be Lord of the world, and that the autoritie of both the swords belongeth unto him by commission from Christ.' (See Appendix 6.)

4 Later in *Julius Caesar* Shakespeare again associates Antony with Revelation 13. Antony's '*Octavius*, Listen great things' (1896–7) mimics Revelation 13:5, and identifies Antony with the 'mouth that spake great things & blasphemies'.

5 I suspect that the Scriptural roots of Antony's prophecy over the dead body of Caesar have been difficult to identify because Shakespeare may be mining St Peter's prophecy of the coming of the Holy Ghost in Acts 2:17–36, which is itself dependent upon the apocalyptic Book of Joel. Where Peter speaks of God 'loosing the sorrowes of hell' (Acts 2:24), Antony speaks of Caesar and Ate 'come hot from Hell'. Antony's reference to a 'Monarkes voice' may be an echo of Joel: 'The Lord shall also roare out of Zion, and utter his voyce from Jerusalem' (Joel 3:16). Antony's 'foule deede' that shall 'smell above the earth' recalls Joel's 'stinke shall come up' (Joel 2:20), etc.

6 Much has been written about the curiously bifurcated character of Shakespeare's *Julius Caesar*. For example: de Gerenday, 1974, and Palmer, 1952. Also Rabkin, 1964.

7 In his *Philippics* Cicero chides Antony for neglecting these duties (Cicero, *Philippics* 353).

8 Shakespeare employs the word in this sense in *MV* 2.2.26, and elsewhere.

9 Shakespeare knew from Ovid that the Lupercii ran naked through the streets of Rome. (Frazer, 1989, 77). In his *Philippics* Cicero chides Antony for offering Caesar a crown and making a public speech while naked and drunk (Bailey, 1986, 85). But Cicero was exaggerating, and Ovid taking poetic licence; the Lupercii wore an apron or thong to cover their privities. The Antony who appeared in Shakespeare's Lupercalian procession was scantily dressed.

10 In Shakespeare's plays of this period (1598–1601) a variation of a character's name is consistently an act of deception. Henry V goes by Hal, Harry, and masquerades as Harry Le Roy (1598–9). Rosalind and Celia conceal their identities and intentions by changing their names to Ganymede and Aliena (1600). Viola poses as a miniature Caesar ('Cesario') to deceive Orsino and Olivia. Sebastian deceives Antonio with the name Roderigo. Feste masquerades as Sir Topas (1599).

11 As the Lupercalian procession enters in 1.2, Casca quiets the rowdy crowd: 'Peace ho, *Caesar* speakes' (88), and 'Bid every noise be still: peace yet againe' (103).

12 I believe this is one of two in-jokes which point to Shakespeare as the actor playing Caesar. The other comes when Cassius complains that Caesar 'bad the Romans / Marke him, and write his Speeches in their Bookes' (223–4). There is no precedent for this claim in Plutarch. If Shakespeare played Caesar, he probably played Polonius, who portrayed Caesar and was accounted a good actor by his own report.

13 Actually, thirty-five words. In *Julius Caesar* Shakespeare rewrites the

political ambush story he exploited in *The Rape of Lucrece* (1593–4). In that tale Lucius Junius Brutus masqueraded as a buffoon (Latin *brutus* adj. = dull, stupid) until Tarquin's rape of Lucrece provided him with a pretext for revolution. In *Julius Caesar* Shakespeare inverts the roles: Marcus Brutus is a bastard masquerading as a man of *gravitas*, while the trivial, marginalized Antony eventually proves to be a 'shrewd contriver'. To his ruin, Tarquin underestimated Lucius Junius just as Shakespeare's Brutus underestimates Antony. As if to emphasize the contrast between the two Bruti, Shakespeare co-opts the elder's name – Lucius – for the invented boy-servant whom Brutus treats with so much kindness. Lucius Junius Brutus had put his boys to death.

14 '*Antonius* very curteously and lovingly did comfort them [his friends], and prayed them to depart: and wrote unto *Theophilus* governor of CORINTHE, that he would see them safe, and helpe to hide them in some secret place, until they had made their way and peace with *Caesar*' (North, 1579, 1002).

15 'This laurel crowne was afterwards put upon the head of one of *Caesars* statues or images, the which one of the Tribunes pluckt off. The people liked his doing therein so well, that they wayted on him home to his house, with great clapping of hands. Howbeit *Caesar* did turne them out of their offices for it. This was a good incoragement for *Brutus* & *Cassius* to conspire his death' (North, 1579, 976).

16 Brutus: 'He [Caesar] would be crown'd: / How that might change his nature, there's the question? / It is the bright day, that brings forth the Adder, / And that craves warie walking: Crowne him that, / And then I graunt we put a Sting in him, / That at his will he may doe danger with' (628–33).

17 Cicero agreed: '*debet vero solvitque praeclare*' (Bailey, 1986, 338).

18 Antony continues, 'Therefore let our Alliance be combin'd, / Our best Friends made, our meanes stretcht, / And let us presently go sit in Councell, / How covert matters may be best disclos'd, / And open Perils surest answered' (1889–93).

19 Deuteronomy 10 was the prescribed reading for the Feast of the Circumcision, observed on 1 January. According to Caesar's and Gregory's calendars, 1 January was the start of the New Year. But in 1599 the English reckoned the start of the new year on Lady Day, 25 March Julian. This concorded with the Ides of March in the Gregorian calendar, the day on which Elizabethans believed Christ was crucified in AD 33.

20 Antony's speech begins, 'Friends, Romans, Countrymen ...'. 'Friends' is something of a keyword with Shakespeare when used by a member of the aristocracy towards commoners. Henry V and Malcolm both use the word towards their social inferiors to suggest a relaxing of the barriers between the classes when no real relaxation exists. Antony's first word, 'Friends', is a clue that he will dissemble with the plebeians. Henry at *HS* 1.3.1, and 4.1.36 and 90; Malcolm at *MAC* 1.2.5.

21 A will is 'a person's formal declaration of his intention as to the disposal of his property or other matters to be performed after his death, most usually made in writing … [and] the document in which such intention is expressed. Formerly properly used only in reference to the disposal of real property, thus distinguished from a "testament" relating to personal property; whence the phrase … last will and testament' (*OED* n.1.IV.23. a). A testament was the document 'by which a person nominates an executor to administer his personal estate after his decease' (*OED* n.I.2).

22 The word derives from the Greek *diatheke*, which incorporated the Latin sense of both 'covenant' and 'will' (*OED* testament n. II).

23 'And when hee was now come neere to the going downe of the mount of Olives, the whole multitude of the disciples began to rejoyce, and to praise God with a loude voyce, for all the great workes that they had seeene, Saying, Blessed be the King that commeth in the Name of the Lord: peace in heaven, and glory in the highest places. Then some of the Pharises of the company said unto him, Master, rebuke thy disciples. But he answered, and said unto them, I tell you, that if these should holde their peace, the stones would cry' (Luke 19:37–40).

24 Matthew's report fulfils the psalmist's prophecy, 'They part my garments among them, and cast lots upon my vesture' (Psalm 22:18). Outside this context, 'vesture' makes only three other appearances in the Bible. Deuteronomy prescribes the wearing of a fringed 'vesture', i.e. the *talith*, worn by orthodox Jews as a sign of their adherence to the old law. And 'vesture' is applied metaphorically in Psalm 102:26, to which St Paul refers at Hebrews 1:12.

25 Shakespeare moves the murder of Cinna from day (North, 1579, 795) to night in order to create this confrontation.

26 See the discussion of the Folio's discrimination between 'state' and 'State' in Chapter 11.

27 Dover Wilson judged that 'there can be no doubt at all that the "copy" for *Julius Caesar* presented Jaggard's compositors with an unusually easy task. The verse-lining – a good touchstone for the quality of a manuscript play – has gone astray in a few instances, but they are very few, almost negligible' (J. D. Wilson, n.d., fol. 4r).

28 Alban probably was an historical figure. A church on the traditional site of his grave dates from AD 429, and his cult is reported in French sources as early as AD 480. Briefly: Alban was raised a pagan and travelled to Rome where he was knighted by Diocletian. On the journey, one of Alban's friends, Amphibalus, was converted to Christianity by Pope Zepherinus. During the violent suppression of the new faith in Roman Britain, Amphibalus took refuge at the home of Alban, and succeeded in converting him. When Roman legionaries came searching for Amphibalus, Alban gallantly exchanged clothes with his friend and allowed himself to be arrested, tried and cruelly martyred in his place.

29 Of Lydgate's first two hundred lines, half are devoted to Caesar's invasion of Britain. For example: 'Overmaystred was Brutis Albion / Bi Julius swerd, remembrid in scriptur. / Record the gospel, wher is division, / Frowarde discencion, of cas or aventur, / Thilk Region may no while endur / In prosperitie; for bi discord of tweyn / To subjeccion was brouht all Briteyn' (134–40).

30 Both Bede and Lydgate emphasize the connection between Alban and John Baptist. Lydgate's Alban performs miracles with water, and his Amphibalus dies praising the virtues of baptism.

31 Conjectural sources examined: Appian, Suetonius, Dio Cassius, Lucan, John of Salisbury's *Polycraticus*, Aquinas's *De Regimine Principum*, Dante, Petrarch, Elyot's *Governour*, Montaigne, and the plays *Il Cesare* (Pescetti, 1594), *Caesar's Revenge* (anon.), *Cornélie* (tr. Kyd, 1594).

32 'There are divers noble mens sonnes, young men, (and some of them Magistrats them selves that governe then) which run naked through the city, striking in sport them they meete in their way, with leather thonges, heare and all on, to make them geve place. And many noble women, and gentle women also, goe of purpose to stand in their way, and doe put forth their handes to be striken, as schollers hold them out to their schoolemaster, to be striken with the ferula: perswading them selves that being with childe, they shall have good deliverie, and also being barren, that it will make them to conceive with child' (North, 1579, 791–2).

33 Previously the Lupercal ceremonies had been in the care of two traditional colleges of priests, the Quinctilii and the Fabii.

34 Holland's translation was begun in 1603 and published in 1606. I use it here for convenience. Suetonius was available to Shakespeare in French (1381, 1541, 1556); Italian (1438 (Caesar only), 1539); Spanish (1547, 1596). The text was also available in Latin and Greek. The relevant passage in Holland's translation reads: '*Q Tubero* writeth, that from his [Caesar's] first Consulship unto the beginning of the Civil war, he was ever wont to write downe for his heire, Cn Pompeius, and to reade the saide will unto his soldiers in their publike assemblie. But in this last Testament of his, he ordained three Coheires, the newphews all of his sisters, To wit C. Octavius, of three fouth parts, L. Pinarius, and Q. Pedius of one fourth part remaining. In the latter end and bottome of this Testamentarie Instrument, he adopted also C. Octavius into his house & name; and many of those that aferwards murdered him [Caesar], he nominated for guardiers to his sonne, if it fortuned he had any borne.'

35. 'But when *Caesar* refused the Diadeame, then all the people together made an outcrie of ioy. Then *Antonius* offering it him againe, there was a second shoute of joy, but yet of a few. But when *Caesar* refused it againe the second time, then all the whole people showted. *Caesar* having made this proofe, found that the people did not like of it, and thereuppon rose out of his chayer, and commaunded the crowne be carried unto *Iupiter* in the Capitoll' (792).

36 An interpolation of an earlier event (North, 1579, 791).

37 'For as he did set his men in battell ray, the falling sickenesse tooke him, whereunto he was geven' (North, 1579, 788). Also in Suetonius: 'also very heathfull, saving that in his latter daies he was given to faint and swoune sodainly ... twice also in the midst of his martiall affaires, he was surprized with the falling sicknes' (Holland, 1606, 19).

38 St Luke begins with his famous four-verse salutation to 'Theophilus' (Luke 1:1–4). Then he turns to the so-called 'infancy narratives', the twinned accounts of the Angel Gabriel's annunciation of the promised birth of John the Baptist to Zacharias, and of the Christ child to the Blessed Virgin Mary. These 'infancy narratives' are uniquely Lucan.

39 The childlessness of Caesar and Calpurnia *was* due to her infertility. According to Plutarch, Caesar had fathered children including Julia, born to his second wife, Cornelia (c. 82 BC). Cleopatra claimed that Caesar had fathered her son Caesarion (b. 47 BC). Plutarch also glances at the gossip that Caesar fathered Marcus Brutus, an insinuation accepted as fact by Suetonious and Appian. Shakespeare appears to accept that Caesar fathered Cleopatra's son. Cf. *Antony and Cleopatra*: 'He [Caesar] ploughed her [Cleopatra], and she cropped' (2.2.235).

40 Luke records that Zacharias and Elisabeth were 'well stricken in age'. Shakespeare employs 'struck' in the sense of 'aged' in *Richard III*: 'We speak no treason, man. We say the King / Is wise and virtuous, and his noble Queen / Well struck in years, fair, and not jealous' (1.1.90–2). The woman described is another Elizabeth, the former Elizabeth Woodville, wife of Edward IV.

41 A linguistic detail in Luke 1:8 may be noteworthy: 'And it came to passe, as hee executed the Priests office before God, as his course came in order' (Luke 1:8). Shakespeare invented Caesar's instructions to Calpurnia: 'Stand you directly in *Antonio's* way, / When he doth run his course.' Shakespeare's use of the word 'course' may be coincidental, or he may have found it in Plutarch: '*Antonius*, who was Consull at that time, was one of them that ranne this holy course' (North, 1579, 792). But Shakespeare also invents Cassius's question to Brutus: 'Will you go see the order of the course?' (116). Shakespeare's two uses of 'run his course' and 'order of the course' are a parallel to the two appearances of 'course' in four verses of Luke. A note on etymology may be relevant. Luke's word for 'course', the Greek *epheemeria*, is rare in the Bible. It appears only three times (Nolland, 1989, 26). The word signifies a 'course' of priests (modern: order), which accounts for the Geneva Bible's awkward 'course came in order'. The translation of this phrase in the Rheims New Testament parallels Shakespeare's language: 'And it came to passe: when he executed the Priestly function in the order of his course.' Likewise, the translators of the 1611 King James Bible rendered the phrase: 'And it came to pass, as he executed the priest's office before God in the order of his course.'

42 The Jewish priesthood was 'divided into twenty-four courses, each of which provided in turn priestly service in the temple for one week, twice in the year' (Nolland, 1989, 26). 'The member of the course who would be privileged to enter the sanctuary to offer the incense was chosen by casting lots' (Fitzmyer, 1985, 323).

43 Luke uses the Greek *naos* to describe that area of the Temple, and to distinguish it from the *hieron*, the outer area which was 'either the Temple in general or the Temple precincts' where the public gathered for prayer. (Fitzmyer, 1985, 324). Plutarch reports the offer of the crown in the *foro Romano*, the central marketplace of Rome. Likewise, in Christ's time the temple precincts were used for commerce (Luke 19:46, Matthew 21:10–17).

44 Luke is careful about the 'blocking' of the scenes he describes. Whereas Matthew 12:9–14, Mark 3:1–6, and Luke 6:6–11 all report that Christ healed a man with a withered hand, only Luke records that the man's 'right hand was dried up'. The same three Gospels report the severing of the ear of the high priest's slave at Gesthesmene (Matthew 26:47–56, Mark 14:43–52, Luke 22:47–53). But only Luke and John (18:10) record 'strooke off his right eare'.

45 Among many others: Daniel's vision of Gabriel (Daniel 8:17); Simon-Peter's revelation (Luke 9:8); Paul's conversion (Acts 9:4).

46 'Although Zacharias would have been in the company of other priests for most of the ceremony, *m. Tamid* 6.3 seems to allow at the end for a brief moment of private prostration before God for the chief officiant. This will be the moment of encounter' with the Angel (Fitzmyer, 1985, 325).

47 For example: 'A line of magisterial finality ... and yet a grave error in judgment', Humphreys, 1984, 104n.

48 Calpurnia's dream of the assassination of Caesar (1069–72); the poet Cinna's dream of Caesar's summons (1814–15); Antony's prophecy after Caesar's death.

49 Shakespeare's third use of 'dreamer' is in *1 Henry IV* (3.1.146). Hotspur is railing against his uncle Owen Glendower: 'Sometime he angers me / With telling me of the moldwarp and the ant, / Of the dreamer Merlin and his prophecies' (3.1.144–6). Merlin is hailed by the Fool in Shakespeare's *King Lear* (3.2.79–96) as an astute judge of men.

50 Sclater, 1619, 229.

51 Luke 9:39 – 'he foameth'. Also: Matthew 17:14–21, and Mark 9:14–29 'hee fell downe on the ground wallowing and foaming' (20).

52 Mark (1:12–13) agrees.

53 In Plutarch's *Antony* the crown offered Caesar is 'a laurell crowne ... having a royall band or diademe wreathed about it, which in old time was the auncient marke and token of a king' (North, 1579, 975). In Plutarch's *Caesar* the crown is 'a Diadeame wreathed about with laurell' (North, 1579, 972).

54 For example: 'Again the irony of the overweening role embodied in the fallible person. Caesar's deafness is Shakespeare's invention' (Humphreys, 1984, 113n). 'Shakespeare's invention, although some critics believe that deafness (especially of the left ear) is associated with epilepsy' (Spevack, 1988, 63n).

55 Cf. Luke's report of Christ's arrest by the Pharisees and the severing of the ear of the high priest's slave (Luke 22:47–53). Luke and John record that the slave's right ear was struck off. Only Luke records that Christ 'touched his eare, & healed him' (Luke 22:51). This would have provided Shakespeare's cue to 'heal' Caesar's deafness in his right ear.

56 'The aged man that coffers up his gold / Is plagued with cramps, and gouts, and painful fits, / And scarce hath eyes his treasure to behold, / But like still-pining Tantalus he sits, / And useless barns the harvest of his wits, / Having no other pleasure of his gain / But torment that it cannot cure his pain', *The Rape of Lucrece* (855–61). Baldwin recognized this as a parody of Christ's parable of the rich man who would pull down his barns and build larger ones (Luke 12:13–21), including the Geneva gloss's reference to 'coffres and barnes' (Baldwin, 1963, 133–6).

57 'The words of Cicero, "Good Even, *Caska*: brought you *Caesar* home?", tend to confirm the impression that it is the night after the Lupercalian festivities, especially as we think of Casca as returning from the engagement that in the second scene he mentioned to Cassius ["I am promised forth"]. On the other hand, [Cicero's] words, "Comes *Caesar* to the Capitoll to morrow?" suggest that it is the eve of the Ides of March, and the storm, which is introduced here, and which is kept so prominently before the mind in the next two scenes, still further leads us to believe that the time of this scene is the night of March 14' (Anonymous, 1899, 277).

58 The depths to which Elizabeth and her bishops would sink to compel conformity – such as Archbishop Whitgift's notorious extralegal Commission and its indefensible *ex officio* oath – still burned bitterly in living memory when *Julius Caesar* came on the boards.

5

Shakespeare's *Corpus Christi* archetype

William Shakespeare was not the first English dramatist to exploit the links between Scripture and the calendar as a mode of discourse. In a finding of tremendous importance Pamela King has demonstrated that in the York Cycle of Corpus Christi Plays, the biblical scenes which are dramatized *and* their order of performance adapt and intergrate the sequence in which these texts are calendared for reading in the missal and breviary (King, 1998, 31ff.). When Shakespeare infused the text of *Julius Caesar* with markers to the liturgical calendar he was employing (or rediscovering) the established technique of the anonymous dramatist of the York Cycle.

In medieval England theatrical performance had been intimately connected with the liturgical calendar. Plays or pageants on religious subjects were regularly performed during the Christmas-Epiphany interval, at Candlemas, Midsummer and during Whitsun week (Furnivall, 1882, xviii ff.). But the principal occasion for theatrics was the feast of Corpus Christi. This medieval holy day of *Natalis Calicis* was rechristened *Corpus Christi* in 1264 by Pope Urban IV (the former Jacques Pantaléon, archdeacon of Liège). Its observance was moved to the Thursday after Trinity Sunday by Pope John XXII in 1317.[1] Within a few years the feast arrived in England.

> In 1322 the archbishop of York ordered it to be kept all over his province, and in 1325 a Corpus Christi guild was founded at Ipswich with the responsibility for a procession ... [The] years 1350–70 saw a surge in the foundation of the guilds. By the early fifteenth century every urban corporation and parish which has left records was observing the processions.
>
> (Hutton, 1994, 54)

Although the first players were clergy, medieval workmen's guilds eventually took up and divided the scenes among them. A number of these so-called 'Mystery plays' survive, including the Chester, York, Towneley and 'N-Town' cycles. 'The records for [Coventry and York] show the plays taking form rapidly in the 1440s, while at York the process occurred between 1433 and 1460. The Chester cycle expanded ... from a single play in 1474 ... into the full three-day sequence which evolved between 1521 and 1532' (Hutton, 1994, 59). Typically, the celebration began with solemn processions of the laity and divines. At York, the procession of divines was moved to the day after Corpus Christi *c.* 1468 (Nelson, 1974, 46). 'Theologically speaking, the feast of Corpus Christi celebrated the Real Presence of the Body of Christ in the Host at Mass' (Beadle and King, 1995, x). After the rejection of the doctrine of transubstantiation by the Reformed Church, the Mystery plays were suppressed in England. 'Between 1572 and 1576 [Grindal's] ecclesiastical commission ... forbade the Corpus Christi plays at Wakefield [and York] on the grounds that they degraded the life of Christ by representing it upon stage' (Hutton, 1994, 126). Some scholars have detected hints that young Will Shakespeare (b. 1564) may have seen the Mystery cycle at Coventry (Kay, 1992, 49). In a few cities – including London – the repressed Corpus Christi festivities recrudesced as secular festivals and Midsummer shows. Laroque cites an instance of a London Midsummer parade 'which included a pageant of Saint John the Baptist ... which was remarkably reminiscent of the Old Corpus Christi pageants' (Laroque, 1993, 58).

In the year of the Bankside's Globe debut, 1599, the date of Corpus Christi was 10 June Gregorian. The nominal date of the suppressed holy day in the Julian calendar would have been 7 June. If Shakespeare were writing *Julius Caesar* for a performance on 12 June one would expect the ghost of the defunct holy day to cast a shadow's shadow over at least some part of the play. In the opening scenes of *Julius Caesar* I believe Shakespeare indeed glances at the Mystery plays of Corpus Christi.

> *Flav.* Hence: home you idle Creatures, get you home:
> Is this a Holiday? What, know you not
> (Being Mechanicall) you ought not walke
> Upon a labouring day, without the signe
> Of your Profession? Speake, what Trade are thou?
> *Car.* Why Sir, a Carpenter.
>
> (5–10)

It is commonplace to note that the first plebeian follows the profession of Christ (Mark 6:3). But the appearance of a carpenter in the van of a band of plebeians had a connection with Corpus Christi which scholars have overlooked. Because of the association of their mystery with Christ, for more than a hundred years the Guild of Carpenters had led 'the general procession of the Feast of Corpus Christi' at Winchester (Gasquet, 1909, 329). On an English stage in 1599, a carpenter in the van of a band of plebeians on a holy day may have presented a marker for Corpus Christi.

The Corpus Christi observances included two processions – one of the laity, another of divines.[2] At line 34 Flavius asks the Cobbler 'Why do'st thou leade these men about the streets?' – which suggests that a loosely organized band rather than a mob is contemplated by the opening direction, '*Enter . . . certaine Commoners over the stage*' (2–3). The next scene opens with a procession led by priests: '*Enter Caesar, Antony for the Course, etc.*' (84–6). Shakespeare would have known that Caesar was *Pontifex Maximus* of Rome and that Antony was appearing as chief priest of the Lupercii. By staging two processions – one of laymen, another of divines – Shakespeare recapitulates the processional of Corpus Christi. The processional was followed by the performance of a series of Biblical playlets which engrossed the period from the Creation to the Resurrection. Shakespeare's processions on the Lupercal are also followed by a theatrical performance: the staging of Caesar's assassination by Brutus's 'Roman actors' – which Cassius indelibly transfigures into a play:

> Cassi. How many Ages hence
> Shall this our lofty Scene be acted over,
> In State unborne, and Accents yet unknowne?
> Bru. How many times shall *Caesar* bleed in sport,
> That now on *Pompeyes* Basis [3] lye along,
> No worthier then the dust?
>
> (1326–31)

Shakespeare's processions and his playlet of the passion of Caesar parody the Corpus Christi festivities. Recognizing this enables us to decipher a remark by Casca which has never been explained. In 1.2 Casca recounts to Brutus and Cassius the events in the marketplace:

> Marry, before he [Caesar] fell downe, when he perceiv'd the common Heard was glad he refus'd the Crowne, he pluckt me ope his Doublet, and offer'd them his Throat to cut:[4] and I had beene a man of any Occupation, if I

would not have taken him at a word, I would I might goe to Hell among
the Rogues, and so hee fell.

(367–72)

Casca is a coward, and we may discount his brag about cutting Caesar's
throat. But why does Casca give *this reason* for inaction? Members of
Shakespeare's audience might have guessed the answer. The Corpus
Christi plays were staged by Guilds of the artisan class. Casca is an
optimate, an aristocrat. He is not a member of a guild. He has no 'occupation'. Therefore, he could not take part in the 'play' he witnessed in
the marketplace.

Notes

1 Corpus Christi can only fall in the interval 21 May to 24 June.
2 As the Corpus Christi observances became increasingingly elaborate the
   festival expanded in a number of English cities to two and three days. See
   Nelson, 1974, for the order of Corpus Christi in other cities. For associations
   of Corpus Christi plays with St Barnabas's Day and Midsummer, see Nelson,
   1974, 59 and 71.
3 Signifying the pedestal, or stage, upon which Pompey's statue stands.
4 Shakespeare has interpolated this moment from an earlier passage in Plutarch (North, 1579, 791).

II

Endemic time confusion in *Julius Caesar*

II

6

The web of Caesar's time

Why, Lewis Theobald wondered, is the Brutus we encounter in his orchard unsure of the date when everyone in the playhouse knows it's the eve of the Ides of March?[1] Why, Thomas Rymer sputtered, are the wily Decius and his fellow conspirators so confused about the point and time of sunrise?[2] It did not occur to these commentators (or to any since) that these perturbations could have been caused by Julius Caesar who, in 45 BC, abolished a calendar by which Romans had marked their births and metered their lives for more than a hundred years. Caesar had reformed an old republican lunar calendar which was so badly flawed that, despite frequent attempts to correct it by intercalating additional days, the Romans' winter festival – the Saturnalia (24/25 December) – had come to be celebrated in early autumn. When the Roman republican calendar said 'winter' the point of sunrise and weather said 'spring'. To correct the sunrise, seasons and holy days, Caesar crammed 445 days into 46 BC. Then he set his new solar calendar in place on 1 January 45 BC. The effect was a titanic dislocation of the year's familiar holidays. Imagine the confusion if a British government suddenly decreed that Shrovetide was Whitsun, Whitsun would be observed on Summer Bank Holiday, and summer vacation would now fall on Hallowe'en ... which would henceforth be celebrated on Christmas Day! To exacerbate the problem, by thrusting ninety days into 46 BC Caesar moved the point of sunrise 28° and altered the time of sunrise by more than an hour. In the wake of Caesar's calendar reform of 1 January 45 BC, *any* Roman – even the noblest of them all – might well have been confused about the day, the date, the hour, or the azimuth or time of sunrise. Like the Romans of Julius Caesar's age, Shakespeare and the Elizabethans were compelled to live, work and worship in Caesar's time. To understand how Shakespeare's first audiences perceived his *Julius Caesar* we must recognize the broad range of calendrical issues which the play raises, and how these related to contemporary Elizabethan experience.

For example, as Brutus paces in his garden, he mutters, 'I cannot, by the progresse of the Starres, / Give guesse how neere to day – ' (617–18). A moment later he summons Lucius and enquires, 'Is not to morrow (Boy) the first of March?' (658). Theobald found 'the *first* of March' insufferable: 'Allowing *Brutus* to be a most contemplative Man, and his Thoughts taken up with high Matters, yet I can never agree, that he so little knew how Time went, as to be mistaken a whole Fortnight in the Reckoning' (6.143n). Theobald concluded that the Folio's '*first*' of March must be a misprint. His explanation is nothing if not ingenious:

> I make no Scruple to assert, the Poet wrote Ides ... contracted thus, *js*: The Players knew the Word well enough in the Contraction; but when the MSS came to the Press, the Compositors were not so well informed in it; they knew that *jst* frequently stood for first; and blunderingly thought that *js* was meant to do so too: and thence was deriv'd the Corruption of the Text.
>
> (Theobald, 1733, 6.143n)

To support his conjecture Theobald cites a 'well known' historical fact: 'But that the Poet wrote *Ides*, we have This in Confirmation. *Brutus* makes the Enquiry on the Dawn of the very Day, in which *Caesar* was kill'd in the Capitol. Now 'tis very well known that this was on the 15th Day, which is the *Ides*, of *March*' (6.143n). Almot all scholarly editions adopt Theobald's emendation: 'Is not to morrow (Boy) *the Ides* of March?' But Theobald's argument is circular, and frivolous. The date of Caesar's assassination was not 'very well known' to Shakespeare's Brutus. In the dramatic universe of the play Caesar's assassination was yet to take place. Theobald's mistake was underestimating Shakespeare's mastery of stagecraft. *The point* is that the whole playhouse knows the date but Brutus doesn't. Brutus's ignorance *is* a howler. But it is not Shakespeare's error, and not a compositor's error. It is *Brutus's* error and reveals him as an 'untimely' man – another of the playwright's unspoken puns.

The key to understanding Brutus's uncertainty about both the date and the time comes when he directs Lucius, 'Looke in the Calender, and bring me word' (660). Brutus cannot tell time 'by the progresse of the Starres' because he doesn't know the date. Constellations rise and set at different times depending on the day of the year. One can tell time by the stars – but only if one knows the date.[3] The calendar Lucius consults is the Julian which still haunted England in 1599. In a way it is Caesar who answers Brutus's question. While Lucius is on his errand Brutus soliloquizes, and resolves himself to Caesar's murder: 'O Rome, I make thee promise, / If the redresse will follow, thou receivest / Thy full Petition at the hand of *Brutus*' (675–7). Brutus's decision to join the conspiracy is Lucius's cue to enter and report, 'Sir, March is wasted fifteene dayes' (679). On the instant, a stage direction commands '*Knocke within*' (680). The hand that knocks is conspiracy. At the very moment Brutus commits himself to Caesar's murder he seems to step across an invisible threshold into Caesar's time.

A few moments later Shakespeare reprises the identical dynamic. Cassius has urged, 'I thinke it is not meet, / *Marke Antony*, so well belov'd of *Caesar*, / Should out-live *Caesar*' (788–90). Brutus expresses his counterview that a double murder of Caesar and Antony will make the conspirators' course 'seeme too bloody' (795). Trebonius capitulates, and the shape of the murder plot is resolved. On the instant, the clock strikes. Cassius says, 'The Clocke hath stricken three' (828). Thanks to Caesar, Brutus and the conspirators now know the date and time. Shakespeare apparently realized that by imposing a new calendar Caesar had reset the clocks of Rome. (See fuller discussion below.)

Time is the subject of every exchange of dialogue between Shakespeare's Caesar and Brutus. When the Soothsayer delivers his warning in 1.2, Caesar turns to Brutus asking, 'What man is that?' Brutus replies, 'A Sooth-sayer bids you beware the Ides of March' (108–9). When the conspirators arrive at Caesar's home on the Ides, it is to Brutus that Caesar turns, asking, 'What is't a Clocke?' Brutus replies, '*Caesar*, 'tis strucken eight' (1110–11). Shakespeare's Caesar seems to rehearse Brutus to confirm that he is aware of the date and the time. When the clock strikes in Brutus's orchard Shakespeare's editors pounce on an 'anachronism, since mechanical clocks were not invented until the thirteenth century. Shakespeare is thinking in terms of modern chronology. Roman hours were divisions of the natural day starting from dawn, and varying with the length of the day at different seasons of the year' (Dorsch, 1983, 44n). This inference that Shakespeare did not understand the Roman practice of timekeeping is not safe. The boy Shakespeare must have understood Roman horology from his grammar school reading of Caesar's *Commentarii* (Baldwin, 1944, 563).[4] It is impossible to follow the narratives of Caesar's campaigns without understanding the Roman system of numbering hours from sunrise.[5] But if Shakespeare and the 'wiser sort' in his audience understood Roman timekeeping practice and were aware that the mechanical clock was a late medieval invention, what was the playwright's purpose in invoking a striking clock in *Julius Caesar*? [6]

Shakespeare's anachronistic clock is a time-shift signal which invites spectators to relate the on-stage action to contemporary English life.[7] Anachronisms were a familiar device in Elizabethan theatre for intruding topical (seditious) comment. In the *Second Shepherd's Play* of the Wakefield Cycle, the First Shepherd sets the scene by remarking on the cold and the condition of shepherds:

> But we simple shepherds that walk on the moor,
> Are soon by richer hands thrust out of door;
> No wonder as it stands, if we be poor,
> For the tilth of our lands lies as fallow as the floor,
> As you know / We are so lamed,
> Overtaxed and maimed, / And cruelly tamed,
> By our gentlemen foe.
>
> (M. Rose, 1962, 207)

An English audience could hardly have failed to recognize that this 'biblical' First Shepherd was lamenting the enclosures controversy.

To understand how Shakespeare's anachronistic clock in *Julius Caesar* relates to the simmering topical issue of calendar reform, we must refer to Elizabethan timekeeping methodology. Renaissance mechanical clocks were notoriously undependable. For sixteenth-century clocks to lose or gain as much as two hours in twelve was common (Burlingame, 1966, 56). Montaigne writes charmingly of the cacophony of church steeple clocks in sixteenth-century Italy. In order to silence a similar cacophony in steeple-bristling Paris, in 1370 Charles V ordered that the bells of all Parisian striking clocks be regulated by the clock at the Palais-Royal, which tolled both hour and quarter-hour (Le Goff, 1980, 50). At the time of the writing of *Julius Caesar* all mechanical clocks required daily regulation by one of the following methods: 'checking with a sundial, *clepsydra*, or stellar clock', or by reference to the sound of a local 'master' striking clock, or by a sexton who observed the sunrise (or moonrise) and manually adjusted the clock to the time provided in the popular almanacs (Burlingame, 1966, 56). Shakespeare glances at this practice in *King John*: 'Old Time the clock-setter, that bald sexton Time' (3.1.250).

When Pope Gregory advanced the calendar ten days he not only altered the date and azimuth of sunrise but the *time* of sunrise as well. Table 3 presents the variations in the observed azimuth and time of sunrise for London in 1599 according to the Gregorian and Julian calendars.

Table 3 *Azimuths and times of sunrise in London, 15 and 25 March 1599, Gregorian (G) and Julian (J), compared*

Date	Azimuth	Time	Variation
15 March G	92°35'	6.16 a.m.	
15 March J	86°26'	5.54 a.m.	+ 22 minutes
25 March G	86°26'	5.54 a.m.	
25 March J	82°03'	5.38 a.m.	+ 16 minutes

Not only was the Protestant calendar ten days behind, but in a manner of speaking the Protestant clocks of England 'ran late' by more than a quarter of an hour. Though it was impossible to observe this variation in Shakespeare's era, mathematicians could and did calculate the disparity. Elizabethan almanacs are extant which catalogue the variations in the times of sun- and moonrise for London, Norwich, Dublin and other cities.[8]

Then again, Gregory advanced his calendar only ten days. Julius Caesar's reform altered the calendar by an aggregate *ninety* days. Consequently, the variations in rising times were much more pronounced

Table 4 *Azimuths and times of sunrise in Rome, 15 March 45 BC (Republican) and 15 March 44 BC (Julian) compared*

Date	Azimuth	Time	Variation
15 March 45 BC[9]	121°26'	7.36 a.m.	
15 March 44 BC	93°32'	6.28 a.m.	− 68 minutes

Caesar's reform had altered the time of sunrise by an hour and eight minutes. This may explain why Cinna wrongly speculates that he detects traces of sunrise although the hour is prior to 3 a.m. Shakespeare and the Elizabethans certainly knew that in mid-March the sun rose after 6 a.m.

Shakespeare's Portia provides a useful example of how his characters become aware of Caesar's time as they become aware of the conspiracy. On the eve of the Ides Portia is unaware of the murder plot. She speculates that Brutus's restlessness is 'an effect of Humor, / Which sometime hath his houre with every man' (891–2). Cato's daughter importunes Brutus to reveal the cause of his preoccupation. He assents: 'All my engagements, I will construe to thee, / All the Charactery of my sad brows' (950–1). Apparently, he does reveal the conspiracy to her. The Portia we meet on the morning of the Ides is a changed woman. Her mask of Stoicism has slipped. She is frenetic, frantic – and obsessed with time. She would have the boy Lucius to the Capitol and back in an instant (1145–50). When the Soothsayer enters she abruptly demands, 'What is 't a clocke?' (1171). The Soothsayer has already predicted Caesar's fall. He knows the time: 'About the ninth houre Lady' (1172). In fact everyone who is aware of Caesar's fate is aware of Caesar's time. '*Trebonius* knowes his time: for look you *Brutus* / He drawes *Mark Antony* out of the way' (1231–2).[10] Intriguingly, 'time' infiltrates the vocabulary of the master-conspirator Cassius only after Caesar's death. Cassius's first reference to time comes in 4.2: 'In such a time as this, it is not meet / That every nice offence should beare his Comment' (1976–7). On the morning of the first battle of Philippi, Cassius confesses, '*Messala*, this is my Birth-day; as this very day / Was *Cassius* borne' (2411–12). Though born under the Republican calendar and ninety days past the actual anniversary of his birth, Cassius finally acknowledges Caesar's calendar – and endues it with the power to circumscribe men's lives: 'This day I breathed first, Time is come round, / And where I did begin, there shall I end, / My life is run his compasse' (2503–5). Even Cassius, 'Last of all the Romans', becomes engulfed by Caesar's time. Brutus's lament over his brother-in-law's corpse rings hollow: 'I shall finde time *Cassius*: I shall finde time' (2593). As Act 5 grinds toward conclusion all the conspirators find 'time'. But it is Caesar's time.

Shakespeare based his Romans' attitude towards Caesar's time on an anecdote he found in Plutarch. Although Caesar's calendar was an important scientific achievement, certain Romans – Cicero being one – regarded the reform as a tyranny:

> But his [Caesar's] enemies notwithstanding that envied his greatnesse, did not sticke to finde fault withall. As Cicero the Orator, when one said, to morow the starre Lyra will rise: Yea, said he, at the commandement of Caesar, as if men were compelled to say and think, by Caesars edict.
>
> (North, 1579, 738)

Sigurd Burkhardt, who takes the palm for being first to identify the connection between the Elizabethan calendar controversy and *Julius*

Caesar, wrote: 'the Roman conservatives felt it [Caesar's calendar] to be an arbitrary and tyrannical interference with the course of nature' (Burkhardt, 1968, 6). Judging from their almanacs and pamphleteering, Elizabethans still felt that way in 1599.

The untimely man

Shakespeare believed that Brutus was the illegitimate son of Julius Caesar. The playwright says so in few words in *2 Henry VI*:

> Great men oft die by vile Besonians;
> A Roman sworder and banditto slave
> Murdered sweet Tully; Brutus' bastard hand
> Stabbed Julius Caesar; savage islanders
> Pompey the Great; and Suffolk dies by pirates.
> (4.1.136–40) [11]

Shakespeare found several reports of Brutus's bastardy in his ancient sources.[12] Seutonius, who revels in retailing Caesar's peccadilloes, records that Brutus's mother, Servilia, was one of Caesar's sexual conquests.[13] Appian, too, shared the view that Brutus was illegitimate, and the natural son of Caesar.[14] Plutarch suggests that fatherly affection was Caesar's motive for sparing Brutus after the battle of Pharsalus: 'Some saye he [Caesar] did this for *Serviliaes* sake, *Brutus* mother. For when he [Caesar] was a young man, he had bene acquainted with *Servilia*, who was extreamelie in love with him. And bicause *Brutus* was borne in that time when their love was hottest, he [Caesar] perswaded him selfe that he begat him' (North, 1579, 1057). Plutarch is certainly unequivocal: Caesar believed *unequivocally* that Brutus was his natural son. This sorts well with Suetonius's report of Caesar's dying words: 'some have written, that as M. Brutus came running upon him he said, Και συ τεκυου; *And thou my sonne*' (Holland, 1606, 33). Although it is impossible to understand *Julius Caesar* without recognizing that Brutus is Caesar's illegitimate son, among the critical literature one can find no Shakespearian who takes up the question of Brutus's bastardy. But Shakespeare's text is rife with unrecognized allusions to it. For example, after the famous 'seduction' scene in Act 1, Brutus has left the stage and Cassius indulges in soliloquy:

> Well *Brutus*, thou art Noble: yet I see,
> Thy Honorable Mettle may be wrought

> From that it is dispos'd: therefore it is meet,
> That Noble mindes keepe ever with their likes:
> For who so firme, that cannot be seduc'd?

(415–19)

Once we recognize Brutus's bastardy, Shakespeare's wordplay becomes accessible. 'Shakespeare frequently puns on metal and *mettle*, [and] there are many places in the plays where the two words coalesce into one significance' (Mahood, 1988, 16). A 'Noble' was a coin of gold, the 'honourable' metal. Cassius compares Brutus to a golden coin which may be 'wrought' from its usual disposition – that is, debased. Counterfeit coins and coining were Shakespeare's habitual metaphors for illicit births and extramarital sex, as in *Measure for Measure* (1.1.49–51 and 2.2.42–6).[15] Cassius's 'Noble' metaphor is completed by Antony's reference in his funeral oration to Brutus as '*Caesars* Angel' (1718). In Shakespeare's day an 'Angel' was an 'old English gold coin, called more fully at first the angel-noble ... having as its device the archangel Michael standing upon, and piercing the dragon' (*OED* angel n.6). Once Cassius's wordplay on Brutus's 'Honorable mettle' is recognized as a glance at Brutus's illegitimacy, another of Cassius's speeches takes on rich new coloration:

> Men at sometime, are Masters of their Fates.
> The fault (deere *Brutus*) is not in our Starres,
> But in our Selves, that we are underlings.

(238–40)

Cassius is dissembling.[16] An illegitimate child's 'fault' is precisely his 'Starres', i.e. the astrology at his nativity. Brutus came into the world under the wrong stars, at the wrong time. His muddle-headedness about politics, intrigue and time flows from that fact. Recognizing Brutus's bastardy lends tremendous poignancy to his prayer as he clutches Portia in his arms: 'O yee Gods, / Render me worthy of this noble wife' (945–6). How could a base-born bastard hope to be a worthy husband for the daughter of Cato?

With the exception of young Faulconbridge of *King John*, Shakespeare's bastards are men of ambiguous social status who have only contempt for a society which marginalizes them. They are enemies of peace and order who lack any comprehension of honour. Most particularly, like Edmund of *King Lear*, their births are untimely. Shakespeare's Brutus is an untimely man. As he wanders in his orchard, he knows neither the date nor the time. During the conflict at Philippi, he sends an ill-timed order calling his army into battle. This is the downfall of the Republican cause; while Brutus's soldiers fall to spoil, Cassius's army is enclosed and defeated. In the aftermath Titinius laments, 'O *Cassius*, *Brutus* gave the word too early' (2483). But of all of Brutus's errors in timing, his most catastrophic is expressed in his most vivid, memorable and persuasive metaphorical figure:

> There is a Tide in the affayres of men,
> Which taken at the Flood, leades on to Fortune:
> Omitted, all the voyage of their life,
> Is bound in Shallowes, and in Miseries.
> On such a full Sea are we now a-float,
> And we must take the current when it serves,
> Or loose our Ventures.
>
> (2217–23)

Norman Rabkin sensed that, somehow, Brutus's metaphor of the tides connected with the universal clock: 'In the world of *Julius Caesar*, the conventions establish a dramatically convincing representation of a universe, governed by inexorable law, in which events are brought about not according to man's idealistic intentions but deterministically by their own logic' (Rabkin, 1964, 251). Rabkin could not quite grasp a phenomenon which would have been perfectly clear to an audience attending a performance of *Julius Caesar* at the Globe on 12 June 1599. As Shakespeare drafted *Julius Caesar* earlier that year, he could easily have ascertained that high tide in the Thames would crest that day at 2 p.m. By the time Shakespeare's Brutus makes his fatal allusion to high tide, the hour would have been between 4 p.m. and 5 p.m., and the tide at Southwark strand was rapidly receding towards its ebb. Brutus is wrong about everything: the date, the time, sparing Antony's life, the decision to march to Philippi, the time to join battle and, as the Globe patrons would realize if they trudged homewards past acres of reeking Thames mud, Brutus was dismally wrong about the tide.

Notes

1 Theobald, 1733, 6.143n.
2 Rymer, 1693, 152–3.
3 How abundantly Shakespeare understood the method of telling time by date-and-stars is apparent from the First Carrier's astronomical time-telling

in *1 Henry IV*: 'Heigh-ho! An 't be not four by the day, I'll be hanged. Charles's Wain is over the new chimney, and yet our horse not packed. What, ostler!' (2.1.1–3). 'Charles's Wain' – literally Charlemagne's chariot – was an Elizabethanism for the constellation we know as *Ursa Major*, the Great Bear. The 'new chimney' may literally be the new chimney of the inn. But it might be slang for the constellation Auriga, the Charioteer, whose principal stars form an awkward sexagon. 'Chimney' is from the Latin *caminus*, signifying an odd-shaped *fossura* or pit – as in *camera caminata*, i.e. a room with a fireplace (*OED* chimney n). That ostlers would be chattering about chariots and charioteers seems a plausible inference.

4 Baldwin cites Cardinal Wolsey's decree (1528) that grammar school students were to read 'History, of Salust, or of Caesar's Commentaries' in the sixth form, and concludes, 'We may regard Sallust and Caesar as universal' in grammar school curricula of the time.

5 The *Commentarii* reveal that Caesar was punctilious about timekeeping. Caesar records having been told that the Isle of Man was in continuous darkness for thirty days during winter. '*Nos nihil de eo percontationibus reperiebamus, nisi certis ex aqua mensuris breviores esse quam in continenti noctes videbamus.*' (Edwards, 1986, 5.13.250–2). Author's translation: 'Though we were unable to make any determination of this fact, we observed by measurement of water that nights in England were shorter than on the Continent.' Caesar apparently carried with him a very accurate *clepsydra* water clock which enabled him to discriminate the variations in the length of night over just a few degrees of longitude. The variation in the length of a winter's night between, say, London and Caen is less than eight minutes in twelve hours

6 The first public striking clocks in Europe had been installed in Milan *c.* 1345.

7 There are many such time-shift signals, the grumbling of the Porter in *Macbeth* being one.

8 For example: W. Gray, *Almanacke, etc. rectified for Dorchester*, Bodley Ashm. 62 (5), and J. Harvey, *Almanacke, etc. referred to London*, Bodley Alm.f. 1589.1(3).

9 For clarity I am referring to the day which fell 455 days prior to 15 March 45 BC.

10 It has been already made clear that 'Trebonius knows his time' from the exchange in Brutus's orchard: '*Cas.* The Clocke hath stricken three. / *Treb.* 'Tis time to part' (828–9).

11. A glance at Shakespeare's source in Plutarch indicates that Suffolk pronounces a precise epitome of Cicero's death: 'So *Ciceroes* gate being shut, they [his murderers] entred the house by force, and missing him, they asked them of the house what was become of him. They aunswered, they could not tell. Howbeit there was a young boy in the house called *Philologus*, a slave ... [and] he told this *Herennius* [a Centurion], that his [Cicero's] ser-

vauntes caried him in a liter towards the sea, through darke narrowe lanes, shadowed with wodde on either side ... *Herennius* did cruelly murder him.' Shakespeare based Suffolk's 'savage islanders' on Plutarch's description of the villainous duo of '*Theophanes* LESBIAN', who persuaded Pompey to land in Egypt, and the rhetorician '*Theodotus* of CHIO', who persuaded the Egyptian court that Pompey should be murdered (North, 1579, 936–7 and 716).

12 On the side of Marcus Brutus's claim to legitimate descent from Lucius Junius Brutus, Plutarch offers this citation: '*Posidonius* the Philosopher wryteth the contrarie, that *Iunius Brutus* in deede slue two of his sonnes which were men growen, as the histories doe declare: howebeit that there was a third sonne, being but a litle childe at that time, from whom the house and family afterwardes was derived' (North, 1579, 1055–6). But there is reason to suspect Posidonius's (135–51 BC) motive for lending his name to this fanciful 'third son' theory. The Stoic philosopher and historian was a teacher and friend of Cicero, who refers to him fondly in his letters and essays, including the *Tusculan Disputations* and *De Natura Deorum*. As Caesar consolidated dictatorial powers, Cicero and his republican faction (including Posidonius) were desperate for a countervailing political figurehead. Posidonius's *apologia* may have been contrived to legitimate Marcus Brutus in the eyes of the Roman citizenry, particularly the nobility. This would hardly be the first time that a famous name brought a mediocrity to political prominence (See King, 1989, 2.25.61).

13 'But above the rest [of Caesar's sexual conquests], he cast affection to Servilia the mother of M. Brutus; for whom both in his last Consulship he had bought a pearle that cost him six millions of Sesterces: and also unto whom during the civill warre [with Pompey], over and above other free gifts, hee sold in open sale, faire Lands and most goodly Manors at a very low price' (Holland, 1606, 21).

14 'It was even thought that Brutus was his son, as Caesar was the lover of his mother, Servilia (Cato's sister) about the time of his birth, for which reason, when he [Caesar] won the victory at Pharsalus, it is said that he gave an immediate order to his officers to save Brutus by all means' (White, 1979, iii. 433).

15 This counterfeit–bastard metaphor remained stable in Shakespeare's mind over a remarkably long period. In *Titus Andronicus* (1592) Nurse presents Tamora's illegitimate child to Aaron, saying, 'The Empress sends it thee, thy stamp, thy seal, / And bids thee christen it with thy dagger's point' (4.2.69–70). Eighteen years later (1610) the same metaphor resurfaces in *Cymbeline*: 'We are all bastards, / And that most venerable man, which I / Did call my father, was I know not where / When I was stamp'd. Some coiner with his tools / Made me a counterfeit' (2.4.154–8).

16 Cassius, an Epicurean, believes in neither fate nor astrology. 'Fates' and 'Starres' suggest that Cassius is dissembling. In fact, Cassius is obliquely touching Brutus's bastardy.

7

Shakespeare's vernal equinox gambit: 'Here lies the East ...'

Just as Brutus is wrong about date, time and tide, Decius is wrong about the azimuth of sunrise, and Cinna about the time of sunrise. It is 'after midnight' (611) and before dawn on the Ides of March when the conspirators arrive at Brutus's orchard in 2.1. After a greeting, Cassius draws Brutus aside – 'Shall I entreat a word?' – and a direction tells us *They whisper* (730). While they do, a peculiar conversation unfolds among Decius Brutus, Casca and Cinna:

> *Decius.* Here lyes the East: doth not the Day breake
> heere?
> *Cask.* No.
> *Cin.* O pardon, Sir, it doth; and yon grey Lines,
> That fret the Clouds, are Messengers of Day.
> *Cask.* You shall confesse, that you are both deceiv'd:
> Heere, as I point my Sword, the Sunne arises,
> Which is a great way growing on the South,
> Weighing the youthfull Season of the yeare.
> Some two moneths hence, up higher toward the North
> He first presents his fire, and the high East
> Stands as the Capitoll, directly heere.
>
> (731–42)

Commentators since Thomas Rymer have been struck, not always with admiration, by 'Casca's almanac': 'Here the *Roman* Senators, the Midnight before *Caesar's* Death, (met in the Garden of *Brutus* to settle the Matter of their Conspiracy,) are gazing up to the Stars, and have no more in their Heads than to wrangle about which is the East and West' (Rymer, 1693, 153). The conspirators' dialogue has no basis in Plutarch. Why, then, did Shakespeare invent it?

Shakespeare's vernal equinox gambit

Alone among Shakespeare's commentators John Dover Wilson recognized that the conspirators' dialogue

> raises a curious point in astronomy. Caska is perfectly correct according
> to the Julian calendar invented in his own day and according to the re
> formed Gregorian calendar introduced into Catholic Europe in 1582. But
> according to the unreformed Julian calendar, still used in Shakespeare's
> England and by then ten days in error, the sun rose north of east on 15
> March. Was Caska astronomically exact by accident or was Shakespeare
> being historically exact to the facts of 44 BC?
>
> (J. D. Wilson, 1948, 128)

To no discredit, Dover Wilson was not an astronomer; Casca's almanac is neither 'perfectly correct' nor astronomically or historically 'exact'. But it is *so close* to being correct that Shakespeare's language could hardly be coincidental. Wilson's hunch – ignored by editors for fifty years – deserves meticulous examination.

Is Casca correct according to the Julian calendar of 44 BC? Yes, as the computer-generated astronomical chart in Figure 5 demonstrates.[1] The disk of the sun (above the planet Mercury) is just rising above the horizon line.[2] The azimuth of sunrise was 94°09′. This is 4°09′ south of east.

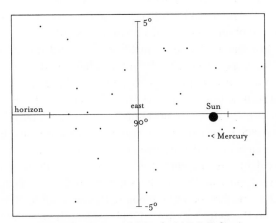

Figure 5. Rome, 15 March 44 BC (Julian)

The horizontal line bisecting the illustration is the horizon. The central vertical line indicates 90° east; the short vertical strokes left

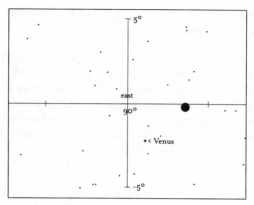

Figure 6. London, 15 March 1599 (Gregorian)

and right indicate ±5° of azimuth. The dots are stars. The planet Mercury appears below the rising line.

Is Casca correct according to the Gregorian calendar which replaced the old Julian calendar in Catholic Europe in 1582? Yes. Figure 6 provides a view of the sky as it would have appeared to a person standing before the eastern façade of the Globe theatre (51°30′ North by 00°10′ West), and looking due east at sunrise (6.16 a.m.) on 15 March 1599 Gregorian. The azimuth of sunrise is 92°35′. This is 2°35′ south of east. In Rome on 15 March 44 BC Julian, and in London on 15 March 1599 Gregorian, the observed point of sunrise was south of east.

Did the sun rise *north* of east on 15 March 1599 Julian? Again, the answer is yes. Pope Gregory's reform had advanced the Catholic calendar ten days. Figure 7 indicates that on 15 March 1599 Julian the azimuth of sunrise in London was 86°26′. That is 3°34′ north of east.

This brings us to Wilson's most important question: was Casca astronomically exact by accident? Or was Shakespeare being historically exact to the facts of 44 BC? Internal evidence in Casca's speech argues against accident. Shakespeare directs Casca not only to point, but *to draw his sword and point* (737). This suggests that Shakespeare ascribed importance to the direction Casca pointed. Even a stubby Roman sword would extend the actor's gesture double its length, and the longer the pointer, the sharper the focus.

But could Shakespeare have known the point of sunrise as observed from Rome on 15 March 44 BC by the Julian calendar? Possibly. An Elizabethan astronomer/astrologer could have supplied the information.

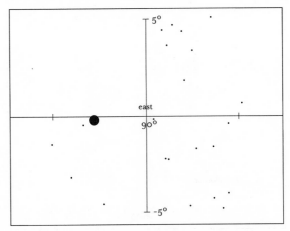

Figure 7. London, 15 March 1599 (Julian)

But even if Shakespeare possessed such arcane information, he could hardly have expected his audience to be aware of it. On the other hand, Shakespeare's audience *was* aware that Elizabeth had rejected the Gregorian calendar reform, and England was living under an antiquated and scientifically discredited Julian calendar. Some members of Shakespeare's audience would certainly have been aware that sunrise on 15 March 1599 was south of east in most of Europe but *north* of east in London. This discrepancy between the Julian and Gregorian calendars was emphasized by the occurrence of one of the year's principal solar events on one of the 'missing' days, 21 March Gregorian. It was well known to Elizabethan mariners, astronomers and almanac readers that the observed azimuth of sunrise on the vernal equinox was virtually 90° east (Figure 8). Since the English Julian calendar was ten days behind the Gregorian, the vernal equinox was observed in London on 11 March 1599 Julian. Casca's almanac analogizes the circumstances of Rome in 44 BC to those in London in AD 1599. Both cities are living by Julius Caesar's calendar. And the citizens of both cities are liable to confusion about the points of sunrise in mid-March.

To sharpen the analogy between Rome in 44 BC and London in 1599, Shakespeare intrudes a reference to the 'high East'. In *The Quest for Shakespeare's Globe*, John Orrell provides mathematical proofs suggesting that Wenceslas Hollar's rendering of the Globe may be reliable within limits of ±3.5 per cent. From these proofs he deduces that the main axis of the Globe was aimed at a point on the horizon 48.7° (±1.7°) east of

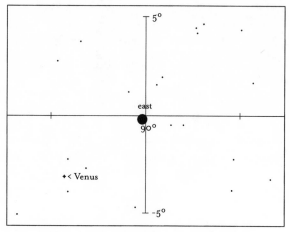

Figure 8. London, 11 March (Julian) 21 March (Gregorian) 1599

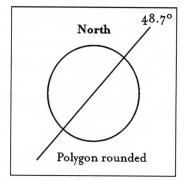

Figure 9.

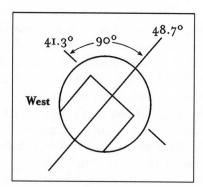

Figure 10.

north (Orrell, 1983, 152–7) (Figure 9). The axis of the Globe closely correlates with the azimuth of sunrise on the summer solstice 12 June 1599 Julian. If Orrell is correct, a stage perpendicular to the axis of the theatre would have been oriented 41.3° west of north (Blatherwick and Gurr, 1992, 315ff.) (Figure 10).

With this schematic in hand we can address the question of where the actor playing Casca pointed as he spoke lines 736–42. Caska's speech is particularized to three points of the compass ('south ... north ... east') and includes an embedded stage direction which requires the actor to draw his sword and point. Casca declares, 'the high East Stands as the Capitoll, directly heere' (741–2). Shakespeare insists on the 'high' east – that is, *precisely east* as the compass points – which had a significance which crystallized Shakespeare's analogy of Rome and London. The conspirators have gathered within the walls of Brutus's orchard. We know they cannot see the city of Rome beyond the walls because Brutus could not see the conspirators before they entered. Therefore any building Casca envisions must retain a presence though invisible beyond the orchard wall. An audience at the Globe would be in an analogous situation. They would not be able to see London beyond the three-storey walls of the theatre. An examination of the geography of Shakespeare's London reveals that if Casca pointed to the *high east* he would have pointed towards a building which dominated its quadrant of the skyline and would have remained a looming presence in the mind of an audience: the Tower of London (Figure 11). The Victorian

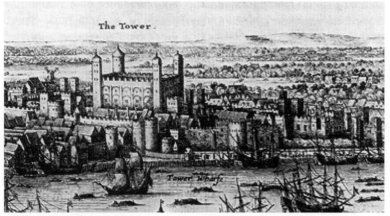

Figure 11. Hollar's view of the Tower of London. © The British Museum

Figure 12. Norden's map of London, 1593. The map has been rotated so that the west–east axis is horizontal

scholar W. A. Wright appears to have been the first to detect this correspondence between the Roman Capitol and the Tower of London: 'It is worth remarking that the Tower, which would be the building in London most resembling the Capitol to Shakespeare's mind, was as nearly as possible due east of the Globe Theatre on Bankside' (cited in Furness, 1913, 89) (Figure 12). In both metaphorical and historical senses the Tower of London is the locus where the Roman and Elizabethan strands of *Julius Caesar* converge. The Tower was the London landmark most closely associated with Julius Caesar.[3] It was the emblem of Elizabeth's power. In the context of Casca's almanac, Shakespeare's glance at the Capitol–Tower analogizes two dictators who imposed the Julian calendar. Understanding where Caska pointed allows us for the first time to visualize a piece of stage business as it was actually played at the Globe.

The Capitol–Tower connection explains another series of anomalies in *Julius Caesar*: Shakespeare's bizarre references to lions wandering the Roman streets and haunting the Capitol. At line 452 Casca reports to Cassius, 'Against the Capitoll I met a Lyon'. At 514 Cassius confirms the presence of lions when he alludes to a man who 'roares, As doth the Lyon in the Capitoll'. At line 1004 we learn that the lion Caska encountered was female. Calpurnia recounts 'A Lionnesse hath whelped in the streets.' No lions were kept in the Roman capitol. They were maintained at the Coliseum. Though scholars have found these references opaque, members of Shakespeare's audiences would have recognized who was signified by the glaring female lion. Stowe's *Annales*

(5 August 1604) records, 'a Lionesse named Elizabeth, in the Tower of London, brought forth a lion's whelp.'[4]

Notes

1 Astronomical charts prepared by the writer using Virtual Reality Laboratories' 'Distant Suns (1.2)' software.

2 There is a difference of opinion even today among astronomers about the meaning of 'sunrise'. Is it the moment when the first rays of the sun appear above the horizon – or when the mid-point of the sun appears – or when the sun is wholly visible? Not to take sides in this question, but merely for consistency, I have used the moment of the appearance of the sun's first rays above the horizon.

3 Shakespeare glances at the tradition that Julius Caesar built the Tower in the dialogue between Prince Edward and the Duke of Buckingham in *Richard III* (3.1.68–74). The present Tower was built on a Roman foundation.

4 A menagerie had been installed there from the time of Henry I in 1125.

8

Why the 'sunne of Rome' set at three o'clock

In *Julius Caesar* there are two references to three o'clock. The first occurs during the scene in Brutus's orchard. An anachronistic clock strikes and Cassius remarks, 'The clocke hath striken three.' This occurs at line 828. In a modern performance of *Julius Caesar*, this line falls approximately 45 minutes into the play. We cannot know how long it took Elizabethans to play 828 lines, but Shakespeare did. If he knew that a performance of *Julius Caesar* at the Globe would begin shortly after 2 p.m. as Platter tells us it did, the playwright would have known Cassius's count of the clock would fall *c*. 3 p.m.[1] The Globe stood only a short walk from St Mary Overy, and across the river from St Bennet's at Paul's Wharf. As erection of the theatre proceeded, the tolling steeple bells of these churches would have been audible on the Bankside construction site.[2] When Shakespeare visited the site it would have been apparent that these bells would be audible within the playhouse. Periodically they would remind audiences of the time of day.[3]

The second reference to three o'clock in *Julius Caesar* occurs between the two battles of Philippi. Brutus remarks, ''Tis three a clocke, and Romans yet ere night, / We shall try Fortune in a second fight' (2599–600). This is a double puzzlement. Only moments before, Titinius discovered the body of Cassius and lamented:

> O setting Sunne:
> As in thy red Rayes thou doest sinke to night;
> So in his red blood *Cassius* day is set.
>
> (2545–7)

This incomprehensible anomaly – a sunset *c*. 3 p.m. – has received scant comment. One might say that of *all* textual cruces in *Julius Caesar*, the sunset at three o'clock at Philippi has been given the widest berth by scholars.[4] Shakespeare found 'three a clocke' in Plutarch: '*Brutus ...* sodainly caused his armie to marche, being past three of the clocke in the after noone' (North, 1579, 1078). What the playwright invented is the sunset. Although the date of the second battle of Philippi had been lost until the discovery of the *Praenestine Fasti* in the twentieth century, we can be confident that Shakespeare and the Globe audience were aware the sun *did not* set at 3 p.m. at Philippi. The earliest sunset of the year in London was 3.50 p.m. Philippi was known to be south of London. Therefore, the earliest sunset of the year at Philippi must have been later than 3.50 p.m.[5] But if Shakespeare knew this, why would he have permitted such a howler during the climactic moments of *Julius Caesar*?

Shakespeare's tactic becomes transparent when we remember that *Brutus* is telling the time. Brutus was wrong about the date in 2.1. Brutus was wrong about the tides in 4.2. At Philippi Brutus is wrong about the time of the second battle. Before Brutus declares, ''Tis three a clocke' at line 2599 of the play, the steeple bells of nearby churches would have chimed four o'clock almost thirty minutes ago. There is a method to this apparent madness. If we accept the level-headed Titinius and Messala as reliable reporters, and take literally their statement that 'the sunne of Rome' is setting at Philippi, there is an astronomical answer to this conundrum which is another of Shakespeare's temporal markers to 12 June 1599. If Cassius's reference to three o'clock was spoken *c.* 3 p.m., Titinius's reference to a setting sun at line 2545 would have been delivered *c.* 4.30 p.m. (Table 5).[6]

Table 5

Line	Play begins 2.00	Play begins 2.15
1	2.00	2.15
828	2.45	3.00
2545	4.18	4.33

While writing *Julius Caesar* in the winter of 1598–9, had Shakespeare consulted an ephemerides for 12 June he would have discovered that the red planet Mars set at 4.26 p.m. on that date. Rome's founder, Romulus, was reputed to have been a son of Mars. After the god Jupiter, Mars was the principal deity of Rome, the protector of the city and, figuratively, the red 'Sun of Rome'. Figure 13 is a view of the sky at

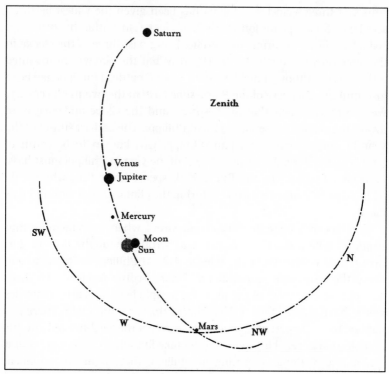

Figure 13. View of the sky looking west-northwest from the Globe at
4.26 p.m. on 12 June 1599 (Julian)

4.26 p.m. on 12 June 1599 Julian looking west-northwest from the
Globe towards the setting point of Mars at 297° azimuth. An Elizabethan
astrologer could have drawn such a chart of the Sun, Moon and known
planets when Mars set at 4.26 p.m. on 12 June. Given what we know
about the orientation of the axis of the Globe and its stage, we can
recreate the panorama of the sky directly behind the stage. Only the
Sun would have been visible, but Figure 14 shows the orientation of
the planets from the point of view of a spectator standing or sitting on
the axis of the playhouse and facing the stage. This was the cyclorama
of the cosmos which formed the invisible backdrop for Titinius's unfor-
gettable lines. The tolling bells of nearby churches would tell the
audience that Brutus was wrong about the time by ninety minutes. But
Elizabethans who knew their astronomy would know that Titinius (and
Shakespeare) were right.

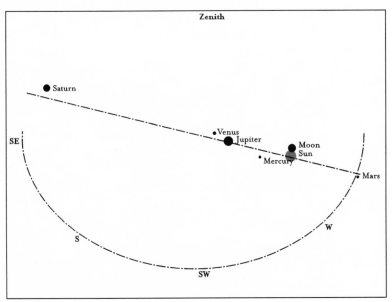

Figure 14. The sky behind the Globe looking south-west at 4.26 p.m. on 12 June 1599 (Julian)

Notes

1 Platter tells us, 'at about two o'clock, I went with my party across the water' (Schanzer, 1956, 466).

2 Shakespeare may be glancing across the river in *Twelfth Night*: 'the belles of S[aint] Bennet sir, may put you in minde, one, two, three' (2189–90).

3 See the discussion of Shakespeare's exploitation of this phenomenon in *Hamlet* in Chapter 18.

4 Perhaps feeling that someone must say *something*, the current Oxford editor suggests that the anachronistic 'image is justified by its poetic appropriateness' (Humphreys, 1984, 221n). The *Variorum* cites Mark Hunter's (desperate) speculation that 'an Elizabethan audience might very well forget that they had just been called upon to imagine sunset'.

5 In fact, the earliest time of sunset at Philippi in 42 BC was 5.00 p.m. on 25 December.

6 Elizabethan mechanical clocks were notoriously unreliable, and liable to lose two hours in twenty-four. Elizabethans knew that the striking of a clock, or the tolling of steeple bells, at best approximated the hour.

III

Shakespeare's *Julius Caesar* and the movable feast discordances of 1599

9

The disrupted Easter cycle of 1599

Midsummer was not the only occasion of discordant holy days in 1599. The Annunciation to the Blessed Virgin Mary was a solar holy day observed on the same date – 25 March – in both Gregorian and Julian calendars. Ironically, since the Gregorian 25 March was the Julian 15 March, Catholics were celebrating the Annunciation on the day on which the English believed Caesar fell and Christ was crucified.

This ten-day offset did not apply to Easter, or to the other lunar-based holy days. In 1599 the Gregorian and Julian calendars differed over the date of Easter by one week. The English observed Easter on 8 April Julian. Catholics observed Easter on 11 April Gregorian. Therefore the Catholic Easter fell on 1 April Julian, All Fools' Day in the English calendar. The solemn occasion of Ash Wednesday – the forty-sixth day before Easter and the first day of Lent – was observed by Catholics on 24 February Gregorian. This fell on 14 February Julian, St Valentine's Day, a holiday of licence and licentiousness. Shrove Tuesday – the day before Ash Wednesday – was the day of *Mardi Gras* and *Carnivale*. In 1599 Shrove Tuesday was observed by Catholics on 23 February Gregorian. Oddly enough, this concorded with 13 February Julian – the eve of St Valentine, and one of the two dates associated with the Roman Lupercal. Throughout the Easter cycle of 1599, the English were confronted by a series of discordances which almost seemed a calculated mockery (Table 6).

It is difficult to believe that such ironic discordances could escape the notice of English folk who thumbed an almanac for 1599. While William Shakespeare was writing *Julius Caesar* these anomalies unfolded around him in real time. As I will indicate in the following chapters, his text contains previously unrecognised allusions to each of these discordances. (See Appendix 10.)

103

The movable feast discordances

Table 6

Julian date	Catholic	Protestant	Roman
13 February	Shrove Tuesday	St Valentine's Eve	Lupercal eve
14 February	Ash Wednesday	St Valentine's Day	Lupercal
15 March	Annunciation	Crucifixion	Ides of March
1 April	Easter	All Fools Day	Fortuna Virilis [1]

1. On the Kalends of April, 'women of the lower sort bathed in the men's public baths, and worshipped *Fortuna Virilis*', Ovid importuned the 'Fairest of goddesses' to 'behold the sons of Aeneas with benign looks' (Frazer, 1989, 198n–201).

10

Shrovetide, St Valentine's Eve and the Roman Lupercal

In February 1599 the rival calendars created a concordance between the Catholic Shrove Tuesday, the Protestant eve of St Valentine, and the old Roman Lupercal. According to the calendar of liturgical readings in the Book of Common Prayer, 2 Corinthians 9–11 was the reading both for 13–15 February and for the period 12–14 June.[1] In the rival calendars for 1599 these two three-day periods engrossed Shrove Tuesday, St Valentine's Day, the Lupercal, Ash Wednesday, the summer solstice, St Anthony's Day, and the Vigil and Nativity of St John Baptist. That is, in 1599 almost every holy day we have so far considered was associated in the liturgical calendar with the Epistles of St Paul to the church at Corinth.[2] Paul had a number of close associations with Rome. He was a Roman citizen. His letter to the Romans began the thrice-yearly cycle of readings of the Epistles. This Epistle contains Paul's argument for justification by faith alone, the battle cry of the Reformation. Arrested, Paul appealed to Caesar for judgement, was transported to Rome and was martyred there – so Elizabethans believed – on the same day as St Peter. Furthermore, the Corinth to which Paul addressed his letters was not the famous city-state which had taken sides with Sparta and defeated Athens in the Peloponnesian War in the fifth century BC; that city had been destroyed by the Romans under Lucius Mummius in 146 BC. The Corinth to which St Paul wrote was *Colonia Laus Julia Corinthensis* – a colony of Roman military veterans founded on the site of the older city by Julius Caesar in 44 BC. Paul wrote his 2 Corinthians while in Macedonia. He went to Macedonia at the command of a vision, which had appeared to him at Troas. Paul founded the first Christian church in Europe at Philippi. Troas lies only some fifty miles north-west of Sardis, where a vision warns Brutus about Philippi. Paul was the Reformers' theologian, often called 'the first Protestant' because of his stubborn independence from the Jerusalem faction led by Peter and James. John Calvin founded the Reformers' claim for equal standing as an independent Church on Paul's quarrel with Peter at Antioch (Galatians 2).[3] All this history was readily available to Shakespeare and the Elizabethans. If our inference is correct that Shakespeare systematically borrowed from Scripture as he drafted *Julius Caesar*, the thought *and the diction* of St Paul's Epistles to the Corinithians should be detectable in the text of the play.

A Pauline cobbler and a Lord of Misrule

Writing about the opening scene of *Julius Caesar*, Richard Wilson has correctly suggested that a Globe audience would have recognized Shakespeare's impudent Mechanicals as emblematic of London's traditional Shrove Tuesday revels (R. Wilson, 1987, 36).[4] Having ascertained that the first plebeian is a carpenter, Tribune Murellus demands of the next man

> You sir, what Trade are you?
> *Cobl.* Truely Sir, in respect of a fine Workman, I am but as you
> would say, a Cobler.
>
> (13–15)[5]

The Guild of Carpenters may have led processions on Corpus Christi, but the cobblers of the Shoemakers' Company had a leading role in Elizabethan Shrove Tuesday celebrations. They sponsored the traditional Shrovetide football game, and provided the ball. On account of excessive violence, football was banned at Chester in 1540, after which 'the Shoemakers' Company were to sponsor a foot race instead' (Hutton, 1994, 41–2). Appropriate to Shrovetide, Shakespeare's Cobbler is in an irreverent carnival mood:

> *Mur.* But what Trade art thou? Answer me directly.
> *Cob.* A Trade Sir, that I hope I may use, with a safe Conscience,
> which is indeed Sir, a Mender of bad soules.
>
> (16–18)

The Cobler's theological punning on 'conscience' and 'bad soules [souls]' has received insufficient comment.[6] The Christian conscience is a Pauline conception. 'Conscience' has only one mention in the Gospel of John and three in the letters of St Peter against more than thirty references by Paul in 1 and 2 Corinthians, Romans, Timothy, Titus, Hebrews and Acts.[7] The Pauline connections of Shakespeare's Cobbler intensify as the man describes himself:

> Truly Sir, all that I live by, is with the Aule: I meddle with no Tradesmans matters, nor womens matters; but withal I am indeed Sir, a Surgeon to old shooes: when they are in great danger, I recover them. As proper men as ever trod upon Neats Leather, have gone upon my handy-worke.
>
> (27–32)[8]

One who 'meddle[s] with no women's matters' suggests a celibate. Paul was unmarried and, likely, celibate. Paul also carried an awl. We moderns are taught that Paul's profession was tentmaker or weaver. But the tents of Paul's day were fashioned of animal skins, not expensive woven cloth.[9] Elizabethans believed that Paul was a leatherworker, one who worked with an awl. The Geneva Bible gloss to Luke's description of Paul's occupation in Acts 18:3 ('to make tentes') reads, 'Or pavillions which then were made of skinnes' (Geneva, QQ.iiii). Unique among the apostles, Paul was present in Jerusalem before Christ made his triumphal entry into that city.

Hearing the Cobbler's declaration that the plebeians 'make Holy-day to see *Caesar*, and to rejoyce', Murellus reprimands them:

> Wherefore rejoyce?
> What Conquest brings he [Caesar] home?
> What Tributaries follow him to Rome,
> To grace in Captive bonds his Chariot Wheeles?
> You Blockes, you stones, you worse then senselesse things
>
> (38–42)

Here for the first time the word 'grace' is associated with Caesar, as it will be each time the word appears in the play. Murellus's castigation of the plebeians as 'blockes' and 'stones' recalls Christ's rebuke to the Pharisees on the day of his entry into Jerusalem on Palm Sunday. Paul was a Pharisee: 'He cried out in the Councill, Men and brethren, I am a Pharise, the sonne of a Pharise' (Acts 23:6). Christ's reference to 'stones' appears only in the Gospel of St Luke – the only Gospel in which Christ is recognized by the people by the name 'king': 'Blessed be the King that cometh in the name of the Lord: peace in heaven, and glory in the highest' (Luke 19:38). Cassius will soon play on Brutus's fear that the Roman plebeians are about to choose Caesar for their king. This is another of Shakespeare's inventions. In Plutarch the commons are firmly opposed to Caesar's royal ambitions. Once we recognize Shakespeare's borrowing from Luke's report of the events on Palm Sunday, a figure in Cassius's description of Caesar previously thought inscrutable becomes transparent:

> it doth amaze me,
> A man of such a feeble temper [Caesar] should
> So get the start of the Majesticke world,
> And beare the Palme alone.
>
> (226–9)

Commentators have concluded that 'start' implies 'outstrip, so gaining the *palm* of victory' (Humphreys, 1984, 109n).[10] This is not safe. The *Oxford English Dictionary* also defines 'start' as 'the footstalk of a fruit ... the stalk of a plant' (*OED* start n.1, 3.a.b). The word is still used in this sense by gardeners in the New England region of the United States. The word 'Majesticke' is closely followed by 'Palm[e]'. Christ's entry into Jerusalem on Palm Sunday began the two weeks of Passiontide (Baldock, 1990, 105). Palm Sunday rituals were known to Elizabethans. Although there were no palm trees in England, the Salisbury rite prescribed an anamnetic ritual: the priest blessed branches 'gathered and presented by the people in memory of the palms said to have been strewn before Jesus' (Hutton, 1994, 20). This custom was one of the few survivals of the Henrican reforms, and persisted into Shakespeare's time (Laroque, 1993, 107). Another survival was the 'prophet' who appeared in English churches on Palm Sunday to read or sing the lessons at Passiontide.[11] On the day of his triumphal entry into Rome, Shakespeare's Caesar encounters a prophet: the Soothsayer. Caesar bears the palm, is destined to be martyred, becomes a god.

Shakespeare's confrontation between the Tribunes and plebeians in 1.1 is entirely the playwright's invention. In Plutarch

> the clash of tribunes and crowd takes place after, not before, the Lupercalia; the tribunes are adherents of Brutus, not Pompey; the crowds come to rejoice at the insult to Caesar's images, not at his triumph; while finally the images are adorned with diadems for the proposed coronation, not, as in Shakespeare, with trophies for the triumph.
>
> (J. D. Wilson, 1948, xvii–xviii)

Why has the playwright rewritten his source, and moved these events to the Lupercal? Richard Wilson has suggested that 'No work of Shakespeare's is more alert to the subversiveness of the traditional festival than *Julius Caesar*, which actually opens in the Roman Carnival' (R. Wilson, 1992, 2). Shrovetide antics were in the Elizabethan theatrical air in the summer of 1599. If *Julius Caesar* were on the boards from 12 June 1599, Shakespeare's Cobbler and his band may have inspired Dekker's *The Shoemaker's Holiday*, which played at the Rose after 15 July, the date of Henslowe's payment for the play. In Dekker's benign and whimsical topsy-turvy, a humble mechanical becomes a wealthy merchant, wins election as Lord Mayor of London, and marries his daughter to a nobleman. But there is a darker side to the tense topsy-turveydom between Shakespeare's well-dressed plebeians and his Tribunes. After the assassination of Caesar, a nightwatch of plebeians turns the tables on their social superiors and catechizes the poet Cinna to death. The principal actor in the Shrovetide topsy-turveydom was the 'Lord of Misrule', a servant momentarily elevated to a position of absolute authority. The archetype of this Misrule myth is the Christ of the Gospel of St Mark who taught, 'For even the Sonne of man came not to be served, but to serve, and to give his life for the raunsome of manie' (Mark 10:45). But in the gaiety of England's traditional pre-Lenten topsy-turvydom the Christ archetype was perverted. The lowly servant becomes a ruler, but he serves man's vice rather than his salvation. *That* is the dark raillery of Elizabethan Shrovetide which Shakespeare captures.

The Lord of Misrule was a familiar figure to Elizabethans.[12] His popularity is attested, and detested, by a sermon preached in St Paul's on St Bartholomew's Day 1578: 'There be now many places where ye word is preached besides the Lords day, yet even that day the better part of it is horriblie prophaned by devellish inventions, as with Lords of Missrule' (cited by Laroque, 1993, 37). As the occasion for (and patron saint of) the plebeians' civil disobedience in *Julius Caesar*, Richard Wilson sees Caesar supplying this function. 'He is the Carnival King, a Lord of Misrule who governs by exploiting his subjects' desire with his "foolery," manipulating "fat, Sleek-headed men," as he indulges Antony in plays and music when he "revels long a nights"' (R. Wilson, 1992, 50). Caesar is the authority cited for an unauthorized 'Holy day', thereby altering the calendar. He presides over the Lupercalian carnival. During his performance in the marketplace he suffers or more likely feigns an epileptic attack (351). The people clap and hiss him as they do actors

(363). The greatest man in secular history addresses common street people as 'Worships' (374).[13] But most important to fulfilling his role as Lord of Misrule, Caesar dies. Chambers (among others) suggests the roots of the Misrule death-imperative are buried in prehistoric village rites surrounding the passage from winter/death to spring/rebirth (Chambers, 1925, 116ff.). But the syncretic thread of man-death-re-birth-god that unites early Christianity and its Mithraic rivals suggests that the roots go deeper, and are so ancient as to be elemental or nearly so. The primitive death-rebirth blood-ritual tradition was familiar to young William Shakespeare in a degenerated, 'civilized' form. Chambers cites 'survivals' within twenty miles of Stratford-upon-Avon in 'the Whitsun "lamb feast" at Kidlington, the Trinity "lamb ale" at Kirtling-ton, and the "Whit hunt" in Wychwood Forest, all three places lying close together in Oxfordshire' (Chambers, 1951, 141). But even if the boy Shakespeare had somehow remained unaware of these festivities, the man could hardly have been unaware of the Elizabethan custom of electing a sacrificial Shrovetide 'king'. 'The Shrovetide Lord of Misrule was an almost universal presence in noble houses in England and em-bodied before the assembled worthies not only good Saturnalian fun but also all of the sins of the flesh, all of the indulgences of carnival, which they would have to repent and give over by the end of Shrovetide and the beginning of Lent' (Hassel, 1979, 74). In 1599 both Lincoln's Inn and the Middle Temple each had its Prince of Misrule. But most germane to our interest in *Julius Caesar* is this report of the festivities at Gray's Inn: 'The next grand Night was intended to be upon *Innocents-Day* at Night [28 December] . . . In regard whereof . . . a Comedy of Errors (like to *Plautus* his *Menechmus*) was played by the Players' (Foakes, 1962, 116). The play is generally believed to have been Sha-kespeare's.[14] If so, Shakespeare was an eyewitness to the antics of the 'Prince of Purpoole'. The colour purple in which the pretender may have been attired had many attributions. Purple was the 'distinguishing colour of the dress of emperors and kings'. But it is also associated with sin and, as early as 1598, with over-flashy prose (*OED* n.a.1.a and 3.a). Purple was also associated with high ecclesiastical office (*OED* 2.b,d). Shakespeare would have known from Plutarch that the Senate accorded Julius Caesar the singular privilege of wearing a purple robe in perpe-tuity. Caesar wore it on the Lupercal in 44 BC, and was wearing it at the time of his murder – as he may have done in Shakespeare's play.

In the twentieth century the vogue for historicizing Shakespeare has emphasized the political dimension – the *obvious* dimension – of *Julius Caesar*. By contrast, the religious dimension of *Julius Caesar* – the profound dimension – has been largely ignored by our learned but secularized age. Francis Douce was first (1807) to detect a connection between the Roman Lupercal and its English homologue, St Valentine's Day (Douce, 1807, ii.252). In respect of sexual licence, Valentine's Day ushered in the season of courtship and love.[15] No one who hears *Julius Caesar* performed can fail to be struck by the play's repeated references to love. The word and its variants ('lover', 'loves', 'loving', 'beloved') appear fifty-seven times – an average of once every fifty lines – an extraordinary total for a play with no 'love story'. Shakespeare's Gaius Cassius Longinus is a man obsessed with love – an appropriate figure for an encounter on a Roman Lupercal which coincides with St Valentine's Eve. Cassius importunes Brutus:

> I have not from your eyes, that gentlenesse
> And shew of Love, as I was wont to have:
> You beare too stubborne, and too strange a hand
> Over your Friend, that loves you.
>
> (124–7)

Brutus hastens to reassure Cassius that his behaviour is only preoccupation which 'Forgets the shewes of Love' (139). But the Cassius who 'loves no plays' is mightily concerned with outward 'shew'. He asks,

> Tell me good *Brutus*, Can you see your face?
> *Bru.* No, *Cassius*:
> For the eye sees not it selfe but by reflection,
> By some other things.
> *Cas.*   'Tis just,
> And it is very much lamented *Brutus*,
> That you have no such Mirrors, as will turne
> Your hidden worthinesse into your eye,
> That you might see your shadow:
>
> (143–51)

Cassius offers to become Brutus's mirror: 'I your Glasse, / Will modestly discover to your selfe, / That of your selfe, which you yet know not of' (162–4). Cassius's subject matter – face, mirror, eye, see, shadow, self-knowledge – is curiously reminiscent of a passage from St Paul's First Epistle to the Corinthians: 'For nowe wee see thorow a glasse darkely: but then shall wee see face to face. Nowe I know in part: but then shall

I knowe even as I am knowen.' (1 Corinthians 13:12).[16] 1 Corinthians 13 is one of Paul's greatest literary passages. It was also a favourite of Shakespeare – who parodied it in Feste's jig which closes *Twelfth Night*,[17] and in *Love's Labour's Lost* (1594/5). Berowne caps his 175-line speech about the primacy of love over oaths: 'It is religion to be thus forsworn; / For charity itself fulfils the law; / And who can sever love from charity' (359–61).[18] This is a paraphrase of 1 Corinthians 13:11 and Paul's colossal claim for Christianity against the Mosaic law: 'For all the Law is fulfilled in one worde, which is this, Thou shalt love thy neighbour as thy self' (Galatians 5:14). Commentators since Edmond Malone (1821) have hypothesized that Shakespeare borrowed Brutus's reply from the poem *Nosce Teipsum*, by Sir John Davies:

> Is it because the mind is like the eye,
> Through which it gathers knowledge by degrees;
> Whose rays reflect not, but spread outwardly;
> Not seeing itself, when other things it sees?
>
> (Malone, 1821, 13n)[19]

This assumption is not safe. More likely, both Shakespeare and Davies borrowed from a common Roman source. In his *Tusculan Disputations* dedicated to Brutus, Cicero wrote, '*Non valet tantum animus, ut se ipsum ipse videat: at ut oculus, sic animus se non videns alia cernit*' (King, 1989, 78). Shakespeare and Davies certainly had access to the English translation of the *Tusculan Disputations* by John Dolman (1561), who renders this passage, 'the soule is not able in this bodye to see him selfe. No more is the eye wyche although he seeth all other thinges, yet (that whiche is one of the leaste) can not discerne his owne shape' (Dolman, 1561, E6v). Cicero was also the author of *De Natura Deorum* and *De Divinatione*, two books riddled with religious scepticism and not a little atheism. Shakespeare's Lupercalian conversation between Brutus and Cassius takes place in those liminal years, 44 BC to AD 33, when a man could become a god. (See Appendix 7.)

Shakespeare's Pauline Cassius

Cassius begins to whet Brutus to the murder of Caesar by touching a subject most dear to him: 'Honor is the subject of my Story' (190).

> I cannot tell, what you and other men
> Thinke of this life: But for my single selfe,

I had as liefe not be, as live to be
In awe of such a Thing, as I my selfe.

(191–4)

The keyword in this speech is 'awe'. It means 'dread mingled with veneration', and 'the attitude of a mind subdued to profound reverence in the presence of mysterious sacredness' (*OED* awe n.1,2).[20] Cassius declares he would rather die than worship a man [Caesar] as a god. He launches into an enumeration of Caesar's all-too-mortal qualities. But as Cassius describes Caesar, he delivers an epitome of himself: 'I was born as free as *Caesar*, so were you' (195). There is a parallel to this declaration in an exchange between Paul and the Centurion who holds him captive in Acts 22: 'And the chiefe captaine answered, With a great summe obtained I this freedome [Roman citizenship]. Then Paul said, But I was so borne' (Acts 22:28). Cassius reminds Brutus 'we can both Endure the Winters cold, as well as hee [Caesar]' (196–7). As an itinerant preacher, Paul was no stranger to inclement weather: 'In wearinesse and painefulnesse, in watching often, in hunger and thirst, fastings often, in colde and nakedness' (2 Corinthians 11:27). This passage was the reading for 14 June. Cassius next describes a swimming match with Caesar:

> For once, upon a Rawe and Gustie day,
> The troubled Tyber, chafing with her Shores,
> *Caesar* saide to me, Dar'st thou *Cassius* now
> Leape in with me into this angry Flood,
> And swim to yonder Point? Upon the word,
> Accoutred as I was, I plunged in,
> And bad him follow: so indeed he did.
> The Torrent roar'd, and we did buffet it
> With lusty Sinewes, throwing it aside,
> And stemming it with hearts of Controversie.
> But ere we could arrive the Point propos'd,
> *Caesar* cride, Helpe me *Cassius*, or I sinke.
> I (as *Aeneas*, our great Ancestor,
> Did from the Flames of *Troy*, upon his shoulder
> The old *Anchyses* beare) so, from the waves of *Tyber*
> Did I the tyred *Caesar*.

(198–213)

The vivid language of Cassius's tale – and his reference to the mythological rescue of Anchises by Aeneas – imbue the anecdote with the force of parable. But Shakespeare and his auditors who had read Plutarch knew Cassius was lying. Caesar was a formidable swimmer. During the battle at Pharos, Caesar escaped an Egyptian encirclement by leaping into the sea in full armour, and swimming away (North, 1579, 787). St Paul was a strong swimmer, too: 'I suffered thrice shipwracke: night & day have I bene in ye depe sea' (2 Corinthians 11:25). In Acts 27:42–3 Paul and others must swim to shore when their ship breaks up off Melita. This is the only appearance of the word 'swimme' in the New Testament.[21]

Cassius now refers to Caesar as a god: 'And this Man, / Is now become a God, and *Cassius* must bend his body, / If *Caesar* carelesly but nod on him' (213–15). Cassius's tone is ironic, as it is each time he declares Caesar's divinity: 'immortall *Caesar*' (153); 'this Man, Is now become a God' (213–14); and ''Tis true, this God did shake' (219). The proclamation of Christ's divinity through the words of a sceptic recurs repeatedly in the New Testament.[22] In medieval and Renaissance hagiography, particularly in *The Golden Legend* (Ryan, 1993, i. 184ff.), a Longinus of Cassius's *gens* was identified with the centurion who stabbed Christ and then declared him the Son of God. 'Nowe when the Centurion [Longinus], which stood over against him, saw that he thus crying gave up the ghost, he say, Truely this man was the Sonne of God' (Mark 15:37). Mark 15 was the reading for the second lesson on 15 June Julian. Cassius repeats the phrase 'give up the ghost' in Act 5 (2428). Cassius insists he and Brutus 'have fed as well [as Caesar]' (196). Paul had a good deal to say about eating, both to his disciples and, pointedly, to Peter during the argument known as the 'Incident at Antioch'. Peter and the Jerusalem faction stood for the fulfilment of the Mosaic Law as a precondition for being a Christian – including both adult circumcision and strict observance of *kosher* dietary restrictions. Paul held that the Mosaic Law was indifferent to salvation, which was through faith alone, saying, 'One beleeveth that hee may eate of all things' (Romans 14:2). The division of opinion climaxed in a confrontation which Paul recounted in Galatians 2:11–21. When Peter reverted to observing the *kosher* laws, Paul argued that Christ's apotheosis had abrogated the law. In their famous confrontation at Sardis in 4.2, Brutus will stand for the law. Cassius will argue that Caesar's calendar and his death have abrogated the law: 'In such a time as this, it is not meet / That every nice offence should beare his Comment' (1976–7). But in Shakespeare's portrait of the Lupercal his most daring allusion to the letters of St Paul occurs in Cassius's image of the decay of republican Rome:

> When went there by an Age, since the great Flood,
> But it was fam'd with more then with one man?
> When could they say (till now) that talk'd of Rome,
> That her wide Walkes incompast but one man?
> Now is it Rome indeed, and Roome enough
> When there is in it but one onely man?
>
> (251–6)

This passage has occasioned lively scholarly debate (Furness, 1913, 40n). Cassius – a pagan – could hardly be making reference to the Old Testament story of the flood (Genesis 5:29–10:32). The conventional wisdom suggests that Cassius is referring to the mythical Deucalion, who escaped the flood of Zeus and founded Greece (Spevack, 1988, 61n). This is not safe. Cassius's reference is another of Shakespeare's anachronisms, but it does not refer to the story of Noah. Noah was not saved alone, but with his sons and family. St Peter refers to Noah as one of 'eight souls' and as 'the eighth man' (1 Peter 3:20, and 2 Peter 2:5).[23] It is not the reference to the 'great Flood' which is the key to identifying Shakespeare's source in Scripture but Cassius's insistence on the solitary individual: 'one man ... one man ... one onely man'. This is an echo of Paul writing to the Romans:

> Wherefore, as by one man sinne entered into the world, and death by sinne, & so death went over all men: in whom all men have sinned ... For if by the offense of one, death reigned through one, much more shall they which receive that abundance of grace, and of that gift of that righteousnesse, reigne in life through one, that is, Jesus Christ. Likewise then, as by the offence of one, the fault came on all men to condemnation, so by the justifying of one, the benefit abounded toward all men ... For as by one mans disobedience many were made sinners, so by that obedience of that one, shall many also be made righteous.
>
> (Romans 5:12–19)

There was, perhaps, no single passage of scripture more closely studied in Shakespeare's time. The Catholic Council of Trent had ratified the so-called Doctrine of Original Sin based on these verses. The Geneva gloss on verse 12 reads: 'From Adam, in whome all have sinned, both guiltinesse and death (which is the punishment of the guiltinesse) came upon all.' The concept of the two Adams was a central precept of Renaissance Christianity. It is a Pauline conception.

To his portrait of a 'Pauline' Cassius on the Lupercal Shakespeare adds a final invention. His Cassius forges the anonymous letters which prod Brutus to join the conspiracy. Again Shakespeare is rewriting a source. Plutarch recorded that various Romans wrote letters to Brutus encouraging him to rise against Caesar's ambition.[24] Shakespeare attributes these forged letters to Cassius alone. Of course, it goes without saying that St Paul was a prodigious letter-writer. The letters Brutus receives call upon him to 'awake', a word Shakespeare never found in Plutarch. There are only three calls to 'awake' in the New Testament – *all three* in the letters of Paul (Romans 13:11; 1 Corinthians 15:34; Ephesians 5:14). The most significant of these appears in the Epistle to the Ephesians: 'Wherefore he saith, Awake thou that sleepest, and arise from the dead, and Christ shall give thee light. See then that ye walk circumspectly, not as fools, but as wise, Redeeming the time, because the days are evil' (Ephesians 5:14–16). Shakespeare had already parodied this passage in *1 Henry IV* (1596/7): 'I'll so offend, to make offence a skill, / Redeeming time when men think least I will' (1.2.211–12).

In February 1599 – when perhaps Shakespeare was hard at work on *Julius Caesar* – the rival calendars created a concordance between St Valentine's Day, Shrove Tuesday and the Roman Lupercal. The playwright seems to infuse the opening scenes of *Julius Caesar* with allusions to these three holy days. He also borrows from the Epistles of St Paul which were read both in mid-February and Midsummer. By so doing Shakespeare instils curious qualities in his Cassius which crystallize during the 'Incident at Sardis' in 4.2, and, in a startling Pauline paradox, on the day of the battle of Philippi.

Notes

1 The Book of Common Prayer prescribed the psalms and passages from the Old and New Testament to be read each day at morning and evening prayer. Broadly speaking, each psalm in the Psalter was read once each month. With certain exclusions, the Old Testament was read through once each year. Except for certain passages from the Book of Revelation, the New Testament was read three times each year. On holy days the quotidian

selections might be superseded by passages of Scripture associated with the observance. (See Appendix 11.)

2　Paul's Epistles to the Corinthians were a favourite source for *Julius Caesar* and for its successor, *Twelfth Night, Or What You Will*. See Chapter 17.

3　A fuller discussion of these issues appears in Chapter 13 below.

4　The Roman Lupercal is never mentioned until the plebeians have left the stage (75).

5　'Cobbler' meant both 'inept workman' and 'leatherworker'.

6　See Kaufmann and Ronan, 1970, 21. Compare: 'Nor does the Christian conception of conscience appear in [Shakespeare's Roman] plays' (Alvis, 1979, 124).

7　St Paul was unique among the authors of the New Testament in that he was already in Jerusalem when Christ arrived on Palm Sunday. As young Saul, Paul had journeyed to Jerusalem from his birthplace in Tarsus to study with Rabbi Gamaliel.

8　A. J. Bate detects a nod to Dekker's *The Shoemaker's Holiday*: 'Let Rafe and his wife stay together, shees a yong new married woman, if you take her husband away from her a night, you undoo her, she may beg in the day time, for hees as good a workman at pricke and awle, as any is in our trade' (Bate, 1986, 461). In addition to punning on 'aule [awl] = prick' Shakespeare adds a comment: a 'Neat' was any horned animal, and associated with cuckoldry.

9　Acts 18:3. Shakespeare's cobbler describes himself as 'a Surgeon to old shooes'; Luke, of course, was a physician. Colossians 4:14.

10　The Riverside editor comments, 'Nearly all commentators gloss [start] as "outstrip," although *OED* "Start" sb^{2}6, citing this instance, gives "priority or position in advance of others in any competitive undertaking."' Also see Spevack, 1988, 60n. Dorsch (1983, 15n) cites *MWW* 5.5.170, 'You have the start of me'.

11　Some churches – like St Peter Cheap – hired a wig or false beard to make their prophet appear more 'patriarchal' (Hutton, 1994, 21). The Chester Cathedral prophet was 'rewarded with a jug of malmsey and a pair of gloves (Hutton, 1994, 97).

12　The 'office' of Lord of Misrule had received official endorsement in 1545 when Henry VIII 'wrote into the statutes of St. John's College, Cambridge ... a clause directing that its Christmas festivities should be supervised by a such a "lord." At neighboring Trinity ... the same office was instituted at once' (Hutton, 1994, 90). Suppressed in the 1570s, the office was revived by the students in 1607–8; the Lord's reign commenced at the beginning of Advent (30 November), and he was allowed 'to die' on Shrove Tuesday (9 February).

13　Caesar 'not only wants the crown; he also wants everyone to want him to have it' (Paris, 1987, 141).

14　In Chapter 17 I will suggest that this play was purpose written for this performance.

15 The association of St Valentine and 14 February with the (haphazard) choosing of a lover was inaugurated by Geoffrey Chaucer in the *Book of St Valentine's Day of the Parliament of Birds*, familiarly known as the *Parliament of Fowls*. Chaucer wove the connection of saint-love-day out of calendar lore. According to ancient tradition, the first day of spring was recognized as 8 February, and the first day of summer on 10 May, 'so that the vernal equinox would fall midway in the season' rather than at the beginning of spring as it does in the modern calendar (Kelly, 1986, 3ff.).

16 1 Corinthians 13 is important as Scripture, and one of the best-known, best-loved, most widely quoted passages in the New Testament. Modern readers may find this link obscure because our King James version of 1 Corinthians is Jacobean: 'And now abideth faith, hope, charity, these three; but the greatest of these is charity' (*agapé*). On Sunday before St Valentine's Day 1599, English Christians would have heard or read: 'And now abideth faith, hope & love, even these thre: but the chiefest of these is love.'

17 See a fuller discussion in Chapter 17. I will suggest that Shakespeare was a particularly close reader of the letters of Paul, and aware of the roots of Paul's travels which took him to Illyria. I will also suggest that Shakespeare played on Paul's self-descriptions as 'a fool' in *TN* and elsewhere.

18 See Shaheen, 1987, 184.

19 Davies's work was registered for publication on 18 April 1599.

20 The word recurs twice in *Julius Caesar*, both times in the diction of Cassius. Again in this speech of Cassius: 'And that same Eye, whose bend doth awe the World' (221). Then as Brutus 'pieces out' the letters written by Cassius: 'Shall Rome stand under one mans awe' (671).

21 'But the Centurion willing to save Paul, stayed them from this counsell, and commaunded that they that could swimme, should cast themselves first into the sea, and goe out to land' (Acts 27:43). Paul was, of course, raised and trained according to Jewish law (Acts 22:3). Under Jewish law, a father has four obligations to his son: to teach him the Torah, to find him a wife, to teach him a craft, to teach him to swim.

22 The Geneva gloss to Luke 23:47 reads: 'Christ causeth his very enemies to give honorable witnesse on his side, so oft as it pleaseth him.' To cite one familiar instance, the interrogation of Christ before the High Priest in the Gospel of Luke: 'Then sayd they all, Art thou then the Sonne of God? And he said unto them, Ye say, that I am' (Luke 22:70). Similar examples may be found in Matthew and Mark and elsewhere in Luke.

23 On the other hand, Shakespeare's Cassius could be making a topical reference to the great flood which inundated Rome at Christmastime 1598, and was reported in an anonymous pamphlet printed in London early in 1599, *A Terrible Deluge or Overflowing in Roome*, London: J. Wolfe, 1599. STC21301.

24 These letters 'did openlie call and procure him to doe that he did. For, under

the image of his auncester *Junius Brutus*, that drave the kinges out of Rome, they wrote: O, that it pleased the goddes thou were now alive, *Brutus*: and againe, that thou were amonge us nowe. His tribunall (or chaire) where he gave audience duringe the time he was Praetor, was full of suche billes: *Brutus*, thou art a sleepe, and art not *Brutus* in deede' (North, 1579, 1059).

11

Ash Wednesday, the night of the Lupercal and the eve of the Ides of March

In February 1599 the rival calendars also created a concordance between the Catholic Vigil of Ash Wednesday and the night of the Roman Lupercal. In the dramatic universe of Shakespeare's *Julius Caesar* the night of the Lupercal is also the eve of the Ides of March. Recognizing the connection between these three important occasions explains a series of cruces which have frustrated commentators (and actors) for centuries. For example, gallons of scholarly ink have been spilt in pursuit of Brutus's motive for refusing to pledge an oath on the eve of the Ides:[1]

> No, not an Oath: if not the Face of men,
> The sufferance of our Soules, the times Abuse;
> If these be Motives weake, breake off betimes,
> And every man hence, to his idle bed:
> So let high-sighted-Tyranny range on,
> Till each man drop by Lottery.
>
> (745–50)

Brutus's reason for refusing an oath is simply calendrical. The Vigil of Ash Wednesday marked the end of Hilary term and the beginning of Lent. Elizabethan courts recessed, and the swearing of oaths was prohibited by the six-hundred-year-old statutes of VI Aethelred 25 and I Canute 17 (Cheney, 1991, 66–7). In 1599, the law courts closed on 20 February and reopened on 12 April. They were closed both on Ash Wednesday and the Ides of March. This temporal marker would certainly have been accessible to members of the Inns of Court.

Our recognition of this temporal link between Ash Wednesday and the Ides also explains Brutus's diffidence about the form of Caesar's murder: 'Let's be Sacrificers, but not Butchers' (799). The butchering of animals was forbidden during Lent, a Catholic holdover which horrified English Puritans (Laroque, 1993, 104).[2] This link also accounts for Brutus's fine distinction between a propitiatory sacrifice and table meat: 'Let's carve him, as a Dish fit for the Gods, / Not hew him as a Carkasse fit for Hounds' (806–7). During Lent there was one allowed form of bloodletting. It entailed the sacrifice of a 'meat' suitable for immortals:

> For my flesh is meate indeede, and my blood is drinke indeede. He that eateth my flesh, and drinketh my blood, dwelleth in me, and I in him. As the living Father hath sent me, so live I by the Father: and he that eateth me, even hee shall live by me. This is that bread which came downe from heaven: not as your fathers have eaten manna, and are dead. He that eateth of this bread [shall live for ever.
>
> (John 6:55–8)

The Lord's Supper was the one 'blood sacrifice' permitted during Lent. In this Lenten mood Brutus's thoughts tend towards repentance:

> And let our Hearts, as subtle Masters do,
> Stirre up their Servants to an acte of Rage,
> And after seeme to chide 'em.
>
> (808–10)[3]

Another Lenten proscription echoes in the encounter between Brutus and Portia: sexual abstinence. It is clear from their dialogue that the couple have not been sharing the conjugal bed. Portia's voluntary wound is, of course, an act of self-mortification.

Another series of textual markers appear as Brutus paces alone in his orchard and receives the conspirators. Shakespeare laces the diction of these scenes with borrowings from St Paul's 1 Thessalonians 5. As the sequence begins, Brutus is concerned about the date and time. He dispatches Lucius to check the date in the calendar. Paul warned the Thessalonians not to be concerned with dates: 'But of the times and the seasons, brethren, ye have no need that I write unto you. For yourselves know perfectly that the day of the Lord so cometh as a thief in the night' (1 Thessalonians 5:1–2). Indeed, like thieves in the night the conspirators will soon arrive with anachronistic hats 'pluckt about their Eares' and faces half-buried in cloaks (696–7). Although it is after midnight,

Brutus says, 'The exhalations, whizzing in the ayre, / Give so much light, that I may reade by them' (662–3). Paul tells the Thessalonians, 'But ye, brethren, are not in darkness. Ye are all the children of light' (1 Thessalonians 4–5). Brutus says 'Since *Cassius* first did whet me against *Caesar*, I have not slept' (682–3). Paul taught, 'Therefore let us not sleep, as do others; but let us watch and be sober' (1 Thessalonians 6). Brutus is determined that the assassination of Caesar should be carried out in a sober demeanour: 'Let not our lookes put on our purposes, / But beare it as our Roman Actors do, / With untyr'd Spirits, and formall Constancie' (862–4). Brutus insists that Caesar's murder must not appear to be 'Wrath in death' (797). Paul wrote that 'God hath not appointed us to wrath' (1 Thessalonians 5:8). Shakespeare's borrowing from 1 Thessalonians 5 was not capricious. The liturgical calendar prescribed these verses for reading for the Ides of March.[4]

A calculated nativity

In Chapter 4 above I suggested that Shakespeare infused his portrait of Caesar on the Lupercal with borrowings from St Luke's narrative of the annunciation to Zacharias and the birth of John Baptist. Lettered Elizabethans could have accepted a link between John Baptist and Caesar's 'son', Octavius. Suetonius gives the birthdate of Octavius (who later took the name Augustus): 'Augustus was borne, when M. Tullius Cicero and Antonie were Consuls, the ninth day before the Calends of October, a little before Sunrising' (Holland, 1606, 39). A marginal note clarifies this date as '23. Of September'. As noted, 23 September is the traditional date of the conception of John Baptist. Shakespeare certainly realized that the births of *both* John Baptist and Octavius were essential preconditions for the coming of Jesus Christ. Octavius Augustus created the *Pax Romana*, the 'time of universal peace' which is the *sine qua non* of the Messiah's birth according to Isaiah 39:8ff. It is commonplace to note that Shakespeare glances at this in *Antony and Cleopatra*: 'The time of universal peace is near' (4.6.4). But it has not been recognized that Shakespeare refers to birth of a new world in the dialogue between Cassius and Casca on the unruly night in *Julius Caesar*:

> You are dull, *Caska*:
> And those sparkes of Life, that should be in a Roman,
> You doe want, or else you use not.

You looke pale, and gaze, and put on feare,
And cast your selfe in wonder,
To see the strange impatience of the Heavens.
But if you would consider the true cause,
Why all these Fires, why all these gliding Ghosts,
Why Birds and Beasts, from qualitie and kinde,
Why Old men, Fooles, and Children calculate,
Why all these things change from their Ordinance,
Their Natures, and pre-formed Faculties,
To monstrous qualitie; why you shall finde,
That Heaven hath infus'd them with these Spirits,
To make them Instruments of feare, and warning,
Unto some monstrous State.

(495–510)

The key phrase in Cassius's speech is 'Why Old men, Fooles, and Children calculate' (504). Dr Johnson explained: '*To calculate a nativity* is the technical term' (Sherbo, 1968, 828). In the morning, Calpurnia will fret that the portents of the unruly night presaged the death of Caesar.[5] But Cassius perceives that the prodigies presage not the death of a man but the birth of 'some monstrous State'. The word 'State' appears six times in the Folio text, twice with a lower-case 's':

The Genius, and the mortall Instruments
Are then in councell; and the state of a man,
Like to a little Kingdome, suffers then
The nature of an Insurrection.

(686–9)

I shall try
In my Oration, how the People take
The cruell issue of these bloody men,
According to the which, thou shalt discourse
To yong Octavius, of the state of things.

(1523–7)

In both instances 'state' refers to 'a combination of circumstances or attributes belonging for the time-being to a person or thing' (*OED* state n. I. 1. a). But on four other occasions the word 'State' appears with an initial capital 'S':

There was a *Brutus* once, that would have brook'd

Th'eternall Divell to keepe his State in Rome,
As easily as a King.

(258–60)

That Heaven hath infus'd them with these Spirits,
To make them Instruments of feare, and warning,
Unto some monstrous State.

(508–10)

[Antony] will follow
The Fortunes and Affayres of Noble *Brutus*,
Thorough the hazards of this untrod State,
With all true Faith.

(1352–5)

How many Ages hence
Shall this our lofty Scene be acted over,
In State unborne, and Accents yet unknowne?

(1326–8)

On each occasion when 'State' is printed with an initial capital, the word appears in conjunction with either metaphysical referents or ritual action. This consistency cannot be dismissed as accidents. The copy for the Folio text almost certainly differentiated these homonyms. Shakespeare wrote 'state' to describe a condition or circumstance, and 'State' to describe a 'system of divine government' (*OED* n.I.5μb).[6] To illuminate the meaning of 'monstrous State' Cassius pronounces Caesar a god for the fourth time:

Now could I (Caska) name to thee a man,
Most like this dreadfull Night,
That Thunders, Lightens, opens Graves, and roares,
As doth the Lyon in the Capitoll:
A man no mightier then thy selfe, or me,
In personall action; yet prodigious growne,
And fearefull, as these strange eruptions are.

(511–17)

Cassius associates Caesar with the symbology of God (thunder and lightning), the Last Judgment (opening of graves) and the resurrection (the lion as a symbol of immortality) (Baldock, 1990, 101–2). These Christian associations are reinforced by Cassius's next figure:

124

> for Romans now
> Have Thewes, and Limbes, like to their Ancestors;
> But woe the while, our Fathers mindes are dead,
> And we are govern'd with our Mothers spirits,
> Our yoake, and sufferance, shew us Womanish.
> (520–4)

It was cliché among Renaissance religious malcontents – Machiavelli being one – to describe Christianity as an effeminate and feminizing religion: '[When] our religion demands that in you there be strength, what it asks for is strength to suffer rather than strength to do bold things ... the world were become effeminate' (Walker, 1983, 277–8). The 'State' which is about to be born is monstrous, godly, suffering, womanish. It is Christianity. It is the 'State of Grace'.

To amplify this Christian connection Shakespeare uses Cassius to introduce the visual image which will dominate the balance of *Julius Caesar*: the dagger, or short Roman broadsword (V. Thomas, 1992, 77). Cassius declares, 'I know where I will weare this Dagger then' (529). In Shakespeare's era unsheathing a weapon was a threatening act; drawing a sword in the presence of the monarch was punishable as treason. Oddly enough, the drawing of weapons in *Julius Caesar* leads to violence on only two occasions: during the assassination of Caesar, and at Philippi. In every other instance where a sword or dagger is unsheathed it is raised as a symbol of deliverance or salvation. Shakespeare carefully embedded stage directions in his dialogue to instruct the actors how to hold their weapons.

Figure 15.

For example, when Casca says, 'Heere, as I point my Sword, the Sunne arises' (737), he must hold his sword by the hilts (Figure 15). But, on the unruly night Cassius is suggesting suicide when he draws his dagger: 'I know where I will weare this Dagger then; / *Cassius* from bondage will deliver *Cassius*' (529–30). To emphasize the threat to himself, Cassius must hold his cruciform dagger by the blade (Figure 16). When Casca and the other conspirators turn their hands against Caesar there can be no question but that they hold

Figure 16.

Figure 17.

their weapons by the hilts. The stage direction is: '*They stab Caesar*' (1287) (Figure 17). But during their famous quarrel, Cassius must offer Brutus his dagger cruciform hilts first (Figure 16):

> There is my Dagger,
> And heere my naked Breast: Within, a Heart
> Deerer then *Pluto's* Mine, Richer then Gold:
> If that thou bee'st a Roman, take it foorth.
> I that deny'd thee Gold, will give my Heart:
> Strike as thou did'st at *Caesar* ...
>
> (2079–84)

This brings us to an intriguing question of stagecraft. During the 'words before blows' prior to the battle of Philippi, Octavius declares, 'Looke, I draw a Sword against Conspirators' (2384). In production, a question always arises: how can Octavius draw his sword without provoking Brutus and Cassius to do the same? By theatrical convention the actor playing Octavius steps back from the group.[7] But this is not supported by the text and not safe. More likely, Shakespeare's Octavius held his sword hilts-up (Figure 16) when he said:

> If arguing make us swet,
> The proofe of it will turne to redder drops:
> Looke, I draw a Sword against Conspirators,
> When thinke you that the Sword goes up againe?

> Never till *Caesars* three and thirtie wounds
> Be well aveng'd.
>
> (2382–7)

This certainly created a stunning tableau for auditors who knew that Christ sweated blood in Gesthesmene and died aged thirty-three.

The next appearance of a drawn sword occurs in Cassius's suicide scene. He offers his sword to Pindarus hilts-first (Figure 16) when he says:

> with this good Sword
> That ran through *Caesars* bowels, search this bosome.
> Stand not to answer: Heere, take thou the Hilts ...
>
> (2522–4)

Titinius soon follows Cassius in a self-inflicted death which requires him to hold his sword-hilt away from his body (Figure 16):

> By your leave Gods: This is a Romans part,
> Come *Cassius* Sword, and finde *Titinius* hart.
>
> (2575–6)

Likewise, Brutus will offer his sword to Volumnius hilts-up (Figure 16):

> Even for that our love of old, I prethee
> Hold thou my Sword Hilts, whilest I runne on it.
>
> (2671–2)

Again and again in *Julius Caesar*, a sword or dagger is raised to exhibit its cruciform hilts. Shakespeare recognized the iconography of cruciform

Figure 18.

sword hilts in *1 Henry IV* and in *Hamlet*. Falstaff swears 'by these hilts' (2.4.206), and Hamlet insists that his fellows should swear by his sword three times (1.5.154, 161, 179). The iconography of the sword vividly explains why Casca shouts, 'Speake hands for me' (1286) before he strikes at Caesar. Standing behind his victim with his weapon raised to stab Caesar 'on the necke', Casca's hands and dagger form the archetypal icon of martyrdom (Figure 18).

Notes

1 For example: Bellringer, 1970, 40, and Rabkin, 1964, 243.
2 Our word 'carnival' derives from the Latin *carnem levare*, 'the putting away or removal of flesh as food' (*OED* carnival n).
3 Laroque relates the vocabulary of food and eating to Carnival festivity; for Elizabethan commoners, one way to 'assimilate the world through language was to (re)convert it into food ... the act of speaking becomes a symbolic kind of consumption' (Laroque, 1993, 44). 'A closer look at some of [Brutus's] lines reveals that there are quasi-Christian elements ... that the sacrifice he envisions is a parody of Christian sacrifice. As "a dish fit for the gods" Caesar becomes like the "banquet of most heavenly good," the "most godly and heavenly feast" described in the Anglican Communion Service' (Kaula, 1981, 207).
4 Shakespeare had another reason to be interested in Paul's correspondence with the Thessalonian church. The city was less than eighty miles from Philippi, and Shakespeare apparently knew that the city had refused aid to Brutus and Cassius, and supported Octavius in the decisive battle of the war. In 4.2 Brutus may be referring to Thessalonica when he grumbles that 'The people 'twixt *Philippi*, and this ground / Do stand but in a forc'd affection: / For they have grug'd us Contribution'(2202–4).
5 The prodigies also 'resemble the chaotic events described in the various biblical accounts of doomsday, a connection Shakespeare makes explicit when he has Trebonius declare: "Men, wives, and children stare, cry out, and run, As it were doomsday"' (Kaula, 1981, 197).
6 This is another of Shakespeare's wordplays in *Julius Caesar* which are detectable only at sight (e.g., the 'Holiday' and 'Holy day' stichomythia in 1.1), suggesting that *Julius Caesar* was written for readers as well as auditors. This is at variance with received opinion that Shakespeare was indifferent to the publication of his plays. But by the time Shakespeare wrote *Julius Caesar*, the poet-playwright was hardly a stranger to print. *Venus and Adonis* had appeared in 1593; *The Rape of Lucrece*, *The Taming of the Shrew*, *Titus Andronicus* and *2 Henry VI* in 1594; *3 Henry VI* in 1595; *Romeo and Juliet* and *Richard II* and *III* in 1597; *1 Henry IV* and *Love's Labour's Lost* in 1598. Some of these editions were certainly pirated memorial texts. But Shakespeare could not have been unaware that his plays were being read. In the year following the writing of *Julius Caesar*, three plays – *2 Henry IV*, *Much Ado About Nothing* and *Henry V* – were registered for publication (in August 1600) and appeared in print within months of each other. On the evidence it seems likely that when Shakespeare wrote *Julius Caesar* he imagined (or even anticipated) that his play would not only be performed but read either in printed quarto or via the prevailing Elizabethan *samizdat*.
7 See the video of *Julius Caesar* in the BBC series, *The Shakespeare Plays*.

12

Good Friday, the Ides of March and the day Christ died

In 1599 the rival calendars created a concordance between the Catholic observance of the Annunciation to the Blessed Virgin Mary on 25 March Gregorian and the Roman Ides of March in the Julian calendar (15 March). As noted, 25 March was the received date of Christ's crucifixion. Recognizing this rich concordance of holy days permits us to recover a number of calendrical markers in Shakespeare's portrayal of the Ides. Nowhere in the canon is Shakespeare's skill at allusion, anamnesis and hieratic art more vigorous than in his portrait of the events on 15 March 44 BC. I have noted above that Shakespeare's ahistorical and unlikely tableau of Caesar and his assassins tasting wine together on the morning of the Ides of March was a textual marker to John 2, the prescribed Gospel reading for the first lesson on the Ides of March 1599. This is the one of a series of markers which link Shakespeare's portrait of events on the Ides with the life and death of Jesus Christ.

Portia encounters the angel

Into his portrait of Caesar on the Lupercal Shakespeare infused more than a dozen details drawn from the first chapter of the Gospel according to St Luke. But Luke's 'infancy narrative' describes not one but two encounters between humans and a supernatural being. The Angel Gabriel's first encounter is with a man, Zacharias. In verses 1:26–56 Luke goes on to describe Gabriel's second encounter with a mortal – the Blessed Virgin Mary. This passage was the Gospel reading for the feast of the Annunciation, 25 March. In 1599, 25 March Gregorian and the Julian Ides of March fell on the same day.

Shakespeare found Portia's anxiety and her messenger in Plutarch.

But her encounter with the Soothsayer on the Ides of March is Shakespeare's invention.[1] Both Portia's and Caesar's conversations with the Soothsayer are about time. The Soothsayer warns Caesar about a date: 'Beware the Ides of March.' Portia enquires about the time: 'What is't a clocke?' The Soothsayer replies, 'About the ninth houre Lady' (1172). By this device Shakespeare involves this numinous character in fixing the date and hour both of Caesar's death and of the 'birth' of his son Octavius.[2] One of the overlooked curiosities of this scene is the Soothsayer's awkward reference to the time as 'the ninth houre'. This scene plays shortly after Caesar and the conspirators left his house for the Capitol. Caesar has not yet arrived at the Capitol, as we learn when he is confronted by Artemidorus and his schedule, and the Soothsayer in 3.1. If the Soothsayer means nine o'clock, why does he not say 'nine a clocke' as Brutus will say 'three a clocke' at Phillipi? Shakespeare certainly knew that in Roman horology the ninth hour meant the ninth after sunrise. On 15 March this would approximate 3:30 p.m. The Soothsayer's 'ninth houre' is a textual marker. Three synoptic Gospels record that Christ died at the 'ninth hour' (Matthew 27:46, Mark 15:34, Luke 23:44). Luke's Gabriel promises Mary that her son 'shalbe great, & shalbe called the Sonne of the moste High'. As the conspirators surround Caesar, Metellus Cimber will greet Caesar as 'Most high' (1239). Moments later, Caesar dies (1288) and Octavius becomes the son of the 'Most high'. While various interpretations of this pattern of borrowings are possible, it rather smacks of impious parody.

Shakespeare provided his audience with a cue to the Portia–Mary connection. As her encounter with the Soothsayer ends, Portia instructs Lucius to go to Brutus and 'Say I am merry' (1197). Phonetically, the pronunciation in Shakespeare's time was: *Sei ai æm mæri*, indistinguishable from 'Say I am Mary'.

The Pontifex Maximus *in the purple robe*

In his reading of Plutarch, Shakespeare would have encountered the historian's judgement that Julius Caesar had been divinely ordained to govern Rome: 'it seemed he was a merciful Phisition, whom God had ordeyned of speciall *grace* to be Governor of the Empire of Rome' (North, 1579, 1081, emphasis added).[3] Although Caesar's pre-eminent position as *Pontifex Maximus* of the Roman state religion goes largely ignored by modern commentators, his status as a divine was conspicuous to

Figure 19. Longleat, Portland Papers, i.59. Reproduced by permission of the Marquess of Bath, Longleat House, Warminster, Wiltshire, Great Britain

Elizabethan readers of Roman history (Weinstock, 1971, 30).[4] The second sentence of Plutarch's *Life* records that Caesar 'made sute unto the people for the Priesthoodshippe that was voyde' (North, 1579, 763). The first sentence of Suetonius's *Historie* records how 'Caesar in the sixteenth yeare of his age, lost his Father: and in the yeare following, [was] elected *Flamen Dialis*' (Holland, 1606, 1).[5] Shakespeare was keenly aware of Caesar's priesthood. His Caesar is all piety, and speaks hardly a line lacking a metaphysical referent. How then might Shakespeare have wardrobed his Caesar? Though scholars have certainly not resolved the question of how Shakespeare's Romans were attired in performance, the famous sketch of *Titus Andronicus* suggests that documentary evidence about Roman dress (from coins, statuary and mosaics) may have been exploited in attiring at least some of the Chamberlain's Men (Figure 19).

Schoenbaum and others speculate that this sketch depicts 'Tamora on her knees, pleading with Titus to spare her two sons. Behind her the sons also kneel, and behind them stands, with sword drawn, the isolated figure of Aaron the Moor' (1975, 122–3). Given that *Titus* may have been performed in this attire as early as 1594, the practice of employing Roman wardrobe might have been followed (and even refined) by the time *Julius Caesar* reached the boards. Elizabethan audiences might have expected this degree of verisimilitude.[6]

As Shakespeare drafted his play, what might he have imagined that his Caesar would wear as he stepped on to the stage at the Globe? From his sources Shakespeare knew that the historical Caesar would have

131

worn the *toga praetexta* of the consul. Uniquely, Caesar was also entitled to wear a purple robe. As a member of the college of augurs, Caesar would carry the *lituus*, the crosier-like staff described by Plutarch in his *Camillus*. Wardrobed this way, Caesar would be instantly recognizable to Elizabethans as a bishop – which sorts well with Shakespeare's pietistic Caesar of 1.2. But what would Caesar wear on his head? This is a subject of intense concern among Shakespeare's Romans. Three times Antony tries to press a 'coronet' upon Caesar. Casca laments that Caesar 'shall weare his Crowne by Sea, and Land, / In every place save here in Italy' (526–8). Brutus frets: 'Crowne him ... And then I graunt we put a Sting in him' (631). But all these passages are Shakespeare's invention. Any reader of Plutarch knows that crowns were *not* anathema to Republican Romans. Wearing a crown did not necessarily signify kingship. Pompey was granted a golden jewelled crown in 61 BC, as was L. Aemilius Paulus in 167 BC (Weinstock, 1971, 108). Among the Romans a golden crown stood third in the hierarchy of honours. More coveted was the oak wreath, the *corona civica*, awarded by the Senate to those who had saved the lives of Roman citizens. It was the Roman custom that when the city bestowed the *corona civica* the people were ever after obliged to honour the recipient as 'savior' and 'father' (North, 1579, 923). After receiving these additions Caesar dispensed with his bodyguard since anyone threatening his person was subject to banishment or death as a parricide (Holland, 1606, 35). From his classical sources Shakespeare would have known that Caesar was deified posthumously by act of the Roman Senate, and that Antony became his *Flamen*. But Shakespeare also would have known that Caesar was revered as a god *during his lifetime*.[7] The 'Greeks often styled him *Deos*, people in Italy called him "*Deus Caesar*", and even in Rome an official inscription [on a statue] had the wording "*Deo Invicto*"' (Weinstock, 1971, 53, 151). The statue of Caesar with the legend *Deo Invicto* stood in the Quirinal temple alongside a statue of old Brutus. In 1.3 Cassius refers to this statue when he orders Cinna to set up one of his letters to Marcus Brutus 'with Waxe Upon old Brutus Statue' (592). By assuming the additions *Deo Invicto* and *pater patriae*, the living Caesar came to be called (as we would say) *god-the-father*. Shakespeare and other readers of Plutarch would have understood that Caesar did not become a god because he conquered the world. He was *recognized* as a god because he had been *born* of a god. A nice detail which enhances our understanding of Caesar's self-fashioning was the dedication of the temple he built to commemorate

132

his triumph over arch-rival Pompey at Pharsalus. The new temple was dedicated not to Venus *Victrix* but to Venus *Genetrix*, a neologism Caesar coined for the goddess-as-mother. Caesar's claim that the Julii had descended from Venus was literally made public currency on coins issued in 47–6 BC. The Julii, it was to be received, had arisen by parthenogenesis from Venus, mother-goddess of love (Cary, 1987, 4.419). No Elizabethan reader of classical history could fail to detect the parallel with the virgin birth of Christ. Brutus and his fellow conspirators were not merely assassins. They were deicides. Like the Pharisees on the Ides of March they killed a living god.

'Are we all ready?'

Elizabethans believed that Christ died on Good Friday 25 March AD 33. In the Gospel for Good Friday, St John explains that Jesus was aware of the fate which awaited him, 'knowing all things that should come' (John 18:4).[8] John 18 was the Gospel reading for the Gregorian Good Friday which fell in 1599 on the eve of the Protestant All Fools' Day, 31 March Julian. Only in John is Christ an active participant in his own betrayal: he gives Judas the sop of wine, after which 'Satan entred into him'. Jesus also gave Judas his cue: 'That thou doest, doe quickly' (John 13:27). Shakespeare's Caesar, too, gives his betrayers wine – a highly suggestive detail. But does Caesar know of his betrayers' intent, and does he abet their crime? Of course, any reader of Plutarch and Appian would know that Caesar Dictator was aware of various disgruntled republicans conspiring against him. But is there any evidence in Shakespeare's text that his Caesar has prior knowledge of *the particular plot* which takes his life?

In 3.1, Shakespeare's Caesar has an opportunity to learn about the Brutus–Cassius plot. Artemidorus attempts to deliver a 'schedule' which discloses the conspiracy. Caesar spurns it with conspicuous grandiloquence: 'What touches us our selfe, shall be last serv'd' (1211). This is Shakespeare's invention. Plutarch reports that Caesar accepted Artemidorus's petition but could not read it because of the press of the crowd (North, 1579, 794). No one has been able to say why Shakespeare alters his source. But I suggest that this device is one of many Shakespeare employs to wrap Caesar's assassination in the colours of a theatrical performance by Brutus and his Roman actors. Artemidorus's schedule must have resembled the scrolls containing actors' parts. By refusing Artemidorus's scroll Caesar demonstrates he 'knows his lines'. This inference is not so fanciful as it may appear. As Brutus and his Roman actors prepare to perform the assassination of Caesar we hear them whisper a series of stage directions. Cassius says, '*Trebonius* knowes his time: for look you *Brutus* / He drawes *Mark Antony* out of the way' (1231–2). Three more stage directions follow in rapid succession:

> *Deci.* Where is *Metellus Cimber*, let him go,
> And presently preferre his suite to *Caesar*.
> *Bru.* He is addrest: presse neere, and second him.
> *Cin.* *Caska*, you are the first that reares your hand.
>
> (1233–6)

As Brutus's actors find their blocking, Caesar impatiently calls: 'Are we all ready?' (1237). Coming at the culmination of a series of stage directions, modern directors find Caesar's interjection problematic and often cut it. But this is a mistake. Shakespeare's Caesar gives the assassins their verbal cue to perform when he says, 'What is now amisse, That *Caesar* and his Senate must *redresse?*' (1237–8, my emphasis). The word 'redresse' is *the* political buzz-word of the faction. Casca introduces it (559), Cassius writes it into the forged letters (666), Brutus parrots it (674, 676) and proselytizes with it (755) – and Caesar uses it for the last time to cue the murder skit.[9] On the fall of 'redresse' Metellus Cimber delivers his salutation:

> Most high, most mighty, and most puisant *Caesar*
> *Metellus Cymber* throwes before thy Seate
> An humble heart.
>
> (1239–41)

This is the diction of bad theatre, and may have provoked laughter. As noted, 'Most high' was an Old Testament epithet for God.[10] In a play characterized by reserved, prosaic diction, Metellus's histrionics alert an audience that Shakespeare's tragedy is shifting keys. The audience at a modern musical experiences the same effect when the orchestra strikes up and the action is suspended while a song is performed. Abruptly, Caesar turns critic. He chides Cimber's verbosity. But as he does, Caesar chillingly pre-empts the conspirators' vocabulary again: 'I must *prevent* thee *Cymber*' (1242, my emphasis). 'Prevent(ion)' is the other political buzz-word of the conspiracy (644, 710, 793, 1224). Caesar rejects Cimber's appeal with a speech that has frustrated commentators:

> These couchings, and these lowly courtesies
> Might fire the blood of ordinary men,
> And turne pre-Ordinance, and first Decree;
> Into the lane of Children.
>
> (1243–6)

Dr Johnson believed the Folio's 'lane' to be a misprint for 'lawe': 'It was, *change pre-ordinance and decree into the law of children*; into such slight determinations as every start of will would alter. *Lane* and *lawe* in some manuscripts are not easily distinguished' (Johnson, 1765, vii.48n). This emendation is generally accepted, and may be correct. However, no scholar has satisfactorily explained the meaning of 'pre-Ordinance, and first Decree', nor the sense in which these 'laws' are the antithesis of 'the lawe of Children'. But Shakespeare's diction becomes transparent when we place these phrases in the context of another of the playwright's inventions. As Brutus joins the supplicants he urges that Cimber's brother, Publius, should be recalled from exile:

> I kisse thy hand, but not in flattery *Caesar*:
> Desiring thee, that *Publius Cymber* may
> Have an immediate freedome of repeale.
>
> (1259–61)

Commentators have puzzled over Brutus's intrusion of the name 'Publius', since the given name of Cimber's brother is not mentioned in either Plutarch's *Caesar* or his *Brutus*.[11] But the commentators have underestimated the range of Shakespeare's classical reading. Certainly Shakespeare had read Cicero's and Sallust's accounts of the Catalinarian conspiracy, as which Elizabethan schoolboy had not? Shakespeare would have known that Cicero erroneously refers in *Cat.* 3.6 to a conspirator as 'Cimber Gabinius' when the man's proper name was Publius Gabinius Capito (MacDonald, 1897, 106). From Cicero's error Shakespeare compounded a 'Publius Gabinius Cimber' and assumed that this was the name of Cimber's banished brother. This inference is confirmed by Caesar's next speech: 'I was constant Cymber should be banish'd, / And constant do remaine to keepe him so' (1280–1). Sallust reports a lengthy speech by Caesar advocating the banishment of the man Publius Gabinius Capito (Rolfe, 1985, 89–101).[12] But Shakespeare and some members of his audience would certainly have been aware that 'Publius Gabinius Cimber' was *not* banished. The man was put to death.[13] By intruding the name 'Publius' Shakespeare has caused his

Brutus to ask Caesar to raise the dead (Rolfe, 1985, 113–15).[14] Caesar refuses, citing the mysterious 'pre-Ordinance, and first Decree'. The word 'ordinance' is rare in Shakespeare. It appears thirteen times, of which five relate to artillery pieces. In virtually all other instances 'ordinance' appears in close concordance with 'God' or Shakespeare's euphemism, 'heaven(s)'. So when we seek the meaning of 'pre-Ordinance, and first Decree' we should think in sacred rather than secular terms. There can hardly be a dispute as to the 'pre-Ordinance' of Scripture. This is the so-called Covenant of Works (or Life) which God made with Adam on the express condition of obedience: 'But of the tree of knowledge of good and evill, thou shalt not eat of it: for in the day that thou eatest thereof thou shalt die the death' (Genesis 2:17).[15] Adam's breach of this covenant called down the 'first Decree' in the Bible – Adam's banishment: 'Therefore the Lord God sent him foorth from the garden, to till the earth from whence he was taken' (Genesis 3:23). Shakespeare's Caesar refuses a request to raise a man from the ultimate banishment of death by asserting that men are mortal and liable to death by the 'first Decree' on account of Adam's breach of the 'pre-Ordinance'. This is another of Shakespeare's textual markers. Caesar was not Christ. Only Christ could raise the dead – as in John 12, the Gospel for 25 March – the date on which Christ was thought to have been crucified – which concorded with the Ides of March in the Julian calendar: 'Then Jesus sixe days before the Passeover, came to Bethania, where Lazarus was, who died, whom he had raised from the dead.'

But why does Caesar deplore Cymber's request on the grounds that it would turn God's pre-ordinance and first decree 'Into the lawe of Children'? This can be explained by reference to a reading for the evening lesson for 15/25 March, 2 Timothy 3: 'and that thou hast knowen the holy Scriptures of a child, which are able to make thee wise unto salvation through faith which is in Christ Jesus' (2 Timothy 3:15). The 'pre-Ordinance, and first Decree' are mandates of the Old Testament God. The 'lawe of Children' is the New Testament of Christ. It was not until the coming of Christ that God's first decree, 'thou shalt surely die', could be redeemed in eternal life. In order for Caesar to recall Publius Cimber from exile, he would have to recall the man from his grave. Only the child born in the manger could do that, and he would not be born for forty-four years. (See Appendix 1.)

Good Friday

Shakespeare's Butchers' Play

Elizabethans who had witnessed Corpus Christi plays knew that the Butchers killed Christ. When Brutus declares, 'Let's be Sacrificers, but not Butchers', when Antony laments, 'That I am meeke and gentle with these Butchers', when a Globe audience heard those words, could Shakespeare's allusion to the Butchers' Play of the old Corpus Christi cycles have been any plainer? Scholars have developed a linguistic detail from *Richard II* which suggests that young Shakespeare may have witnessed one of the final performances of the mystery plays.[16] But it is beyond dispute that many members of the Globe audience had seen the Coventry, York or Chester plays, or other cycles since lost. We cannot be certain why the Worshipful Company of Butchers was designated to perform the crucifixion pageant, but the tradition might have arisen out of the story of the Centurion Longinus thrusting his lance into the body of Christ. The York Cycle declares this the *coup de grace*. As the York Guild of Sledmen portray the journey to Emmaus, Cleophas tells the disguised Christ, 'A blind knight – such was his good hap – / In with a spear point at the pap / To the heart full throughly he thrust him.'[17] A glance at the Butchers' Play in the York Cycle may enrich our understanding of Shakespeare's method in *Julius Caesar*. I have suggested that Caesar's words before Casca strikes – 'Doth not *Brutus* bootlesse kneele?' (1285) – parody the ritual of Creeping to the Cross on Good Friday. The parallel epiphany in the Butchers' Play begins as Pilate calls forth Longeus:

> Sir Longeus, step forth in this stead;
> This spear, lo, hold here in thy hand.
> To Jesus now set forth with speed,
> And stay not till stiffly thou stand.
> In Jesus' side / Shove it this tide. / No longer bide,
> But go thou directly at hand.
>
> (Purvis, 1957, 297)

When the blind knight Longeus strikes, his sight is suddenly and miraculously restored:

> O maker unmade, full of might,
> O Jesus so gentle and kind,
> That sudden has sent me my sight –
> Lord, loving to thee be assigned.

137

Longeus declares that Christ is Lord. Shakespeare would have known from Plutarch that Cassius's full name was Gaius Cassius Longinus, and that he was a member of the same clan as the Longeus of the Butcher's Play. The story of Longinus is recorded in *The Golden Legend* (Ryan, 1993, i. 184). It describes him as 'almost blind' and records that 'the blood that ran down the shaft of his spear touched his eyes and at once he saw clearly'. Shakespeare vexes his Gaius Cassius Longinus with weak eyesight – his 'sight was ever thicke' (2501) – a characteristic not found in Plutarch. Of course, only members of the Globe audience who knew their Roman history could make the connection between Shakespeare's Cassius, the Longinus of *The Golden Legend*, and the Longeus of the Butcher's Play. Shakespeare wrote for two audiences, which is why his occasional *Julius Caesar* still stands today.

The sacrament of baptism, and the coming of grace

In the aftermath of Caesar's assassination, Brutus suddenly conceives an inspired idea:

> Stoope Romans, stoope,
> And let us bathe our hands in *Caesars* blood
> Up to the Elbowes ...
>
> (1320–2)

There is a complex and unrecognized Shakespearean wordplay in Brutus's 'Stoope Romans, stoope'. In the ethical sense, 'stoop' means 'to lower or degrade oneself morally; to descend to something unworthy' (*OED* v1.I.1.d). We generally use 'stoop' to describe a lowering of the body 'by inclining the trunk or the head and shoulders forward, sometimes bending the knee at the same time' (*OED* v1.I.1.a). But anyone who watches this scene in performance recognizes that in order to bathe their hands in Caesar's blood 'up to the Elbowes' Brutus and his colleagues cannot stoop – they must *kneel*. This produces one of the memorable tableaux of the play: the assassins kneeling about the corpse of Caesar. The attitude of supplication which the kneeling murderers assume, coupled with the reference to 'bathe', would certainly remind some Elizabethan Christians that 'stoop' has a homonym – 'stoup' – 'a vessel to contain holy water, set in or against the wall of the church porch' (*OED* n.3). This basin of holy water is provided so that worshippers may sprinkle themselves as they enter, a gesture which re-enacts the rite of purification through baptism.[18] This notion of cleansing and purifying is sharpened by Cassius's intrusion of the word 'wash' – 'Stoop then, and wash' (1326). 'The "bathing" and "washing" of the hands in blood echoes the biblical cleansing and washing in the blood of Christ (1 Jn 1:17, Rev 1:5) and the words of the Communion Service: "our souls washed through his most precious blood"' (Kaula, 1981, 208). Shakespeare apparently had the epithet 'precious blood' fixed in his mind; Caesar's blood is variously described as 'Noble' (1377), 'costly' (1486) and 'sacred' (1670). Brutus analogizes 'blood = Drachmaes' (2050).

Christ's death made possible the baptism of grace. Except for his baptism of Christ (Mark 10:11), John Baptist performed only 'baptisms of repentance' (Matthew 3:11, Mark 1:4, Luke 3:16, Acts 13:24). St Luke records how Paul explained the distinction between these forms of baptism in Acts 18:25–19:6. If Shakespeare's Caesar is an *imagunculum* of Christ, we *must* be able to detect the presence of grace after his death. Of course, we do. After Caesar's death the word 'grace' infiltrates the vocabulary of Cassius ('grace his heels' (1337)), Brutus ('Do grace to *Caesars* Corpes, and grace his Speech' (1591)), and Antony ('These are gracious droppes' (1731)). This new perspective helps resolve a crux in Cassius's rumination as he washes in the blood of Caesar:

> How many Ages hence
> Shall this our lofty Scene be acted over,
> In State unborne, and Accents yet unknowne?
>
> (1326–8)

Scholars have long disputed whether the singular 'State' is a misprint for 'States', which would parallel 'Accents' and refer to nations and languages yet unknown.[19] But I have suggested that Shakespeare consistently employs the upper-case 'State' to describe a 'system of divine government' (*OED* state n.I.5μ.b). Cassius's 'State unborne' could refer to the state of grace which will be born with Christ.

The inference that Shakespeare is parodying the ritual of baptism is supported by the action immediately following: a mock rite of confirmation. Antony was a priest. I have suggested that Antony dressed in his priestly garments and carried his *lituus* when he went to the Capitol to confront the assassins – which explains why Brutus greets him with 'reverence'. In Shakespeare's time (and our own) the baptism of adults differs from infant baptism. Adult baptism is immediately followed by ritual confirmation. This rite has two elements: the laying-on of hands and the calling of the individual by name (Livingstone, 1977, 48).[20] Priest Antony conducts a laying-on of hands and calls the name of each assassin:

> Let each man render me his bloody hand.
> First *Marcus Brutus* will I shake with you;
> Next *Caius Cassius* do I take your hand;
> Now *Decius Brutus* yours; now yours *Metellus*;
> Yours *Cinna*; and my valiant *Caska*, yours;
> Though last, not least in love, yours good *Trebonius* ...
>
> (1406–11)[21]

Antony shaking the hands and calling the names of the conspirators washed in the blood of Caesar is a parodic ritual of confirmation. Although there were eight conspirators, Shakespeare has contrived for only seven to be present to take Antony's hand. There are 'Seven Steps' in the Catholic rite of Confirmation (Anonymous, 1966, 721–7).

Recognizing the scene of Caesar's assassins washing in his blood as a parody of baptism, and the handshaking scene as a parody of confirmation, allows us to explain a crux in Antony's encomium over the body of Caesar:

> Heere did'st thou fall, and heere thy Hunters stand
> Sign'd in thy Spoyle, and Crimson'd in thy Lethee.
> O World! thou wast the Forrest to this Hart,
> And this indeed, O World, the Hart of thee.
>
> (1427–30)

Antony's reference to 'Lethee' has been 'much discussed since Capell's unconfirmed definition of it (in *Notes*) as a hunting term for the quarry's blood used to anoint its killers' (Humphreys, 1984, 170n). This cannot be correct. Even a patient researcher cannot find support for Capell's citation. On the other hand, Shakespeare uses 'Lethe' in *Hamlet* (1.5.33) and *Richard III* (4.4.250) in its familiar sense as 'A river in Hades, the water of which produced, in those who drank it, forgetfulness of the past' (*OED* Lethe 1). Shakespeare's Antony employs 'Lethee' to convey that Caesar's blood is a fluid which has the power to extirpate the past. The holy water which was used in the ritual of baptism was thought to wash away past sins. St Augustine wrote that baptism removed the stain of original sin which bars even the new-born child from Heaven.

Good Friday

But Caesar is not Christ. Washing in Caesar's blood does not extirpate the assassins' guilt. Antony's ritual handshaking is its confirmation.

Notes

1 'For *Porcia* being verie carefull and pensive for that which was to come, and being too weake to away with so great and inward griefe of minde: she coulde hardlie keepe within, but was frighted with everie litle noyse and crie she heard, as those that are taken and possest with the furie of the Bacchantes, asking every man that came from the market place, what *Brutus* did, and still sent messenger after messenger, to knowe what newes' (North, 1579, 1062).
2 Caesar's final encounter with the Soothsayer also has a temporal dimension. '*Caes.* The Ides of March are come. / *Sooth.* I *Caesar*, but not gone' (1204–5).
3 This perhaps suggested the association between Caesar and 'grace' which appears repeatedly in Shakespeare's *Julius Caesar*.
4 Caesar was a priest from age thirteen until his death at fifty-six.
5 The *flamen* was the 'kindler' who officiated in the lighting of sacrificial fires. The *Flamen Dialis* was the officiating priest at the rites of Jupiter.
6 The fact that some of the characters depicted in Figure 19 are in Roman and others in anachronistic Elizabethan dress may suggest that funds for wardrobing were limited. On the other hand, the performance of old plays in modern dress tends to underscore the timelessness of art, and the relevance of the events portrayed on the stage to all time. Perhaps this device was known to Elizabethans as it is to us.
7 Reflecting on the dead Caesar in *De Officiis*, Cicero wrote, '*ecce tibi, qui rex populi Romani dominusque omnium gentium esse concuriverit idque perfecerit!*' (Miller, 1990, xxi. 357). Remarkably, in his lifetime Caesar made the transition from political to religious *dominus omnium gentium*.
8 The other Gospel accounts concur (Matthew 26, Mark 14, Luke 22).
9 Caesar also repeatedly mentions 'blood': 'blood of ordinary men ... rebel blood ... flesh and blood' as if to provoke the bloody act of murder (Charney, 1961, 51).
10 First in Genesis 14:18, most conspicuously in the Psalms and the Book of Daniel.
11 Some commentators conclude that Shakespeare was careless about names. Preferring the *Caesar* as his source, the playwright had named one of his conspirators *Metellus* Cimber, whereas the name *Tullius* Cimber in the *Brutus* is correct. In the *Caesar*: 'and parte of them [the conspirators] also came towards him [Caesar], as though they made sute with Metellus Cimber, to call home his brother againe from banishment' (North, 1579, 794). In the *Brutus*: 'So when he [Caesar] was set, the conspirators flocked

about him, & amongst them they presented one Tullius Cimber, who made humble sute for the calling home againe of his brother that was banished' (North, 1579, 1062).

12 Cato, who spoke after Caesar, advocated a death sentence for Publius Gabinius Cimber, and prevailed.

13 The strangling of these conspirators is graphically described in Sallust *BC* 55.1–6 (Rolf, 1985, 113–15).

14 When Caesar refuses to raise the dead, he is himself killed. For the ritual killing of a 'man-god' whose powers have failed see Frazer, 1956, 309ff. On his cross, the archetypal Lord of Misrule, Christ, was called upon to have his God save him. Like Caesar at his moment of death, Christ called out in a foreign language, and was stabbed by a Roman.

15 *OED* covenant n.8.a. After Adam's fall, Christ brought the 'Covenant of Grace (or of Redemption)', i.e. the New Covenant or Testament.

16 When Richard II 'in the process of being deposed, is called to appear before the assembled peers, he notes the silence of his sometime followers, and asks: "Did they not sometime cry 'All hail!' to me?" So Judas did to Christ' (Kay, 1992, 49).

17 Christ conceals his wound and does not correct him. Cleophas and his aconanical fellow-traveller, Luke, exaggerate as they tell Christ the story of his crucifixion: 'They shook him and shot him his limbs all asunder. His brains thus brake they and burst him' (Purvis, 1957, 330). In fact, St Luke never met Christ, nor was he an eye-witness to either Christ's life or death. Like Christ's successors in the York Cycle, Caesar's successors will rewrite the facts of his martyrdom in Acts 4 and 5.

18 Shakespeare uses 'stoupe' for a container of fluid in *TN* 2.3.14 and *Ham.* 5.2.267.

19 By 'State unborne' and 'Accents yet unknowne' most commentators since Theobald have assumed that the singular 'State' was a misprint for the plural 'States', and Cassius is simply referring to nations and languages which will succeed Rome and Latin (with a glance at England, and English). But in the context of baptism we ought to reconsider whether 'State unborn' is a misprint. Malone favored the singular, and took the phrase to mean 'In theatric pomp yet undisplayed', i.e. ceremony (Malone, 1821, xii.81). Steevens and most subsequent critics emended 'State' to its plural, reasoning 'our author must have meant – "communities which as yet have no existence"'. But this emendation is not safe.

20 The service for the baptism of adults differs from that for children in that holy water is employed, but chrismation is omitted.

21 Antony's two ironic epithets suggest how deeply he is dissembling. He addresses a notorious coward and backstabber as 'valiant *Caska*'. Then he smiles 'good *Trebonius*' at the conspirator who lured him aside so that he could not come to Caesar's aid.

13

Shakespeare's third day, the Books of Samuel and the Mass of the Catechumens

In 1599 Catholics observed the Vigil of Easter on the night of Saturday 10 April Gregorian. This concorded with the eve of the English All Fools' Day, 31 March Julian. Holy Saturday commemorates the resting of Christ in his tomb. In the early Church, no Mass was performed on this sombre day. Instead, a Mass of the Catechumens was performed at the evening service and followed immediately by a ritual of adult baptism (Leduc and Baudot, 266ff.). Catechumens were new converts undergoing instruction which culminated in admission to the Church. The celebration of their mass on the night before the resurrection signifies that in the time of Christ all his followers were novices entering a new Church. To honour the hour of the resurrection, this high mass was celebrated in the pre-dawn hours of Sunday morning. The Mass of the Catechumens was a sung service, and specifically included the lighting of the Paschal candle with fresh fire struck from a flint, and the Twelve Lessons from the Old Testament which predicted the coming of the Messiah.[1] I will suggest that this ritual, and passages from Galatians 2, provide a subtext for Shakespeare's 'incident at Sardis' in *Julius Caesar* 4.2.

Shakespeare's third day

Shakespeare parodied the notion of parthenogenesis when he exploited Luke 1:5–25 in his Lupercalian portrait of a Caesar who gains a son (Octavius) without copulating with his mother. When Shakespeare fashions his version of Brutus's encounter with the Ghost of Caesar, the playwright interrogates the truth of the resurrection. In order to cause his Ghost of Caesar to walk on the third day following his death, Shakespeare alters Plutarch's report of the murder of Cinna the Poet. This is the anecdote as Shakespeare found it in his source:

> There was one of Caesars frends called Cinna, that had a marvelous straunge & terrible dreame the night before. He dreamed that Caesar bad him to supper, & that he refused, and woulde not goe: then that Caesar tooke him by the hand, and led him against his will. Now Cinna hearing at that time, that they burnt Caesars body in the market place, notwithstanding that he feared his dreame, and had an agew on him besides: he went into the market place to honor his funeralls. When he came thither, one of the meane sorte asked what his name was? He was straight called by his name. The first man told it to an other, and that other unto an other, so that it ranne straight through them all, that he was one of them that murdered Caesar: (for in deede one of the traitors to Caesar, was also called Cinna as him selfe) wherefore taking him for Cinna the murderer, they fell upon him with such furie, that they presently dispatched him in the market place.

> (North, 1579, 795)

Plutarch sets Caesar's funeral and Cinna's murder during daylight hours some days after the assassination. Shakespeare removes Cinna's death to the night of the Ides. Shakespeare also substitutes a band of Elizabethan rowdies for Plutarch's Roman 'meane sort'. By inserting this night scene in 3.3, Shakespeare contrives for his play to comprise dramatic time of four days (and three intervening nights). Although Plutarch recorded that Caesar's Ghost appeared to Brutus more than two years after his death (summer 42 BC), Shakespeare's Ghost appears to Brutus before dawn on the morning of the third day of dramatic time after his assassination. Table 7 segregates the principal scenes of *Julius Caesar* according to the dramatic time in the play. In the dramatic universe of Shakespeare's play, Caesar is slain on Day two. Caesar's Ghost appears to Brutus before dawn on Day four. By the Roman system of inclusive reckoning, Caesar rises on the third day.

Table 7

Dramatic time	Principal actions
Day one	Tribunes encounter plebians
	Caesar offered crown
	Cassius 'seduces' Brutus
Night of day one	Encounters on the unruly night
Morn of day two	Conspirators visit Brutus
	Brutus speaks with Portia
Day two	Scenes at Caesar's house
	Portia encounters the Soothsayer
	Caesar journeys to the Capitol
	Caesar slain
	Antony meets the Conspirators
	Funeral orations
Night of day two	Murder of Cinna the poet
Day three	Black proscriptions
Night of day three	Brutus and Cassius argue
Morn of day four	Caesar's Ghost appears to Brutus
Day four	Two battles of Philippi

The vigil of Caesar's Ghost

After the decision to march to Philippi has been taken and Cassius, Messala and the others have left Brutus alone in his tent, Lucius enters carrying a dressing gown:

> *Bru.* Give me the Gowne. Where is thy Instrument?
> *Luc.* Heere in the Tent.
> *Bru.* What, thou speak'st drowsily:
> Poore knave I blame thee not, thou art ore-watch'd.
> (2246–9)

Lucius is literally 'ore-watch'd'. The hour is after midnight. It is no longer the second night after Caesar's death but the wee hours before dawn of the third day. It was a Roman convention that watches changed at midnight, and we meet new guards. Brutus says: 'Call *Claudio*, and some other of my men, Ile have them sleepe on Cushions in my Tent' (2250–1). This is Shakespeare's invention. In Plutarch, Brutus is alone during his encounter with Caesar's Ghost.

When the guards have entered and settled themselves, Brutus asks Lucius to play a tune: 'Canst thou hold up thy heavie eyes a-while, / And touch thy Instrument a straine or two' (2266–7). The tableau of

a boy playing an instrument for a general on the eve of battle is Shakespeare's invention. For the Elizabethans as for us, it could hardly fail
to call to mind the Old Testament story of Saul and David. Both Brutus
and Saul have made a god their enemy. Both are on the eve of destruction. Both are in extremity because they failed to kill an adversary while
he was in their power: Brutus failed to take Cassius's advice in 2.1 and
kill Antony on the Ides of March; Saul refused to kill Agag as God had
commanded. As noted, Elizabethans had a powerful reason to connect
the Books of Samuel with the calendar in Lent and Eastertide. Each year
the reading of 1 Samuel began with the evening lesson on 29 March,
the earliest possible date for the Octave of Easter. Each year the reading
of 2 Samuel continued to 24 April, the latest possible date for the Vigil
of Easter. The Books of Samuel were *de facto* the Old Testament scriptures
Elizabethans identified with the preparations for Easter.

The association of Lucius with David is heightened by the identity of
Lucius's instrument. That Shakespeare had a lyre in mind is clear from
an unspoken pun: 'The [lyre] strings my Lord, are false [liar]' (2305).
A synonym for 'lyre' is 'psalter', from which we derive the words 'Psalm'
and 'Psalter'. King David is traditionally the author of the Book of Psalms
of the Old Testament. The Greek word for harp – *psalter* – is the root of
'psalm', and is found in both the Septuagint and Greek New Testament
(*OED* psalm n). The Book of Psalms was called 'the Psalter' after the
Latin *psalterium* and Greek *ψalterion*, 'a stringed instrument played by
twanging' (*OED* psalter n). As to the nature of Lucius's song, the Folio
stage direction says only: '*Musicke. and a Song*' (2278). Brutus adds,
'This is a sleepy Tune' (2279). The absence of a lyric from the Folio text
is in itself suggestive. It is rare in the Shakespeare canon that a song is
indicated by a stage direction but not provided in the text.[2] Although
Lucius's song has been thought irretrievable, recognizing the connection with David and the Psalter suggests it may have been the
thirty-ninth Psalm, and another of Shakespeare's temporal markers. At
Philippi Brutus will sigh, 'O that a man might know / The end of this
dayes businesse, ere it come' (2466). This is a paraphrase of the thirty-
ninth Psalm: 'Lord, let me know mine end, & the measure of my dayes,
what it is: let me know how long I have to live' (Psalm 39:4). This Psalm
is strikingly appropriate as Lucius's pre-dawn song at Sardis. In the
Book of Common Prayer the thirty-ninth Psalm was prescribed for the
morning of the eighth day of the month. In 1599, 8 April Julian was
Christ's third day, the English Easter Sunday.

The three questions

Recognizing that Shakespeare is exploiting the Book of Samuel finally explains one of the most bizarre and problematic cruces of 4.2. As Caesar's Ghost departs, Brutus rouses the sleepers:

> *Bru.* Did'st thou dreame *Lucus*, that thou so cryedst out?
> *Luc.* My Lord, I do not know that I did cry.
> *Bru.* Yes thou did'st: Did'st thou see any thing?
> *Luc.* Nothing my Lord.
> *Bru.* Sleepe againe *Lucius*: Sirra *Claudio*, Fellow.
> Thou: Awake.
> *Var.* My Lord.
> *Clau.* My Lord.
> *Bru.* Why did you so cry out sirs, in your sleepe?
> *Both.* Did we my Lord?
> *Bru.* I: saw you any thing?
> *Var.* No my Lord, I saw nothing.
> *Clau.* Nor I my Lord.
>
> (2309–22)

Brutus interrogates three people – Lucius, Varrus and Claudio. He suggests that each cried out in his sleep. Since *no one* had cried out, this passage has puzzled audiences and scholars alike.[3] But the crux can be explained by reference to 1 Samuel. Brutus's interrogation of the three sleepers parallels the calling of young Samuel by the Lord three times in 1 Samuel 3. The boy Samuel had been placed in training with Eli, the high priest. One night as Eli and Samuel slept in the temple, Samuel heard a voice:

> Then the Lord called Samuel: and he said, Here I am. And he ranne unto Eli, and said, Here I am, for thou calledst me. But he [Eli] said, I called thee not: go againe and sleepe. And he went and slept. And the Lord called once againe, Samuel. And Samuel arose, and went to Eli, and said, I am here: for thou diddest call me. And he answered, I called the not, my sonne: go againe and sleepe. Thus did Samuel, before he knewe the Lord, and before the worde of the Lord was reveiled unto him. And the Lord called Samuel againe the third time: and he arose, and went to Eli, and said, I am here: for thou hast called me. Then Eli perceived that the Lord had called the child.
>
> (1 Samuel 3:4–8)

Like Brutus, three times Samuel asks the sleepy Eli if he called out. Like Brutus, three times Samuel receives a negative reply. After the third rebuff, Samuel realizes he has heard the voice of God. Brutus is sceptical as he begins his encounter with Caesar's Ghost: 'I thinke it is the weak-nesse of mine eyes / That shapes this mostrous Apparition' (2289–90). But three rebuffs change Brutus's opinion, too. At Philippi Brutus will blame Caesar for the death of Cassius (2583), and use his dying breath to call out to Caesar (2696–8). This passage of 1 Samuel 3 was the prescribed reading for the evening lesson on 30 March 1599, the eve of Holy Saturday.

Brutus's interrogation of the sleepers contains another mo-ment which has been overlooked by commentators. At line 2310 Brutus addresses his boy: 'Did'st thou dreame *Lucus*, that thou so crydest out?' Editors invariably dismiss 'Lucus' as a compositor's error for 'Lucius'. But, given our new perspective on the context, this dismissal is not safe.[4] Shakespeare and his audience were aware that a man named *Lucus* or *Lucas* wrote one-fourth of the New Testament. The word 'dream' occurs only twice in Luke's writings, both in the Pentecostal prophecy of St Peter: 'And it shalbe in y[e] last dayes, saith God, I wil powre out of my Spirit upon all flesh, and your sonnes, and your daughters shal prophecie, and your yong me[n] shal se visions, and your olde men shal dreame dreames' (Acts 2:17).[5] In Acts 16, Luke recounts Paul's dream at Troas:

> Where a vision appeared to Paul in the night. There stode a man of Macedonia, & prayed him saying, Come into Macedonia, and helpe us. And after he had sene the vision, immediatly we prepared to go ... to Philippi, which is the chief citie in the partes of Macedonia, and whose inhabitants came from Rome to dwell there, and we were in that citie abiding certeine dayes.
>
> (Acts 16:9–12)

Shakespeare and the Elizabethans knew the Holy Ghost had appeared to Paul in the guise of a 'man of Macedonia' and summoned him to Philippi where Paul would found the first Christian church in Europe. A link between this spectre and Caesar's Ghost is a nice conceit.

Brutus's book, and Caesar's holey ghost

Plutarch twice describes Brutus's encounter with Caesar's Ghost, once in his *Life of Caesar*, and again in his *Brutus*. Shakespeare used the version in Plutarch's *Brutus* as his principal source:

> So, being ready to goe into EUROPE, one night very late (when all the campe tooke quiet rest) as he [Brutus] was in his tent with a litle light, thinking of waighty matters: he thought he heard one come in to him, and casting his eye towards the doore of his tent, that he saw a wondefull straunge and monstruous shape of a body comming towards him, and sayd never a word. So Brutus boldly asked what he was, a god, or a man, and what cause brought him thither. The spirit aunswered him, I am thy evill spirit, Brutus: and thou shalt see me by the citie of PHILIPPES. Brutus beeing no otherwise affrayd, replyed againe unto it: well, then I shall see thee agayne.
>
> (North, 1579, 1072)

Plutarch's Brutus was sitting up late by candlelight ('litle light'), and thinking of 'waighty matters'. But Shakespeare contrives for his Brutus to be reading. He says,

> Let me see, let me see; is not the Leafe turn'd downe
> Where I left reading? Heere it is I thinke.
> *Enter the Ghost of Caesar.*
> (2285–7)

Brutus's book is the Ghost's cue to enter. The book's presence – and its identity – have puzzled scholars. Why would Shakespeare introduce an invented, anachronistic book, and make it the Ghost's cue to enter?

The effect of the written word on suggestible people was proverbial in Shakespeare's time as it is in ours. Dante employs the device to trigger the incestuous affair between Francesca of Rimini and her brother-in-law Paolo in Canto 5 of *Inferno*. Shakespeare's Brutus is a highly suggestible man.[6] Throughout the play he exhibits an extravagant dependence on the written word. Brutus is moved to join the conspiracy against Caesar by anonymous letters which would have put a wiser man on guard (675–7).[7] After his reasons for Caesar's murder have been writ and 'inroll'd in the Capitoll', Brutus wrongly assumes that the plebeians must be satisfied (1567). Brutus is picayune about the number of senators proscribed in Messala's letters (2170–2).[8] Since

149

there are no ghosts, I suggest that Shakespeare introduced Brutus's book to imply that his vision was inspired by something he was reading. Obviously, this inference might be strengthened if we could identify Brutus's anachronistic book. Its identity has been thought irretrievable, but perhaps not. (See Appendix 3.)

Readers of the classics, Shakespeare being one, would have known that Cicero dedicated several of his chief works to Brutus. The dates of these books are significant: *Brutus (Orator)* appeared in 46 BC; *De Finibus, Disputationes Tusculanae,* and *De Natura Deorum* in 45 BC – all before the death of Caesar. But Cicero's second treatise on religion, *De Divinatione,* was written and published *after* the death of Caesar.[9] Shakespeare knew Brutus was an augur, and would have been interested in divination.[10] *De Divinatione* contains an incident so similar to Brutus's encounter with Caesar's Ghost as to be uncanny: the execution of Callanus by Alexander the Great. We can be confident that Shakespeare was familiar with this tale. Kenneth Muir (1960) and J. C. Maxwell (1956) demonstrated that the playwright borrowed from a passage in *Tusculan Disputations* which alludes to Callanus. In *Richard II*, as Bollinbroke anticipates his banishment he ruminates:

> O, who can hold a fire in his hand
> By thinking on the frosty Caucasus,
> Or cloy the hungry edge of appetite
> By bare imagination of a feast,
> Or wallow naked in December snow
> By thinking on fantastic summer's heat?
> O no, the apprehension of the good
> Gives but the greater feeling to the worse.
> Fell sorrow's tooth doth never rankle more
> Than when he bites, but lanceth not the sore.
>
> (1.3.257–66)

Muir and Maxwell (283ff.) cite this passage of Cicero as Shakespeare's source:

> *Quae barbaria India vastior aut agrestior? in ea tamen gente primum ei, qui sapientes habentur, nudi aetatem agunt et Caucasi nives hiemalemque vim perferunt sine dolore, cumque ad flammam se applicaverunt, sine gemitu aduruntur ...*

What barbarous country more rude and wild than India? Yet amongst its people those, to begin with, who are reckoned sages pass their lives unclad and endure without show of pain the snows of the Hindu Kush and the rigour of winter, and when they throw themselves into the flames they let themselves be burnt without a moan.

(King, 1989a, 505)

It was Callanus who was burnt alive by Alexander. He is the man who threw himself into the fire 'without a moan'. Cicero was fascinated by this episode – an extraordinary example of Stoicism – and wrote of it in both *Tusculan Disputations* and *De Divinatione*. But in the latter book Cicero also recorded that, as Callanus ascended his pyre, Alexander enquired whether the condemned man had anything to say. Callanus replied: '"Thank you, nothing, except that I shall see you very soon." So it turned out, for Alexander died in Babylon a few days later' (Cicero, *Divinatione*; King, 1989, 277). Caesar was compared to Alexander, both in his own mind and by Plutarch, who paired the men in his *Lives*. The plebeians had resolved to burn the body of Caesar at the end of 3.2: 'Wee'l burne his body in the holy place, / And with the Brands fire the Traitors houses' (1792–3). It is possible that Shakespeare imagined his Brutus alone at night at Sardis reading of the death of Callanus in Cicero's *De Divinatione*. Brutus finding this place in Cicero's theological text cues the entrance of Caesar's Ghost.

Bru.	Ha! Who comes heere?
	I thinke it is the weakenesse of mine eyes
	That shapes this monstrous Apparition.
	It comes upon me: Art thou any thing?
	Art thou some God, some Angell, or some Divell,
	That mak'st my blood cold, and my haire to stare?
	Speake to me, what thou art.
Ghost.	Thy evill Spirit *Brutus?*
Bru.	Why com'st thou?
Ghost.	To tell thee thou shalt see me at *Philippi.*
Brut.	Well: then I shall see thee againe?
Ghost.	I, at *Philippi.*
Brut.	Why I will see at *Philippi* then:
	Now I have taken heart, thou Vanishest.
	Ill Spirit, I would hold more talke with thee.

(2288–302)

Shakespeare found Brutus's description of the Ghost as a 'monstrous Apparition' in Plutarch. But how could the playwright make these words ring true for members of the Globe audience who had not read Plutarch? The answer may be found in Shakespeare's stagecraft and his Ghost's wardrobe. The playhouse had already seen Caesar's bloody mantle, and heard it described by Antony (1711–17). Caesar's body, too, was a ghastly sight to judge by the reactions of the plebeians:

Ant.	Heere is Himselfe, marr'd as you see with Traitors.
1	O pitteous spectacle!
2	O Noble *Caesar*!
3	O wofull day!
4	O Traitors, Villaines!
1	O most bloody sight!

(1734–9)

But most of the Globe audience had to take the plebeians' word for the condition of Caesar's body. The corpse was brought on-stage in 'a hearse'. Supine and surrounded by plebeians, Caesar's body may not have been visible to the groundlings – perhaps only to spectators in the uppermost tier of the Globe. But when the Ghost enters Brutus's tent, the spectre stands erect. Caesar's body and wounds would be visible to the groundlings and lower tiers for the first time. Caesar would certainly present a 'monstrous Apparition' of a priest-victim swathed in a bloody 'vesture', perhaps carrying his *lituus* crook and wearing his coronet of thorns. This would have been extraordinarily daring theatre. But it was entirely justified within the dramatic framework of the play. A Ghost of Caesar who appeared to Brutus with its stigmata revealed was literally a holey ghost.

Caesar's Ghost declares that he is Brutus's 'evill Spirit'. Shakespeare made a choice when he recorded this epithet. In his *Life of Caesar*, Plutarch characterizes the Ghost as Brutus's 'ill angell'. In his *Brutus*, the epithet is 'evill Spirit', the version which Shakespeare adopted. His choice may have been influenced by the five appearances of the phrase 'evil spirit'[11] in 1 Samuel's account of David playing the harp for Saul:

But the Spirit of the Lord departed from Saul, and an *evil spirit* sent of the Lord vexed him. And Sauls serva[n]ts said unto hi[m], Behold now, ye *evil spirit* of God vexeth thee. Let our lord therefore commande thy servants, that are before thee, to seke a man, that is a conning player upon the harpe: that when the *evil spirit* of God commeth upon thee, he may playe with his hand, & thou maiest be eased ... And so when the *evil spirit* of

God came upon Saul, David toke an harpe and plaied with his hand, & Saul was refreshed, & was eased: for the *evil spirit* departed from him.

(1 Samuel 16:14–16, 23; emphasis added)

Like wicked King Saul, Brutus was visited by an evil spirit who promised not eternal life, but doom.

The private mass of Caesar's catechumens

The calendar was not the only part of the Elizabethan liturgy which Shakespeare exploited as he created *Julius Caesar* 4.2. The two received sacraments of Elizabeth's Church were baptism and the Lord's Supper. In the aftermath of the death of Caesar, Shakespeare parodied the sacrament of baptism (and confirmation) as the assassins washed in blood and shook hands with the priest Antony. In Brutus's tent at Sardis, Shakespeare's Romans perform a mock-communion. The ritual takes place *before* the changing of guards which signals midnight. In Shakespeare's dramatic time-scheme this correlates with the night of Holy Saturday. In the early Church, no Mass was said during daylight hours of this sombre day. Instead, the Mass of the Catechumens was performed at night. This included the kindling and blessing of the Paschal candle, and the recitation of the Twelve Lessons – a number equal to the apostles who spread the Gospel. In 4.2 we are very much among 'the Twelve'. Scene 4.2 is not a single scene but a sequence comprising twelve distinct scenes:

A Brutus–Lucillius (1910–14)

B Brutus–Pindarus (1915–22)

C Brutus–Lucillius (1923–42)

D Brutus–Cassius–Lucillius/Lucius–Pindarus–Titinius (1943–68)

E Brutus–Cassius (1969–2107)

F Brutus–Cassius–Cynicke Poet–Lucillius–Titinius (2108–28)

G Brutus–Cassius (2129–48)

H Brutus–Cassius–Lucius (2149–53)

I Brutus–Cassius–Messala–Titinius (2154–245)

J Brutus–Lucius–Varrus–Claudio (2246–86)

K Brutus–Caesar's Ghost (2287–302)

L Brutus–Lucius–Varro–Claudius (2303–26)

Although the first two thousand lines of *Julius Caesar* are remarkably free of props, 4.2 also requires the employment of twelve props.[12]

1 tent (1961)
2 dagger (2079)
3 wine (2148)
4 tapers (2148)
5 bowl/cup (for wine) (2149)
6 carafe or decanter (2152)
7 table and chairs (2256–7)
8 Brutus's gown (2240)
9 letters (2161)
10 instrument (lyre) (2247)
11 cushions (2251)
12 book (2263)

Intriguingly, each of the physical properties required for the performance of 4.2 has a homologue in the Elizabethans' communion service.

1. Tent. The word 'tent' is derived from the Latin *tabernaculum*, i.e. 'a temporary dwelling ... constructed of branches, boards, or canvas' (*OED* tabernacle n.1). History's most famous tabernacle was the curtained tent containing the Ark of the Covenant borne by the Jews during the Exodus. Eventually, 'tabernacle' came to denote any portable religious shrine. But the word also describes the 'little tent (or pavilion) placed in the middle of the altar ... which serves for the reservation of the Blessed Sacrament' during the Mass (Leduc and Baudot, n.d., 5).[13]

2. Dagger. When Cassius offers his dagger to Brutus, he must present the dagger with its cruciform hilts forward (Figure 16). This recreates the familiar tableau of the cross.

3. Wine. Shakespeare contrives for wine to make two appearances in *Julius Caesar*. The first is at Caesar's house on the morning of his assassination when Caesar invites the conspirators to 'taste some wine with me' (1125). The second comes in 4.2 as Brutus and Cassius share a bowl of wine (2148). The Lord's Supper is anamnetic for the Passover meal Christ shared with his disciples, as the communion wine is anamnetic for his blood.

4–6. Tapers, bowl, carafe. Candlesticks, a chalice and a cruet are among the furnishings necessary to perform the ritual of the Lord's Supper. At line 2148 a stage direction signals, '*Enter Boy with Wine, and Tapers.*' Although the tapers Lucius carries are an Elizabethan stage convention to suggest the drawing-on of darkness, they are uncalled for. Lucius apparently bears only a single cup or bowl. Brutus says, 'Give me a bowl of wine, / In this I bury all unkindnesse *Cassius*'(2149–50). While Brutus drinks, Cassius protests his thirst: 'My heart is thirsty for that Noble pledge' (2151). Cassius must wait for Lucius to refill the bowl before he can satisfy himself.[14] Drinking from a common cup was part of the communion rite.

7. Table and chairs. The 'communion table' was the focal point of the ritual of the Lord's Supper. In Elizabethan churches the north or right side of the table was referred to as the 'Gospel' side. Chair(s) were often set on the south or left side, which was referred to as the 'Epistle' side (Figure 3). The table and chairs used in 4.2 were brought on-stage for the 'black proscription' scene. That is, Antony, Octavius and Lepidus sat at this very table when they damned men.

8. Brutus's 'gown'. This is not a robe; Caesar wears a 'robe'. Brutus puts his 'gown' on over his daytime attire. The garment must be something like an alb or surplice – 'A loose vestment of white linen having wide sleeves and, in its amplest form, reaching to the feet, worn (usually over a cassock) by clerics, choristers, and others taking part in church services' (*OED*).[15]

9. Letters. When Messala and Titinius enter, Brutus says, 'Now sit we close about this Taper heere' (2157). Once seated at the table the group immediately falls to discussion of their letters (epistles). Brutus says, 'I have heere received Letters' (2161). Messala responds, 'My selfe have Letters of the selfe-same Tenure' (2165). Reading from the Epistles was a focal point of the sacred service.

10. Instrument (lyre). The playwright's choice of Lucius's instrument and its association with psalms has been discussed above.

11. Cushion(s). In Shakespeare's time, and in English usage down to the early nineteenth century, the word 'cushion' could describe the pillow 'set on the book-board of a pulpit ... to support the bible' (*OED* n.1.b). The epithet 'cushion-thumper' signified 'a preacher who indulges in violent action' (*OED* n.11).

12. Book. Although the formula for the communion service was contained in the Book of Common Prayer, the celebrants had recourse to the Bible for the reading of the Gospel and Epistle.

Given this enumeration, it is now possible to construct a table of homologues between the props in 4.2 and the artefacts of the communion service (Table 8).

Table 8

4.2 properties	Line	Communion item
1 tent	1961	tabernacle
2 dagger	2079	cross
3 wine	2148	communion wine
4 tapers	2148	candlesticks
5 bowl/cup (for wine)	2149	chalice
6 carafe or decanter	2152	cruet
7 table and chairs	2257	communion table
8 Brutus's gown	2257	alb or surplice
9 letters	2161	epistles
10 instrument	2247	psalter (*yaltarion*)
11 cushions	2251	cushion
12 book	2263	Bible or prayer book

Each of the twelve properties in 4.2 has a parallel among the furnishings necessary for the communion service.[16]

After a series of greetings, the action of 4.2 moves inside Brutus's tent, and the great confrontation begins. Cassius declares:

> That you have wrong'd me, doth appear in this
> You have condemn'd, and noted *Lucius Pella*
> For taking Bribes heere of the Sardians;
> Wherein my Letters, praying on his side,
> Because I knew the man was slighted off.
>
> (1970–4)

Shakespeare knew that the historical Brutus condemned and stigmatized a Lucius Pella for abusing his office of praetor (Plutarch 1071). But Cassius's 'praying' letters are the playwright's invention. Like St Paul, Shakespeare's Cassius is a chronic letter-writer. Like Paul, Cassius believes that a great man's death has abrogated the law: 'In such a time as this, it is not meet / That every nice offence should beare his Comment' (1976–7). There is no question but that Shakespeare was on page 1071 of Plutarch's *Brutus* when he wrote this couplet. North's translation reads: '[Cassius] greatly reproved Brutus, for that he would shew him selfe so straight and seveare in such a tyme, as was meete to beare a litle, then to take thinges at the worst' (North, 1579, 1071). Shakespeare also follows Plutarch when his Brutus alleges:

> Let me tell you *Cassius*, you your selfe

Are much condemn'd to have an itching Palme.
To sell, and Mart your Offices for Gold
To Undeservers.
Cassi. I, an itching Palme?

(1978–82)

Although Brutus's allegation is an invention, Shakespeare would have found Cassius's appetite for gain in Plutarch: 'And as for *Cassius*, a hot, chollerick, & cruell man, that would oftentymes be caried away from iustice for gayne' (North, 1579, 1068).[17] Brutus chastises Cassius for greed:

I did send to you
For certaine summes of Gold, which you deny'd me,
For I can raise no money by vile meanes:
By Heaven, I had rather Coine my Heart,
And drop my blood for Drachmaes, then to wring
From the hard hands of Peazants, their vile trash
By any indirection. I did send
To you for Gold to pay my Legions,
Which you deny'd me: was that done like *Cassius*?
Should I have answer'd *Caius Cassius* so?
When *Marcus Brutus* growes so Covetous,
To locke such Rascall Counters from his Friends,
Be ready Gods with all your Thunder-bolts,
Dash him to peeces.

(2046–59)

Readers of Cicero would know that Shakespeare's Brutus is lying. The historical Brutus was not above usury. In 50 BC Brutus had used his influence to exempt from the usury laws a loan made to the people of Salamis at the confiscatory interest rate of 48 per cent. Brutus also notoriously concealed the fact that he himself was the lender.[18] In letters to Atticus, Cicero roundly deplored Brutus's behaviour on both counts. The argument over money between Brutus and Cassius is entirely Shakespeare's invention.[19] It reveals Brutus as a hypocrite, and prepares his hypocrisy in the so-called 'double-report of Portia's death'. The argument also reveals something new about Cassius: he has developed a genuine love for Brutus, and is vulnerable to Brutus's scorn. Cassius laments,

Brutus hath riv'd my hart:

A Friend should beare his Friends infirmities;
But *Brutus* makes mine greater then they are.

(2063–5)

Cassius is again paraphrasing St Paul: 'We which are strong ought to beare the infirmities of the weake and not to please ourselves' (Romans 15:1). Brutus is unmoved:

Bru. I do not, till you practice them on me.
Cassi. You love me not.
Bru. I do not like your faults.
Cassi. A friendly eye could never see such faults.
Bru. A Flatterers would not, though they do appeare
As huge as high Olympus.

(2066–71)

At the fall of the word 'Olympus' – the last word Caesar spoke before his assassins struck – Cassius's façade crumbles:

Come, *Antony*, and yong *Octavius* come,
Revenge your selves alone on *Cassius*,
For *Cassius* is a-weary of the World:
Hated by one he loves, brav'd by his Brother,
Check'd like a bondman, all his faults observ'd,
Set in a Note-booke, learn'd, and con'd by roate
To cast into my Teeth. O I could weepe
My Spirit from mine eyes.

(2072–9)

He draws his dagger, proclaiming

There is my Dagger,
And heere my naked Breast: Within, a Heart
Deerer then *Pluto*'s Mine, Richer then Gold:
If that thou bee'st a Roman, take it foorth.
I that deny'd thee Gold, will give my Heart:
Strike as thou did'st at *Caesar*: For I know,
When thou did'st hate him worst, you loved'st him better
Then ever thou loved'st *Cassius*.

(2079–86)

Cassius's display of dagger-hilts (Figure 16) has a sudden, transforming effect on Brutus:

> Sheath your Dagger:
> Be angry when you will, it shall have scope:
> Do what you will, Dishonor, shall be Humour.
> O *Cassius*, you are yoaked with a Lambe [20]
> That carries Anger, as the Flint beares fire,
> Who much is inforced, shewes a hastie Sparke,
> And straite is cold agen.
>
> (2087–93)

On seeing the cruciform hilts Brutus recants and introduces the figures of a 'Lambe' and a flint striking fire – iconographic for the lighting of the Paschal candle during the Mass of the Catechumens, which included 'striking fresh fire from a flint' (Leduc and Baudot, n.d., 267). This triggers a startling exchange:

> *Bru.* When I spoke that, I was ill temper'd too.
> *Cassi.* Do you confesse so much? Give me your hand.
> *Bru.* And my heart too.
>
> (2097–9)

According to the Elizabethans' prayer book, when two members of the congregation had become estranged they were required to exchange mutual confessions and perform an act of reconciliation before they could receive communion: 'The same order shall the curate use with those betwixt whom he perceiveth malice and hatred to reigne, not suffering them to be partakers of the Lords table, untill he knew them to be reconciled' (C3v). Cassius identifies the source of his bad temper:

> Have not you love enough to beare with me,
> When that rash humour which my Mother gave me
> Makes me forgetfull.
> *Bru.* Yes, *Cassius*, and from henceforth
> When you are over-earnest with your *Brutus*,
> Hee'l thinke your Mother chides, and leave you so.
>
> (2102–7)

An audience can hardly fail to connect this confession with Cassius's declaration on the unruly night:

> our Fathers mindes are dead,
> And we are govern'd with our Mothers spirits,
> Our yoake, and sufferance, shew us Womanish.
>
> (522–4)

The motherish 'age's yoke' – the effeminate, un-Roman spirit of Christianity – has brought Brutus and Cassius to exchange mutual
confessions. This is the Cynicke Poet's cue to enter and paraphrase the
Gospel of John 15, Christ's womanish commandment to love one another. As the Cynicke Poet departs, Brutus calls out, '*Lucius*, a bowle of
Wine' – and a ritual ensues. At line 2148 Lucius enters with candles,
one cup and a jug of wine.

> *Brut.* Give me a bowl of wine.
>   In this I bury all unkindnesse *Cassius*.   *Drinkes*
> *Cas.* My heart is thirsty for that Noble pledge.
>   Fill *Lucius*, till the Wine ore-swell the Cup:
>   I cannot drinke too much of *Brutus* love.
>
>   (2149–53)

The stage direction, '*Drinkes*', is important. While Brutus drinks Cassius
speaks and awaits his turn at the cup. Lucius has brought only one cup,
and Cassius must wait for Brutus to finish before he can drink. To the
extent that an Elizabethan audience might have recognized that a parodic communion service was under way in Brutus's tent, this was a
clearly a Catholic rite. The Protestant ritual required communion 'in
both kinds' by the taking of both bread and wine. Elizabethans would
also recognize that Brutus and Cassius are sharing a 'private mass'.
While Catholic doctrine (Council of Trent, session xxx.6) permitted a
priest to take the sacrament of Communion with only one other person
present, private communion was forbidden by the Church of England.
The Primer of 1549 provided 'There shall be no celebration of the Lord's
Supper except there be some to communicate with the Priest ...' By
1552 the minimum number of communicants in addition to the priest
is expressly 'four, or three at the least' (Book of Common Prayer, C7v).
The Mass of the Catechumens at Sardis will have its effect. At Philippi
both Brutus and Cassius reveal that they believe in the immortality of
Caesar.

Incident at Sardis, incident at Antioch

One aspect of 4.2 which has excited intense scholarly debate is the
so-called 'double report' of Portia's death. The first report comes as
Brutus and Cassius await the entrance of Lucius with the wine:

> *Bru.* O *Cassius*, I am sicke of many greefes.

Cas. Of your Philosophy you make no use,
      If you give place to accidentall evils.
Bru. No man beares sorrow better. *Portia* is dead.
Cas. Ha? *Portia*?
Bru. She is dead.
      How scap'd I killing, when I crost you so?

                                    (2131–7)

Cassius *literally* 'crossed' Brutus (Figure 16) at line 2079, when he said, 'There is my Dagger, / And heere my naked Breast' (2079–80). On learning of Portia's death, Cassius expresses grief – and curiosity: 'O insupportable, and touching losse! / Upon what sicknesse!' (2138–9). Brutus explains that Portia was a suicide:

                    Impatient of my absence,
      And greefe, that yong *Octavius* with *Mark Antony*
      Have made themselves so strong: For with her death
      That tydings came. With this she fell distract,
      And (her Attendants absent) swallow'd fire.

                                    (2140–4)

In medieval iconography the Stoical spirit was often depicted as a woman patiently holding her hand in a fire. Cassius is flabbergasted to hear the means of Portia's death:

Cas. And dy'd so?
Bru. Even so.
Cas. O ye immortall Gods!

                                    (2145–7)

This is the first use of 'immortall' to characterize 'Gods'. Previously, only Caesar was declared immortal (153, 1145). Cassius's invocation of the immortal Gods is Lucius's cue to enter with the properties for communion.

The second report of Portia's death comes as Brutus and Cassius confer with Messala and Titinius.

      Had you your Letters from your wife, my Lord
Bru.   No *Messala*.
Messa. Nor nothing in your Letters writ of her?
Bru.   Nothing *Messala*.
Messa. That me thinkes is strange.

Bru.   Why aske you?

         Heare you ought of her, in yours?

Messa. No my Lord.

Bru.   Now as you are a Roman tell me true.

Messa. Then like a Roman, beare the truth I tell,

         For certaine she is dead, and by strange manner.

Bru.   Why farewell *Portia*: We must die *Messala*:

         With meditating that she must dye once,

         I have the patience to endure it now.

Messa. Even so great men, great losses should indure.

Cassi. I have as much of this in Art as you,

         But yet my Nature could not beare it so.

                                 (2175–91)

Commentators in general – and Brutophiles in particular – have been distressed by Brutus's counterfeit Stoicism.[21] Shakespeare's source in Plutarch is equivocal as to whether Brutus learned of Portia's death by letter, or whether the information arrived after Brutus was already dead (North, 1579, 1080). Shakespeare employs both possibilities to make his Brutus appear a hypocrite. The Stoical manner of Portia's death underscores Brutus's 'Art' as he enacts the part of a Stoic before his generals. In the argument about money – and in the double report of Portia's death – why does Shakespeare go to such lengths to paint his Brutus as a hypocrite? I suggest that, in framing his confrontation between Brutus and Cassius at Sardis, Shakespeare is writing a parody of the so-called 'incident at Antioch' recounted by Paul in his Epistle to the Galatians:

> And when Peter was come to Antiochia, I withstode him to his face: for he was to be blamed. For before that certeine came from James, he ate with the Gentiles: but when they were come, he withdrewe & separated him self, fearing them which were of the Circumcision. And the other Jewes dissembled likewise with him, in somuche that Barnabas was broght into their dissimulation also. But when I sawe, that they went not the right way to the trueth of the Gospel, I said unto Peter before all men, If you being a Jewe, livest as the Gentiles, & not like the Jewes, why constrainest thou the Gentiles to do like the Jewes? We which are Jewes by nature, and not sinners of the Gentiles, Knowe that a man is not justified by the workes of the Law, but by the faith of Jesus Christ: even we, I say, have beleved in Jesus Christ, that we might be justified by the faith of Christ, and not

by the workes of the Law, because that by the workes of the Law no flesh
shalbe justified.

(Galatians, 2:11–16)

Peter and the Jerusalem faction believed that Christ's coming had fulfilled the law. Paul preached that Christ's crucifixion had abrogated the
law, and that the law and works were indifferent to salvation. Galatians
2 was a favourite of the Reformers. Calvin cited this passage when he
argued that the Petrine wing of Christianity – the Roman Catholic
papacy – should not have precedence over other Christian churches.
As Brutus and Cassius become Caesar's 'believers', Shakespeare endues
these characters with remarkable qualities: Brutus becomes more dependent on the written word, more literal and picayune; Cassius
preaches the end of the law, and proclaims love. I suggest that these
two modes of belief are anamnetic for Catholicism and Protestantism.
In Act 5, Brutus will urge his men to 'rest on this Rocke' (2640–1).[22]
And Cassius's bondman, Pindarus, will deliver a stunning Pauline
paradox.

Notes

1 They teach the catechumens that the coming of Christ was repeatedly
  prophesied from Genesis 1 to Daniel 3.
2 Compare the presence of songs in Shakespeare's contemporary plays, i.e.
  As You Like It and *Twelfth Night*.
3 Stirling suggests that Brutus is attempting to conceal his own fear of the
  spectre (1959, 215–17).
4 That Shakespeare attached significance to the name 'Lucius' can be illus-
  trated by considering another [invented] boy named Lucius, the grandson
  of Titus Andronicus. And a well-read boy he is. Aunt Lavinia has read
  Cicero's *Brutus* to him (4.1.14); on his own, Young Lucius has read of
  Hecuba either in Homer or Euripides (4.1.20); he also knows Ovid's *Meta-
  morphoses* (4.1.42). This Lucius figures prominently in the 'book scene' of
  Titus Andronicus; however, no one can hear the boy's presentation of weapons to Demetrius and Chiron (4.2.1–17) without recognizing the
  paradigm for the young Duke of York in *Richard III*. After Titus is slain, it
  is left to Young Lucius to be a teller of tales: 'Many a story hath he [Titus]
  told to thee, / And bid thee bear his pretty tales in mind, / And talk of them
  when he was dead and gone' (5.3.163–5). That is, not to retell the story
  of Titus, but to retell stories *told by* Titus. The name Lucius–Lucus was
  connected in Shakespeare's mind with the promulgation of myth from
  generation to generation.

5 Shakespeare parodied these passages when he created Antony's prophecy over the fallen Caesar.

6 Bowden (1966, 61) calls attention to Brutus's first line which parrots someone else's idea: '*Sooth*. Beware the Ides of March. / *Caes*. What man is that? / *Bru*. A Sooth-sayer bids you beware the Ides of March' (107–9).

7 'It is hard to believe that if Shakespeare had wanted to stress Brutus' intelligence, he would thus have introduced, unnecessarily, a trick which at about this same time he was allowing Maria to play on Malvolio' (Bowden, 1966, 60).

8 'The uncertainty as to whether it was seventy or a hundred senators that the triumvirs had put to death is a kind of gruesome pedantry' (Bellringer, 1970, 46).

9 'the latter part of Book I and all of Book II were written after March 15, 44 BC.' Falconer, 1992, 214.

10 In Shakespeare's text Brutus's friends described him as capable of 'Alchymie' (607), and described him as an 'Exorcist' who 'conjur'd up' the 'mortified Spirit' of Caius Ligarius (968–9). See Addington, 1993, 116–18.

11 There are nine appearances of the phrase in the Old and New Testaments, six in 1 Samuel.

12 The properties necessary to the performance of the first nineteen-hundred-plus lines of *Julius Caesar* are seven swords or daggers, seven written documents (three might do), one statue, and pen-ink-paper. Firebrands are also called for in dialogue (1848), though not mentioned in stage directions. The presence of a table and three chairs may be inferred in the 'black proscription' scene 4.1; it may be that the table and chairs were brought out at the beginning of Act 4 and remain throughout 4.2.

13 From the consanguinity of 'tent' and 'tabernacle' came the Elizabethan pejorative 'tent wine' to denote a ruddy Spanish *vino tinto* frequently used in the tabernacle as sacramental wine (*OED* tent n.4).

14 The stage direction '*Enter Boy with Wine, and Tapers*' (2148) deserves scrutiny. Elsewhere Lucius is always referred to by name, e.g. '*Enter Lucius*' (621, 651, 678, etc.). The other two directions to Lucius in 4.2 are '*Enter Lucius*' (2232) and '*Enter Lucius with the Gowne*' (2240). Shakespeare may have imagined an altar-boy carrying wine and tapers.

15 In *All's Well that Ends Well*, Shakespeare describes the wearing of such a gown: 'Though honestie be no Puritan, yet it will doe no hurt, it will weare the Surplis of humilities over the blacke-Gowne of a bigge heart' (1.3.99).

16 Early in 4.2 Brutus enquires about the whereabouts of Cassius and his army. Lucillius replies, 'They meane this night in Sardis to be quarter'd.' The only mention of Sardis in the Bible comes in the Book of Revelation. This is the great 'hear-say' book of the New Testament. The Geneva gloss explains that God revealed his revelation to Christ; Christ revealed it to his Angel; the Angel revealed it to John; and John revealed it to the seven churches in Asia, including Sardis. This is the book which declares: 'I am

Alpha and Omega, the beginning and the ending ... the first and the last' (Revelation 1:8–11). That is, God *is* time.

17 Shakespeare's invented dialogue emphasizes the phrase 'itching Palme' by repetition (1979, 1982). The word 'itching' appears only once in the Bible, in St Paul's second letter to Timothy: 'For the time wil come, when they wil not suffer wholsome doctrine: but having their eares itching, shal after their owne lustes get them an heape of teachers, And shal turne their eares fro[m] the trueth, and shal be given unto fables' (2 Timothy 4:3–4). The Edwardian Arden editor detected a possible connection between Shakespeare's text and this passage from St Paul (Macmillan, 1902, 125n).

18 Cicero *Ad Atticus*, v.21 and vi.2 (Winstedt, 1956, 407ff. and 443ff.).

19 Plutarch recorded that when Brutus requested funds Cassius had first hesitated, but eventually provided the money willingly: '*Brutus* prayed *Cassius* to let him have some parte of his money wherof he had great store, bicause all that he could rappe and and rend of his side, he had bestowed it in making so great a number of shippes, that by meanes of them they should keepe all the sea at their commaundement. *Cassius* friends hindered this request, and earnestly disswaded him from it: perswading him, that it was no reason that *Brutus* should have the money which *Cassius* had gotten together by sparing, and leavied with great evill will of the people their subjects, for him to bestowe liberally uppon his souldiers, and by this meanes to winne their good willes, by *Cassius* charge. This notwithstanding, *Cassius* gave him [Brutus] the thirde parte of his totall summe' (North, 1579, 1069).

20 The Proper Preface in the communion service on Easter Day and seven days after offers praise 'for the glorious resurrection of thy Sonne Jesus Christ our Lord: for he is the very paschal Lambe', etc. (Book of Common Prayer, C6r).

21 For example: W. D. Smith, 1953, 153–61, and Stirling, 1959, 211–17.

22 Jesus renamed the fisherman Simon as Peter: 'thou shalt be called Cephas, which is by interpretation, A stone' (John 1:42). In Matthew 16, Jesus puns on the name Peter, which also means 'rock': 'And I say also unto thee, That thou art Peter, and upon this rock I will build my church; and the gates of hell shall not prevail against it. And I will give unto thee the keys of the kingdom of heaven: and whatsoever thou shalt bind on earth shall be bound in heaven: and whatsoever thou shalt loose on earth shall be loosed in heaven' (Matthew 16:18–19). This passage was cited by Catholic theologians to demonstrate that Peter's Church, the papacy, was the one true Church, and that the Pope and his clergy had the right and power to forgive sin – issues hotly disputed by Protestants.

14

Holy Easter and Shakespeare's April Fools

The most jarring of all holy day discordances in 1599 occurred when the Catholic (and correct) date of Easter, 11 April Gregorian, fell on the English Protestant All Fools' Day.[1] Easter is the holiest of Christian feasts. It celebrates the resurrection of Jesus Christ, and Christianity depends on its truth. One can hardly be a Christian without believing that a man born by parthenogenesis died and was restored to life. If this belief is false, the Gospels are a lie, and there is no hope of salvation or eternal life through Christ. In stark contrast to Easter's truth, All Fools' Day was characterized by false reports, practical jokes and the dispatch of underlings on 'fools' errands'. Intriguingly, the holiday had its roots in the Roman *Hilaria*, 25 March – the date of the Annunciation and the received date of Christ's crucifixion.[2] Shakespeare infuses the action of Act 5 with misconstruing, bad intelligence, broken metaphors, false reports, distortions, confusion and fatal misjudgements – every manner of foolish behaviour – to interrogate the concordance of Easter and All Fools' Day.[3] (See Appendix 8.)

The opening direction *'Enter Octavius, Antony, and their Army'* (2328) is Shakespeare's invention. The playwright knew that Octavius was ill and absent from the first battle, and had been carried from his tent on account of the ominous dream of one of his captains (North, 1579, 1074). A brief, invented exchange ensues:

> *Octa.* Now *Antony*, our hopes are answered,
> You said the Enemy would not come downe,
> But keepe the Hilles and upper Regions:
> It proves not so: their battailes are at hand,
> They meane to warne us at *Philippi* heere:
> Answering before we do demand of them.

Ant. Tut I am in their bosomes, and I know
Wherefore they do it: They could be content
To visit other places, and come downe
With fearefull bravery: thinking by this face
To fasten in our thoughts that they have Courage;
But 'tis not so.

(2329–40)

Octavius chides Antony for misconstruing the enemy's intention. Antony responds with another misjudgement. From listening to the council of war in 4.2, the audience knows that Brutus and Cassius had decided to force the battle for tactical reasons ('good reasons must ... give place to better'). Octavius's phrase 'upper Regions' is a clue to the hieratic drama underlying Act 5.[4] By characterizing the forces of Brutus and Cassius as coming down from the 'upper Regions', Shakespeare casts them in the role of the forces of light. This is ironic. Brutus and Cassius murdered Caesar, but both have come to believe in his immortality. Brutus has seen Caesar's Ghost. Both Brutus and Cassius will directly address Caesar with their dying words. Their enemies, Octavius and Antony, will deify *Divus Julius*. But there is no hint in Shakespeare's text that either Octavius or Antony believes in the immortality of Caesar. Both Brutus and Cassius sense a supernatural power shaping the outcome at Philippi. Antony attributes his success to chance here (2637)[5] and elsewhere (1517). Shakespeare saw tremendous irony in the draw for the battle of Philippi. What was at stake was not merely the form of civil government of Rome but the godhead of Julius Caesar – who would hardly have been deified had Brutus and Cassius prevailed. Shakespeare is also placing another textual marker. The Gospel for Easter Day, Colossians 3, warns Christ's adherents to keep to the upper regions: 'If ye then be risen with Christ, seek those things which are above, where Christ sitteth on the right hand of God. Set your affection on things above, not on things on the earth' (Colossians 3:1–2). Brutus – who was wrong about the date, the time and the tides – will be wrong to abandon the upper regions at Philippi when he orders, 'Let them all come down.' In the battle's aftermath Antony will declare that the vanquished assassins acted 'in envy of great Caesar' (2719). Colossians 3 also warned that envy will be punished: 'Mortify therefore your members which are upon the earth ... and covetousness, which is idolatry: For which things' sake the wrath of God cometh on the children of disobedience' (Colossians 3:5–6).

As Antony and Octavius speak together, a messenger enters:

The movable feast discordances

> Prepare you Generals,
> The Enemy comes on in gallant shew:
> Their bloody signe of Battell is hung out,
> And something to be done immediately.
>
> (2342–5)

This is another false report. The battle will not be joined until the generals have exchanged 'words before blows'. But Antony seizes the moment to set the order of the army:

> *Octavius*, leade your Battaile softly on
> Upon the left hand of the even Field.
> *Octa.* Upon the right hand I, keepe thou the left.
> *Ant.* Why do you crosse me in this exigent.
> *Octa.* I do not crosse you: but I will do so.
>
> (2346–50)

Most men being right-handed, a sword-wielding army's right flank was more aggressive. Antony suggests that Octavius should lead the lesser left flank. But Octavius insists on the more honourable right. In fact this exchange took place between Brutus and Cassius (North, 1579, 1074). Shakespeare interpolates it here, and invents the striking 'crosse me … crosse you' exchange to cue the entrance of Brutus and Cassius. Catching sight of the enemy, Brutus infers, 'They stand, and would have parley' (2352). This is not correct. Octavius is eager to fall to blows and must be restrained:

> *Mark Antony*, shall we give signe of Battaile?
> *Ant.* No *Caesar*, we will answer on their Charge.
> Make forth, the Generals would have some words.
>
> (2354–6)

The mutual misconstruance of the parties leads to this exchange:

> *Bru.* Words before blowes: is it so Countrymen?
> *Octa.* Not that we love words better, as you do.
> *Bru.* Good words are better then bad strokes *Octavius*.
>
> (2358–60)

Brutus attempts (and fails) to produce an epigram. His phrase 'Good words' – a synonym for 'Gospel' – cues one of the most perplexing passages in the play, the 'rewrite' of Caesar's assassination. Antony begins this exchange by delivering yet another false report:

168

> In your bad strokes *Brutus*, you give good words
> Witnesse the hole you made in *Caesars* heart,
> Crying long live, Haile *Caesar*.

(2361–3)

Shakespeare and his audience knew that Antony's allegation was false. The audience had only just witnessed the assassination of Caesar. It was nothing like Antony describes. Readers of Plutarch would also know that Brutus did not stab Caesar in the heart but in the 'privities'. Nor did Shakespeare's Brutus cry 'long live, Haile' as Judas does in the Mystery plays. This is another of Shakespeare's textual markers. The hailing of Jesus by the Romans was recorded by Matthew, by Mark and by John, whose version reads

> And the soldiers platted a crown of thorns, and put it on his head, and they put on him a purple robe. And said, Hail, King of the Jews! and they smote him with their hands. Pilate therefore went forth again, and saith unto them, Behold, I bring him forth to you, that ye may know that I find no fault in him. Then came Jesus forth, wearing the crown of thorns, and the purple robe. And Pilate saith unto them, Behold the man!
>
> (John 19:2–5; cf. Matthew 27:29, Mark 15:17)

The most revered and most coveted of all Roman crowns was not the oak wreath *corona civica* but the *corona obsidionalis*. This 'was given by the soldiers themselves to those who saved the whole army or part of it. The grass was taken from the battlefield' (Weinstock, 1971, 148). With such a crown Titinius garlands dead Cassius. Ironically, the Roman soldiers have given Jesus the coronet of a saviour. In 1.2 Casca reported that Antony offered Caesar a 'coronet', i.e. a circlet of thorny nettles. In 1599 John 19 was the Protestant Gospel reading for All Fools' Day, 1 April, the correct date of Easter.[6]

Cassius now introduces the perplexing image of bees:

> Antony,
> The posture of your blowes are yet unknowne;
> But for your words, they rob the Hibla Bees,
> And leave them Hony-lesse.
> *Ant.*   Not stinglesse too.

(2364–8)

Brutus Malapropus over-extends the metaphor, and breaks its back:

169

O yes, and soundlesse too:
For you have stolne their buzzing *Antony*,
And very wisely threat before you sting.

(2369–71)

Elizabethans believed that bees were born through parthenogenesis. But 'buzz' also meant a false rumour.[7] Antony was not present at the assassination, and he is 'buzzing' (lying). Brutus and Cassius were there, and they call him on it. Nevertheless, Antony presses on with his rewrite of the assassination in a flurry of invented details:

when your vile daggers
Hackt one another in the sides of *Caesar*:
You shew'd your teethes like Apes,
And fawn'd like Hounds,
And bow'd like Bondmen, kissing *Caesars* feete.

(2372–6)

The Globe audience knew that Brutus had kissed Caesar's hand, not his foot.

Then, suddenly, Antony strikes on an exact and correct detail: 'Whil'st damned *Caska*, like a Curre, behinde / Strooke *Caesar* on the necke' (2376–7). This snaps us back to the tableau of Caska standing behind Caesar with his cruciform dagger raised (Figure 18). Octavius grows irritable: 'Come, come, the cause. If arguing make us swet, / The proofe of it will turne to redder drops' (2382–3). Plutarch wrote of a soldier who sweated rose oil during the battle of Philippi (North, 1579, 1078). The transmuting of 'rose' to 'redder drops' calls to mind Luke's description of Christ's passion: 'and his sweat was as it were great drops of blood falling down to the ground.' (Luke 22:44). On this note Octavius draws his sword, demanding.

When thinke you that the Sword goes up againe?
Never till *Caesars* three and thirtie wounds
Be well aveng'd ...

(2385–7)

As he holds his cruciform sword aloft (Figure 16) Octavius delivers the final trope in the rewrite of Caesar's assassination. Plutarch, Appian and Suetonius all record that Caesar received twenty-three wounds, not thirty-three. Almost all our contemporary editions adopt Theobald's erroneous emendation, 'twenty-three' (Theobald, 1733, 196–7n). The

Cambridge editor retains 'three and thirty', but cites Kittredge: 'Such mistakes in copying and printing were very common on account of the practice of using Roman numerals' (Spevack, 1988, 135). Kittredge apparently did not have access to a copy of North's Plutarch. The number is spelt out in the text as 'three and twenty', and is accompanied by an unequivocal marginal gloss employing Arabic numerals: '*Caesar slaine and had 23. wounds upon him*' (North, 1579, 794). I see no reason to doubt that Shakespeare intentionally altered his sources and changed Caesar's 'three and twenty' wounds to 'three-and-thirtie'.[8]

The changed man

As the opposing armies form for battle, Cassius confides to Messala, '*Messala*, this is my Birth-day: as this very day / Was *Cassius* borne' (2411–12). Cassius had been born under the old Republican calendar, and his actual birthday was ninety days past. But, suddenly, the instigator of the conspiracy against Caesar has begun to reckon in Caesar's time. On the instant Cassius is touched with metaphysical doubts.

> You know, that I held *Epicurus* strong,
> And his Opinion: Now I change my minde,
> And partly credit things that do presage.
>
> (2416–18)

Like the villains of the old revenge tragedies, Cassius has become the object of his crime. Like Caesar, Cassius 'is Superstitious growne of late'.

> Comming from *Sardis*, on our former Ensigne
> Two mighty Eagles fell, and there they pearch'd,
> Gorging and feeding from our Soldiers hands,
> Who to *Philippi* heere consorted us:
> This Morning are they fled away, and gone,
> And in their steeds, do Ravens, Crowes, and Kites
> Fly ore our heads, and downward looke on us
> As we were sickely prey; their shadowes seeme
> A Conopy most fatall, under which
> Our Army lies, ready to give up the Ghost.
>
> (2419–28)

The phrase 'give up the Ghost' was proverbial, but appears only once in the Shakespearean canon. Its presence seems to seal the connection between the on-stage action and All Fools' Day. Cassius is quoting the

171

Gospel of John 19:30: 'When Jesus therefore had received the vinegar, he said, It is finished: and he bowed his head, and gave up the ghost.' As noted, John 19 was the prescribed Gospel for 1 April – the Protestants' All Fools' Day – the correct date of Easter.

Messala tries to cheer his commander, and Cassius responds: 'I but beleeve it partly, / For I am fresh of spirit, and resolv'd / To meete all perils, very constantly' (2430–2). In his 'fresh' spirit Cassius turns to Brutus with a prayer: '[May] The Gods to day stand friendly, that we may / Lovers in peace, leade on our dayes to age' (2435–6). This leads to a startling exchange:

> And whether we shall meete againe, I know not:
> Therefore our everlasting farewell take:
> For ever, and for ever, farewell *Cassius*.
>
> (2458–60)

To which Cassius responds: 'For ever, and for ever, farewell *Brutus*' (2461) The repeated phrase, 'For ever, and for ever', derives from Paul's Epistle to the Hebrews: 'Make you perfect in every good work to do his will, working in you that which is wellpleasing in his sight, through Jesus Christ; to whom be glory for ever and ever. Amen' (Hebrews 13:21). Hebrews 13 was the Gospel reading for 11 April Julian. There is a stinging irony here; 11 April Gregorian was the (correct) Catholic Easter. The phrase 'for ever, and for ever' is also closely associated with the Catholic Eucharistic Prayer (Anonymous, 1966, 140).[9] Tertullian considered the original Greek so sacred that he specifically deplored its repetition *in a playhouse* as the height of blasphemy:

> *Quale est enim de ecclesia dei in diaboli ecclesiam tendere, de caelo, quod aiunt, in caenum? Illas manus quas ad deum extuleris postmodum laudando historionem fatigare? Ex ore, quo Amen in Sanctum protuleris, gladiatori testimonium reddere, εἰς αἰῶνας ἀπ' αἰῶος alii omnino dicere nisi deo et Christo?*

> What sort of conduct is it to go from the assembly of God [church] to the assembly of the devil [theatre]? from sky to stye, as the proverb has it? those hands you have uplifted to God, to tire them out clapping an actor? with those lips, with which you have uttered Amen over the Holy Thing to cheer for a gladiator? to say for ever and ever to any other whatever but to God and Christ?
>
> (Tertullian; Glover, 1984, xxv. 290–1)

In the Elizabethan prayer book the phrase 'for ever, and for ever' was associated with the Visitation of the Sick, itself a descendant of the Catholic rite of Extreme Unction. Shakespeare had parodied the Visitation of the Sick in *Henry V*. Before the dawn of the battle of Agincourt Hal prays, 'Not today, O Lord, / O not today, think not upon the fault / My father made in compassing the crown' (4.1.289–91). The formula in the Elizabethan prayer book is: 'Remember not Lord our iniquities, nor the iniquities of our forefathers. Spare us good Lord, spare thy people whom thou hast redeemed with thy most precious bloud, and be not angry with us for ever' (Book of Common Prayer, D.5v).

The great Pauline paradox

As the first battle of Philippi begins, Brutus dispatches a written order to his army to attack.

> *Alarum. Enter Brutus and Messala*
> Bru. Ride, ride *Messala*, ride and give these Billes
>   Unto the Legions, on the other side.
> > *Lowd Alarum*
> >   Let them set on at once: for I perceive
> >   But cold demeanor in *Octavio*'s wing:
> >   And sodaine push gives them the overthrow:
> >   Ride, ride *Messala* and let them all come downe.
> > > *Exeunt*
> > > (2470–7)

Here Shakespeare weds two of the central themes of *Julius Caesar*: the untimeliness of Brutus and the unreliability of written documents. Brutus's ill-timed order has an immediate and pernicious effect. As Brutus and Messala leave the stage, Cassius and Titinius enter in distress:

> *Alarums. Enter Cassius and Titinius.*
> Cassi. O looke *Titinius*, looke, the Villianes flye:
>   My selfe have to mine owne turn'd Enemy:
>   This Ensigne heere of mine was turning backe,
>   I slew the Coward, and did take it from him.
> Titin. O *Cassius*, *Brutus* gave the word too early,
>   Who having some advantage on *Octavius*,
>   Tooke it too eagerly: his Soldiers fell to spoyle.
>   Whil'st we by *Antony* are all inclos'd.
> > (2478–86)

In the confusion of battle, Ate has been busy. Cassius's own soldiers have become 'Villaines' and he their 'Enemy'. Brutus's misperception of the strategic situation and his ill-timed 'Billes' have lost the battle. At this moment Pindarus enters in panic:

> Fly further off my Lord: flye further off,
> *Mark Antony* is in your Tents my Lord:
> Flye therefore *Noble Cassius*, flye farre off.
>
> (2488–90)

In the name of love, Cassius dispatches Titinius to reconnoiter:

> *Cassi.* *Titinius*, if thou lovest me,
> Mount thou my horse, and hide thy spurres in him,
> Till he have brought thee up to yonder Troopes
> And heere againe, that I may rest assur'd
> Whether yond Troopes, are Friend or Enemy.
> *Tit.*   I will be heere againe, even with a thought.   *Exit*
>
> (2494–9)

Then Cassius makes a fatal misjudgement. He asks Pindarus to be his eyes and describe the ride of Titinius:

> Go *Pindarus*, get higher on that hill,
> My sight was ever thicke: regard *Titinius*,
> And tell me what thou not'st about the Field.
>
> (2500–2)

Like Paul, Cassius confesses poor eyesight. Paul was blinded on the Damascus road, and subsequently refers to problems with his eyes (Galatians 4:13–15).[10] From above Pindarus shouts the chilling news that Titinius has been taken prisoner. His report is false. It is also Shakespeare's invention. In Plutarch, Cassius hears the shouting from the field of battle and deduces for himself that Titinius was 'take of the enemies' (North, 1579, 1075). Destitute, Shakespeare's Cassius turns to Pindarus.

> Come hither sirrah: In *Parthia* did I take thee Prisoner,
> And then I swore thee, saving of thy life,
> That whatsoever I did bid thee do,
> Thou should'st attempt it. Come now, keepe thine oath,
> Now be a Free-man, and with this good Sword
> That ran through *Caesars* bowels, search this bosome.
> Stand not to answer: Heere, take thou the Hilts,

And when my face is cover'd, as 'tis now,
Guide thou the Sword – *Caesar*, thou art reveng'd,
Even with the Sword that kill'd thee.

(2518–27)

Shakespeare found Cassius's death-scene in Plutarch. But the playwright invented Cassius's last words of direct address to Julius Caesar. Shakespeare also rewrote Plutarch's scene in two other important ways. In Plutarch, Cassius's head was stricken off.[11] Shakespeare leaves Cassius's head intact to wear Titinius's coronet. In Plutarch, Pindarus is a 'freed bondman' when he assists in Cassius's suicide. Shakespeare's Pindarus is freed by Cassius's death. Shakespeare rewrites his source to allow his Pindarus to express a remarkable paradox:

So, I am free,
Yet would not so have beene
Durst I have done my will.

(2528–30)

Pindarus is free because he was a slave to Cassius's will. Had Pindarus not been slave to Cassius's will, Pindarus would be a slave still. This antilogy of 'free will' and 'slavery' is the great paradox of Pauline theology. Again and again Paul returns to the themes of the bondage of the flesh and liberation through Christ (Romans 5:18, 6:18ff., etc.). Paradoxically, Paul argues that liberation can be achieved only through bondage: 'For he that is called in the Lord being a servant, is the Lords freman: likewise also he that is called being fre, is Christs serva(n)t' (1 Corinthians 7:22). Paul's paradoxical view of freedom and predestination (Romans 8:29) form the basis for the Christian debate of free will which began with St Augustine's controversy with the Pelagians (AD 416–30) and continued into Shakespeare's day and ours. Implicitly Pindarus becomes anamnetic for Paul's disciple Timothy. This is another of Shakespeare's textual markers. The Gospel for the correct date of Easter, 11 April Gregorian, was Hebrews 13:1–25. This passage begins, 'Let brotherly love continue' (Hebrews 13:1). Paul emphasizes bondage: 'Remember them that are in bonds, as bound with them' (Hebrews 13:3). And he concludes with freedom from bondage: 'Know ye that our brother Timothy is set at liberty' (Hebrews 13:23). Timothy went off to teach the Gospel to the heathens, and was stoned to death in Constantinople. Shakespeare's Pindarus vanishes to a place where 'never Roman will take note of him'.

There is one more colossal Pauline trope in Shakespeare's portrayal of the events at Philippi. When Brutus discovers the body of Cassius he attributes Cassius's death to Caesar's invisible power:

> O *Julius Caesar*, thou art mighty yet.
> Thy Spirit walkes abroad, and turnes our Swords
> In our owne proper Entrailes.
>
> (2583–5)

Brutus then pronounces one of the most startling lines – if not *the* most startling line – of the play: 'Come therefore, and to *Tharsus* send his body' (2594). Since 1733 editors have adopted Theobald's emendation, 'Thassos'. Plutarch records that Brutus 'caused his [Cassius's] body to be buried, and sent it to the citie of Thassos' (North, 1579, 1076). Theobald reasoned:

> the whole Tenor of History warrants us to write … *Thassos. Tharsos* [Tarsus] was a Town of *Cilicia*, in *Asia Minor*: and is it probable, *Brutus* could think of sending *Cassius's* Body thither out of *Thrace*, where they were now incamp'd? *Thassos*, on the contrary, was a little Isle lying close upon *Thrace*, and at but a small Distance from *Philippi*, to which the Body might very commodiously be transported.
>
> (Theobald, 1733, 203n)

But there is an important reason to believe that Shakespeare wrote and intended 'Tharsus' – and it was a reason widely known. St Paul was born at Tarsus. I have no doubt that Shakespeare wrote 'Tarsus', and the Folio text should be restored.

Hateful error, and the setting sunne of Rome

When Titinius and Messala discover the dead Cassius a remarkable poetical duet ensues. First, Titinius:

> O setting Sunne:
> As in thy red Rayes thou doest sinke to night;
> So in his red blood *Cassius* day is set.
> The Sunne of Rome is set. Our day is gone,
> Clowds, Dewes, and Dangers come; our deeds are done:
> Mistrust of my successe hath done this deed.
>
> (2545–50)

Messala picks up Titinius's final words as though they were a refrain:

> Mistrust of good successe hath done this deed.
> O hatefull Error, Melancholies Childe:
> Why do'st thou shew to the apt thoughts of men
> The things that are not? O Error soone conceyv'd,
> Thou never com'st unto a happy byrth,
> But kil'st the Mother that engendered thee.
>
> (2551–6)

No passage in *Julius Caesar* has engendered more critical confusion. The *Variorum* citation is typical:

> It is to be regretted that Shakespeare did not 'blot' these lines. The fancy becomes a conceit and the conceit is followed too far ... The Mother of error is said to be Melancholy; but, obviously Error is not reproached for slaying Melancholy, but for slaying Cassius ... [Therefore] should we read *father* [in place of *mother*]?
>
> (Furness, 1913, 262n)

Modern editors try to explain away the 'gender confusion' by suggesting that Mother–Melancholy was the intended effect.[12] This is not safe. The commentators have overlooked the (erroneous) connotation which Julius Caesar's name carried in Shakespeare's time. Elizabethans believed that the Roman dictator was born by Cesarean section, a procedure which invariably resulted in the death of the mother.[13] The 'Error' of whom Messala speaks is not Cassius or an abstraction but Julius Caesar himself. Antony has prophesied that Caesar's spirit will range for revenge in the company of Ate, goddess of error, whose special gift is blinding men to the difference between good and evil.

But there is a secondary meaning to 'Error' which must not be overlooked. In Shakespeare's time 'error' described heretical practices and the 'holding of mistaken notions or beliefs ... false beliefs collectively' (*OED* n. III.3.a). The Elizabethan prayer book identifies Christianity as the means by which 'we are brought out of darkness and error' (127). Shakespeare uses 'error' in the sense of heresy in *The Merchant of Venice*, 'In religion, / What damned error, but some sober brow / Will bless it?' (3.2.77–9). As the sun of Rome sets we may hear Shakespeare's judgement of Julius Caesar's antiquated calendar – and Queen Elizabeth's autocracy. For England to celebrate All Fools' Day instead of Easter on 1 April 1599 qualified as 'damned error'. (See Appendix 2.)

The triumph of Caesar's time

Shakespeare alters his Plutarchan source to stage the two battles of Philippi on the same day. By this device Shakespeare causes Cassius and Brutus to die on the same day as it was thought Sts Paul and Peter died on 29 June AD 64. As the battle slips through his fingers, Brutus summons his adherents: 'Come poore remaines of friends, rest on this Rocke' (2640). Though Shakespeare found this 'rocke' in his source, most of his Globe audience had not read Plutarch. Christ renamed Peter *Cephas*, the Greek word for 'rock'. Brutus's rock, in association with the Cassius–Tarsus trope, recalls this Peter-Cephas connection. Brutus is suddenly afflicted by the same fatalism that brought Cassius to ruin. As Cassius did, Brutus attributes his distress to the power of immortal Caesar:

> The Ghost of *Caesar* hath appear'd to me
> Two severall times by Night: at *Sardis*, once;
> And this last Night, here in *Philippi* fields:
> I know my houre is come.
>
> (2660–3)

Brutus's reference to 'my houre' calls to mind the Gospel of John: 'when Jesus knewe that his houre was come, that he shulde departe out of this worlde unto the Father' (John 13:1). As noted, only in John 13 does Christ give the sop of wine to Judas and abet his betrayal. Brutus pledges his love to his followers as Jesus does in John 13:1: 'for as much as he loved his owne which were in the world, unto the end he loved them.' Three times a friend denies Brutus's request to slay him. At last Strato agrees to the deed. Like Cassius before him, in his last extremity Brutus makes a direct address to Caesar: 'Caesar, now be still, / I kill'd not thee with halfe so good a will. *Dyes*' (2696–8).

As Strato stands over the dead Brutus, Antony, Octavius, Messala, Lucillius and the army enter. Octavius demands, 'What man is that?' and Messala replies, 'My Masters man. / *Strato*, where is thy Master?' (2701–2). Strato's answer is sharp, frank:

> Free from the Bondage you are in *Messala*,
> The Conquerors can but make a fire of him:
> For *Brutus* onely overcame himselfe,
> And no man else hath Honor by his death.
>
> (2703–6)

In performance this speech of Strato cuts through with profound effect. It is the first accurate report in Act 5. Octavius makes a magnanimous offer of a general amnesty: 'All that serv'd *Brutus*, I will entertaine them' (2709). But there is a price for Octavius's clemency, as he explains to Strato: 'Fellow, wilt thou bestow thy time with me?' (2710). To be Octavius's man one must surrender to his time. Strato is willing, if Messala will permit him. Messala asks, 'How dyed my Master *Strato?*' (2713). Strato raises Brutus's sword as he replies: 'I held the Sword, and he did run on it' (Figure 16) (2714). This is the final tableau of *Julius Caesar*. Strato holding aloft the cruciform sword hilts as the great liar, Antony, delivers Brutus's epitaph. Shakespeare knew that history was written by the victors.

Notes

1 It was also the Roman festival of *Fortuna Virilis*. On the Kalends of April 'women of the lower sort bathed in the men's public baths, and worshipped *Fortuna Virilis* (Virile Fortune)'. Ovid importuned the 'Fairest of goddesses' to 'behold the sons of Aeneas with benign looks' (Frazer, 1989, 198n–201).

2 Cicero's prophetic words spoken on the unruly night seem to typify the action of Act 5: 'Indeed, it is a strange disposed time: / But men may construe things after their fashion, / Cleane from the purpose of the things themselves' (465–7).

3 St Paul's letters to the Corinthians are laced with references to fools, foolishness and foolery. These are keywords in *Julius Caesar*. Casca describes the offstage events in the marketplace as 'Foolerie' at lines 339 and 391. Cassius sneers that inclement weather causes 'Fooles [to] calculate' (504). Calpurnia's well-founded fears seem 'foolish' to Caesar (1098), as do the conspirators' fawning 'which [might] melteth Fooles' (1249). The Second Plebeian bristles when Cinna implies those who marry 'are fooles' (1830). Cassius disavows his own messenger as 'a Foole' (2062). Brutus characterizes the Cynicke Poet as a 'Jigging Foole' (2122).

4 Shakespeare rarely applies a modifier of height or depth to the word 'region(s)'. When he does, the word takes on a metaphysical overtone, as when Jupiter chides the dead relatives of Posthumus, 'no more, you petty spirits of region low' (*Cym*. 5.4.93), or when Joan of Arc calls out for help to the devils in 'the powerful regions under earth' (*1H6* 5.3.11).

5 Perhaps a glance at the Roman holy day *Fortuna Virilis*.

6 The connection between Caesar's coronet and Christ's is alive in the concordance of 'Crowne' and 'mocke' when Decius woos Caesar to accompany him to the Capitol: 'the Senate have concluded / To give this day, a Crowne to mighty *Caesar*. / If you shall send them word you will not come, / Their

mindes may change. Besides, it were a mocke' (1086–9). Christ predicted His own mocking by the Romans in the Gospel of St Mark: 'Behold, we go up to Jerusalem; and the Son of man shall be delivered unto the chief priests, and unto the scribes; and they shall condemn him to death, and shall deliver him to the Gentiles: And they shall mock him, and shall scourge him, and shall spit upon him, and shall kill him: and the third day he shall rise again' (Mark 10:34).

7 Shakespeare uses the word in this sense in *King Lear* (1.4.348). To buzz was to make false insinuations, or express untrue ideas (*OED* buzz v.1.4). Shakespeare employs the word 'buzzers' in this sense in *Hamlet* (4.5.90).

8 Untruthful Roman soldiers had a role in the Gospel accounts of Easter. The Catholic Gospel for Holy Saturday was Matthew 28:1–7. The verses immediately following tell the story of the Roman guards who were bribed to lie by the Pharisees, and told the people that Christ was not resurrected but stolen from the tomb by his adherents (Matthew 28:11–15). Matthew concludes that the Romans took the money and lied, 'and this story has been spread among the Jews to this day'.

9 The Latin version is '*Per ipsum, et cum ipso, et in ipso, est tibi Deo Patri ominipotenti, in unitate Spiritus Sancti, omnis honor et gloria, per omina saecula saeculorum. Amen.*'

10 Cassius claims to have slain his Ensigne: 'My selfe have to mine owne turn'd Enemy' (2480). Paul frequently writes of man as his own enemy, for example in Romans 7:18–24.

11 Plutarch records that Cassius went 'into a tent where no bodie was, and tooke *Pyndarus* with him, one of his freed bondmen, whom he reserved ever for suche a pinche … then casting his cloke over his head, & holding out his bare neck unto *Pindarus*, he gave him his head to be striken of. So the head was found severed from the bodie: but after that time *Pindarus* was never seene more. Whereupon, some tooke occasion to say, that he had slaine his master, without his commaundement' (North, 1579, 1075–6).

12 For example: Dorsch, 1983, 122n, and Humphreys, 1984, 222n.

13 Plutarch records that Julius Caesar's mother, Aurelia, survived his birth and lived to take a hand in his advancement through the Roman priesthood.

IV

Shakespeare among the assassins

15

The writer who changed the world

If Samuel Schoenbaum is correct is suggesting that William Shakespeare's parents delayed his baptism because of superstition, the playwright's preoccupation with the calendar may have been congenital. On the other hand, François Laroque reasons,

> Given that one of the greatest problems of the theatre and dramatic representation generally is to find visual and gestural equivalents to the abstract categories of thought and speech, it is easy to see how Shakespeare seized upon ... the medium of the calendar linked with the various traditions and games of the major festivals [to] endow his plays with the extra semantic dimension of temporal symbolism.
>
> (Laroque, 1993, 203)

Literate English men and women were aware of Elizabeth's rejection of the Gregorian calendar reform of 1582. They knew they were being compelled to live and worship according to an antiquated and scientifically discredited calendar. As he created *Julius Caesar*, Shakespeare harnessed the energy of the bubbling calendar controversy. He seized upon the public's awareness of the bizarre discordances of holy days in 1599 as a means of creating a new mode of discourse with an audience. By staging a *Julius Caesar* rife with calendrical markers and Scriptural allusions, Shakespeare and Company put their London public on notice that their playhouse would be not only a place of entertainment but a venue where simmering issues of the day would be interrogated. Through *Julius Caesar* Shakespeare proclaimed the new Globe a theatre of courage and ideas, and a place where one must observe with the inner eye, listen with the inner ear.

Like Shakespeare's portrait of *Richard III*, his Julius Caesar has eclipsed the historical man in the popular consciousness. One has to remind oneself that Caesar did not gasp, '*Et tu, Brute?*' Shakespeare did.

Shakespeare among the assassins

[The] part played by Shakespeare himself in creating our notions of the ancient Romans should not be forgotten. It has become difficult to see [*Julius Caesar*] straight, to see the thing in itself as it really is, because we are all in the power of Shakespeare's imagination, a power which has been exercised for several generations and from which it is scarcely possible to extricate ourselves.

(Spencer, 1957, 37–8)

This dilemma is particularly problematic for Shakespeare scholars. In our compartmentalized twentieth century it is a rare mind which combines the *bona fides* of Shakespearian, Latinist, classical historian, astronomer, astrologer and biblical scholar. Our specialization as Shakespearians defines not only our competency but our limitations. The eminent John Dover Wilson suspected some arcane connection between 'Caska's almanac' and Elizabeth I's rejection of the Gregorian calendar reform. Not being an astronomer, Wilson turned for advice to Professor Greaves, Astronomer Royal of Scotland (J. D. Wilson, n.d., 128n). And while the astronomer confirmed Wilson's hunch, the Shakespearian was not competent to interpret its relevance to the play. Wilson's quandary is emblematic. All of Shakespeare's modern commentators are specialists, whereas Shakespeare himself was a generalist, and a man of superbly refined intelligence.

Julius Caesar is also the work of a writer coming into the full flower of genius. The play marks the crossroads of the dramatist's career. Its text is Roman, English, ancient, Elizabethan, pagan, Christian. It engrosses history, philosophy, politics, religion and science. Its sweep of thought embraces the Bible, the ancient historians, time and the calendar, Renaissance humanism and Elizabethan *realpolitik*. No other play in the canon more vividly displays Shakespeare's phenomenal erudition, insatiable curiosity and command of language, tableau and audience response. In the 1950s Ernest Schanzer proselytized the view that Shakespeare intended *Julius Caesar* as a 'problem play'.

There is widespread disagreement among critics about who is the play's principal character or whether it has a principal character, on whether it is a tragedy and if so whose, on whether Shakespeare wants us to consider the assassination as damnable or praiseworthy, while of all the chief characters in the play violently contradictory interpretations have been offered.

(Schanzer, 1955, 297)[1]

The present essay offers an alternative view. It suggests that scholars have found Shakespeare's *Julius Caesar* opaque because they have underestimated the playwright's intellect and the range of his classical reading – and that they have failed to discriminate the awesome undertaking he had in hand. The key to understanding Shakespeare's *Julius Caesar* is seeing this play through Elizabethan eyes in 1599 by the corrupt Julian calendar. When Shakespeare moved on from *Henry V* to *Julius Caesar* the playwright did more than shift ground from the old Curtain to the new Bankside Globe. He ratcheted up the level of discourse. Modern commentators share the opinion that 'no play of consequence devoted to an avowedly religious subject was written for public performance by professional actors after Marlowe's *Dr Faustus*' (Wickham, 1981, ii.94).[2] It is also a scholarly commonplace that representations of the sacraments disappeared from English playbooks and London playhouses after the Star Chamber ban of 12 November 1589.[3] This essay suggests that these prejudices must be discarded. Plays about religious subjects and depictions of the sacraments did not vanish from the Elizabethan stage. Rather, they sublimated to a new level of discourse. Every Shakespearean scholar knows there is *something* different about Shakespeare's plays after *Henry V*. Beginning with *Julius Caesar*, the plays seem to cast transcendental shadows which elude interpretation. This essay suggests that a key to unlocking this elusive level of meaning is the calendar and liturgy.

Like a number of Shakespeare's later plays, *Julius Caesar* is hieratic art. It presents a superficial, exoteric narrative with a minimum of puzzling cruces. But the play also has a secondary meaning which has become impenetrable to modern audiences who do not live by the church and its calendar, and do not read the Bible. An Elizabethan audience's capacity to digest *Julius Caesar*'s hieratic diction of words and tableaux depended on a shared body of knowledge: knowledge of Scripture, of the Elizabethan church calendar and of a common typological vocabulary of sacred persons, events and rituals. Even the faintest of Shakespeare's calendrical markers in *Julius Caesar* would have been accessible to some members of his audience. Many Elizabethans knew large sections of the Bible by heart. They memorized the order of feast days through repetitive recitation of mnemonic doggerels. The temporal and textual markers in *Julius Caesar* were as apparent to Shakespeare's first audience as they should be now to the present reader.

But there is another reason why we have found it difficult to penetrate to the heart of Shakespeare's *Julius Caesar*. We do not live under a censorious regime. We have lost the habit of sifting for recondite meanings in contemporary plays because our contemporary playwrights work under no strictures of ideas, language, piety or modesty. Our playwrights can be as lewd, vulgar and impious as they wish. Shakespeare developed a novel form of discourse in *Julius Caesar* because he lived and thought and wrote under an intensely censorious regime. When young William Shakespeare arrived in London – arguably in the late 1580s – the three avatars of the English theatre were Lyly, Kyd and Marlowe. Before *Julius Caesar* was written, Lyly had been silenced,[4] Marlowe murdered, Kyd racked and broken – all, so it was thought, by a vindictive, violent central government. What impression the brutal suppression of these *glitterati* might have made on an apprentice playwright is a nice question. In the spring of 1599 – at the very moment Shakespeare was writing *Julius Caesar* – John Hayward nearly lost his life to savage, arbitrary censorship. Other Renaissance writers, Machiavelli and Milton, worked in equally noxious environments. They found refuge in what James Joyce would come to call 'silence, exile, and cunning'.

Julius Caesar was written in an environment of religious tyranny of which the absurd Julian calendar was merely one manifestation. The text of *Julius Caesar* must be encountered as a response to that tyranny. Queen Elizabeth's refusal to accept the reformed Gregorian calendar turned the English Easter observances of 1598 into a theatre of the absurd. Being compelled to celebrate Easter on the wrong day would humiliate and enrage any devout Christian. Then again there has hardly been an enforced state religion without its idiosyncrasies. An illustration can be framed around the lifespan of John Shakespeare (*c.* 1529–1602). Had William Shakespeare's father wished to live in conformity with the state religion of England he would have been born Catholic, and lived

Catholic (1529–33)
'Henrican' (1534–47)
Protestant (1547–53)
Catholic (1553–58)
Protestant (1559–1602).

Over a single lifetime the incumbent priesthood taught that the Eucharist was the body and blood of Christ in so many years, and merely crackers and wine in others. Over time the effect of this uncertainty would be to disjoin ceremony from faith. While lipservers might drift with the dogma *en vogue*, the devout would cling ever more tenaciously to their personal relationship with God. As *Julius Caesar* moves into Act 4, Shakespeare winks at the priesthood through his portrait of the new elders of Rome. During the black proscriptions scene 4.1, Antony scolds Octavius: 'I have seene more dayes then you' (1873). In Suetonius, Cicero's *Philippics* and other sources Shakespeare learned that Antony, who was twice as old as Octavius's nineteen years, keenly resented his jejune partner. Antony's theme – broadly, 'listen to your elders' – recurs three times in Act 4: Antony to Octavius (1873); Cassius to Brutus: 'I am a Souldier, I, Older in practice' (2002); the Cynicke Poet to Brutus–Cassius: 'I have seene more yeeres I'm sure then yee' (2117). An 'elder' was a man 'venerable for age, or conventionally supposed to be' (*OED* n.3.3). Its ecclesiastical sense evolved from the Greek *presbyteros*, which became the Latin *presbyter*, from which the English 'priest' derived (*OED* elder n.3.4). After the death of Christ, his apostles fashioned themselves as elders of his new church. Peter declared himself an elder (1 Peter 5:1). Paul instructed Timothy: 'Rebuke not an elder, but exhort him as a father' (1 Timothy 5:1). Luke repeatedly refers to the Jerusalem faction as 'the elders' to distinguish the Petrines from Paul and his adherents in Acts 15:2 and elsewhere. The three men who claim to be elders in *Julius Caesar* have something important in common. Cassius, the Cynicke Poet and Antony are all *writers*. Cassius forged letters to Brutus in 1.2, and complains in 4.2 that his letters 'praying' on behalf of Lucius Pella were 'slighted off'. The Cynicke Poet rewrites Homer and Christ's commandment in the Gospel of John. Antony 'authors' the principal actions of the play, participates in the rewrite of Caesar's assassination, delivers Brutus's epitaph and holds the pen in the black proscriptions scene. Shakespeare and his audience knew that Christ's legacy – his Word – was entrusted to the writers. In the closing play of the York Mysteries Christ instructs his disciples

> Now all fare forth, my brethren dear,
> On all sides in each country clear;
> My rising tell both far and near;
>   Preach it shall ye.
> And my blessing I give you here,
>   And this company.

> (Purvis 344)

This was the Escriveners' Play, the play of the writers. Elizabethans believed that eight men wrote the book that changed the world: Matthew, Mark, Luke, John, Peter, James, Paul and Jude.[5] Shakespeare was mindful of this, and he parodies it. Though he knew from Plutarch and Suetonius that more than sixty men took part in the conspiracy against Caesar, Shakespeare turns out exactly eight: Cassius, Brutus, Casca, Cinna, Trebonius, Caius Ligarius, Metellus Cimber and Decius Brutus. Casca proclaims a writer's battle cry when he shouts, 'Speake hands for me.'

In our time it has become commonplace to read *Julius Caesar* as a political play. Elizabeth's continued imposition of the discredited Julian calendar was, indeed, political. The question of who would succeed the old Queen was the burning political question. Shakespeare – who had named his children Susannah, Hamnet and Judith – was certainly no admirer of tyrants. Indeed, *Julius Caesar* may be the play we have always been taught it is: a political potboiler of murder and revenge. But I suggest that something more important than politics is at stake in *Julius Caesar*. It is an issue more consequential than calendar reform, and more important than whether Essex or the Infanta, or James VI of Scotland would succeed to England's throne. When Shakespeare decided to compound the martyrdom of Christ and the murder of Caesar he set out to interrogate the truth of the Gospels – mimetically – the way an artist writing for the stage interrogates things. Competent scholars have, in so many words, told me that 'such a thing wasn't done' – 'it wasn't proper' – 'it wasn't British' – 'it was too dangerous' – 'Shakespeare was a man of discretion' – 'he wouldn't have done it' – 'the man wrote for money – why would he risk everything?' – etc. But I respond: this is what writers of literature do. They define themselves by challenging their society to doubt its fundamental beliefs. And this indeed is dangerous. In our own century, when Alexander Solzhenitzen wrote *The Gulag Archipelago* – when Günter Grass wrote *The Tin Drum* – when Arthur Miller wrote *The Crucible* – when Nadine Gordimer wrote *July's People* – each was aware of the possible consequences of challenging a society to doubt its most tenaciously held beliefs. Why would Shakespeare do it?

Why

This essay has suggested that after contemplating the story of Caesar's fall for a decade, Shakespeare was moved to write *Julius Caesar* by the

Elizabethan calendar controversy, an extraordinary disparity between the Protestant and Catholic dates of Easter in 1598, and an even more bizarre series of holy day discordances in 1599. While these pages have addressed Shakespeare's *occasion*, this essay has remained pointedly silent about Shakespeare's *intention*. It is perilous to speculate about a writer's intentions – particularly when that writer is universally revered as an avatar, cherished by the English as a national treasure, and has recently been misappropriated by a multitude of factions to support narrow political and social agendas.[6] But the moral and ethical question – why do we find Shakespeare among Caesar's assassins? – *must* be addressed if we are to ever know *Julius Caesar* all the way through.

A clue may be found in the play's title. Shakespeare called his play *The Tragedie of Julius Caesar*, and a 'tragedy'

> to define it very simply – is a killing poem; it is designed toward the end of bringing a man to some sort of destruction. And the killer is, quite literally, the poet; it is he, and no one else, who devises the deadly plot; it is he, therefore, who must in some sense accept responsibility for it. Even if the events of the plot are drawn from history – as with Julius Caesar they obviously are – what is the poet's purpose in reenacting them and shaping them as he does, at that particular time and place? Why does he not leave history to the historians? Why, and how, does he represent as a living reality what is, or seems to be, a dead past? In other words, what is he, the plotter, doing when he has Caesar killed? These questions are not simply speculative. It is always true that a poem – especially a dramatic poem – is an act, not just a report; this truth used to be felt more concretely in Shakespeare's day than it is in ours.
>
> (Burkhardt, 1968, 15)

Aspects of *Julius Caesar* suggest that the playwright was moved by an ingrained hostility toward dogmatic faith. Shakespeare repeatedly imbues his Romans with a foolhardy, blind trust in the written word. This essay has also inferred that Shakespeare took note of the similarities between the careers of two men with the initials JC who became the greatest figures in secular and sacred history. Shakespeare must also have noticed the dissimilarities, too: Julius Caesar owed his greatness to arms, Jesus Christ to words. Both achieved godhead. But the immortality of only one endured. And, curiously enough, that was Christ, whose godhead was perpetuated by the most ephemeral of all monuments: human breath made written characters. This essay has noted that Elizabethan Christians believed that theirs was the true religion because the events described in the New Testament actually happened. In his *Arte of Rhetorique* (1553) Thomas Wilson wrote: 'The Historie of God's booke to the Christian is infallible' (Muir, 1909, 190). This is paradoxical. Protestants who rejected the infallibility of the Pope – a man – were expected to believe that *a book* was infallible? *A book*, which every writer knew had gone through countless drafts and numerous translations, was infallible? *A book* written, transcribed, copied, typeset and printed by men was infallible? If a man is fallible, how can a book created by a man be infallible? The Christian's answer in Shakespeare's day as in ours is that *this book is the word of God*. And this might have been the sticking point for William Shakespeare: the foundation for believing the divinity of Christ is believing that the Gospels are infallibly true. This test of faith – which challenges every believer down to our own day – was in 1599 compounded by the fact that there was not one universally accepted edition of the Word of God. Just as there were two rival calendars, there were two New Testaments in English: the Protestant Geneva (1560) and its successors, and the rival Catholic Rheims (1582). While the variations between the two texts may seem insignificant to secular modern readers, we must remember that the Bible had become widely available in English only within the lifetime of Shakespeare's father – since which time Englishmen had not ceased to butcher one another over variations in its text and interpretations thereof.[7]

In the era when Shakespeare wrote *Julius Caesar* the Renaissance mind was struggling to digest the new vernacular Bible as literal history. But it was also simultaneously grappling with fundamental questions of historiography. In a variety of commentaries ranging from the essays of Montaigne (1580, 1588) to Machiavelli's *Florentine Histories* (tr. 1595) to Raleigh's *History of the World* (1614) one can trace the growing dissatisfaction with the Christian interpretative historiography typified by St Augustine's *Civitas Dei* (AD 413–26) and Orosius's *History Against the Pagans* (AD 417).[8] Shakespeare's *Julius Caesar* represents a blunt rejection of Christian historiography.[9] According to Augustine it was God's will which brought Augustus to the empery of Rome.[10] According to Shakespeare, it was Mark Antony's guile.

Shakespeare's rejection of Christian historiography did not end with the writing of *Julius Caesar*. In 1610 the rival calendars again presented the playwright – for the last time during his active life in the theatre –

with *precisely* the same bizarre concordance of holy days which occurred in 1599. And in 1610 Shakespeare turned to the subject of Cymbeline:

> Perhaps the most impressive evidence that Shakespeare was preoccupied with the crucial factors of Christian historiography lies ... in the complex of motivations that led Shakespeare, uniquely, to fix his attention upon the reign of King Cymbeline. Once more Shakespeare turns to Holinshed ... [where] the only unequivocal evidence about Cymbeline to be picked up ... was that 'during his reign, the Saviour of the world our Lord Jesus Christ the onelie sonne of God was borne of a virgine, about the 23 yeare of the reigne of this Kymbeline, and in the 42 yeare of the emperour Octavius Augustus, that is to wit, in the yeare of the world 3966, in the second yeare of the 195 Olympiad, after the building of the citie of Rome 750 nigh at an end' (Holinshed i.32). There again, even in a single phrase anticipating the fall of Rome, history is shaped in the way that most captured Shakespeare's imagination.
>
> (Simmons, 1973, 165)

In *Cymbeline* we encounter a world in which Britain is the last hold-out against Octavius Caesar Augustus's *Pax Romana*. In the end a British king pays tribute, and the time of universal peace begins. *Cymbeline* is a good-natured romance of history as revelation. *Julius Caesar* is a cold-eyed inquisition against revelation as history.

The writer Shakespeare knew that writers of history couldn't be trusted. One can see this idea at work in his treatment of 'writers' in *Julius Caesar*. Caesar is a Lord of Misrule who 'bad the Romans / Marke him, and write his Speeches in their Bookes' (223–4) in the hope of becoming a king; instead he became a corpse and a god. Cassius tried to use the written word to whet Marcus Brutus against Caesar, but succeeds only in ruining the republic and sealing his own awful death. Brutus eradicates the last hope of the republic with the ill-timed 'bille' which calls the armies of the upper regions down to defeat. Artemidorus alone writes truth. He is ignored. Cinna, a benign poet, is murdered for bad verses. The Cynicke Poet who brings the Gospel of John is reviled and kicked off the stage. In Shakespeare's *Julius Caesar* the legitimate chroniclers of history are slain, silenced or dismissed.[11] In their place Antony, Octavius and Lepidus use pen-and-ink to murder the innocent. Another poet's namesake, Pindar(us), is a flatterer – and blinder than Cassius. Caesar's only true believers are Cassius – a forger who stoops to writing letters on behalf of an extortionist – and the suggestible *Brutus*

Malapropus, slave of the proverbial idiom, slave of the book. In the end the writing of the history of Caesar and the honourable men is left to ruthless Octavius, to the great liar, Antony … and to William Shakespeare – poet, playwright, purveyor of doubt.

Which brings me to that moment which William Shakespeare apparently believed to be *the* turning-point in the secular history of Western civilization. Caesar is dead. The plebeians have heard Brutus' explanation of the causes for Caesar's assassination and seem satisfied withal. Then a stage direction orders, *'Enter Mark Antony, with Caesars body'* (1570). Visualize the scene. Caesar's body is brought onstage in a hearse. Behind it follows the writer, Antony – perhaps dressed in his priestly robes, carrying his augur's *lituus* crook, his hands stained red from shaking the bloody hands of Caesar's killers. The prosaic Brutus departs. Priest Antony ascends to the pulpit. He speaks verses. His listeners are rapt, then moved, then imbued. The *perousia* begins. But the writer lies. And his lies – well, they change the world for ever.

Notes

1 Among other questions Schanzer raises: Who is the play's principal character? Why is *Julius Caesar* entitled 'The Tragedie of'? What is Shakespeare's attitude towards the assassination and assassins? Also, Rees, 1955, 135: 'It has at one time or another been argued that the play is broken-backed because its titular hero is murdered in Act III; that the play is wrongly named and should have been called *Marcus Brutus*; that the quarrel scene is irrelevant; and that, since the presentation of Caesar is in many ways unexpected, Shakespeare deliberately "wrote Caesar down" for the purpose of "writing Brutus up" [G. B. Shaw].'

2 In particular, it has been thought that *Julius Caesar* had little or nothing to do with the Bible. 'There are hardly any direct references to Biblical texts or subjects in the play' (Carter, 1905, 343).

3 Minutes of the Privy Council, 12 November 1589: 'whereas there hathe growne some inconvenience by comon playes and enterludes … in that the players take upon themselves to handle in their plaies certen matters of Divinytie and of State unfitt to be suffred' (cited in Chambers, 1923, iv. 306.) On the other hand, Richard Dutton, 1991, has argued that the censorious Revels Office was actually a benign lacuna of benevolence and *laissez-faire*.

4 'Lyly's ineptitude in polemic, coupled probably with an over-eagerness to please authority, seems to have led to some gaffe … the Paul's boys were inhibited from acting for the period 1590–1600 (approx.); and when

silence falls on the Paul's boys, silence is not far from the dramatic voice of John Lyly' (Hunter, 1962, 80–1).

5 In fact there were probably nine – but Elizabethans believed that the authors of the Gospel of John, the letters of John and the Book of Revelations were the same John.

6 The writer of the present essay is a secular humanist *sans* portfolio.

7 An English Protestant view of the magnitude and significance of the variations between the two translations can be found in Fulke's parallel texts and commentary, which went through many editions between 1588 and 1633.

8 Montaigne admired the work of Machiavelli's friend and colleague Guicciardini, who 'never referreth any one unto vertue, religion, or conscience: as if they were all extinguished and banished the world' (Henley, 1893, ii. 107).

9 '*Julius Caesar* exploits for dramatic purposes the growing awareness among Renaissance historians and others that the past is difficult to retrieve, and that the ends of history are best served by scrupulous objectivity' (Chang, 1970, 63).

10 Green, 1944, 315–22.

11 'But the murder of a poet also symbolizes Antony's willful distortion of the end [objective] of art. Murdering poets, as Orpheus was dismembered by the Bacchic women, signals the destruction of those charged with chronicling ... history' (F. W. Willson, 1990, 24).

V

Evidence of calendrical markers in other plays of Shakespeare

16

Prolegomenon for a mode of criticism

In addition to *The Tragedie of Julius Caesar*, in the years 1599–1601 William Shakespeare wrote three other plays which interrogate aspects of the Elizabethan calendar controversy: *Twelfth Night*, *As You Like It*, and *Hamlet*. In the final chapters of this book I wish to lay a plan for the study of these plays by offering certain general remarks. Then I will provide introductory essays about calendrical design in two of these plays.

In *Julius Caesar* Shakespeare asked a series of questions of faith, and then answered them mimetically. *How can a man become a god? Are his gospels reliable? Can his priests (and writers) be trusted?* I have inferred that Shakespeare's answers to these questions entail a religious sensibility which is informed, sophisticated and sceptical. This is not to imply that the playwright was an unbeliever. But it does suggest that as William Shakespeare entered his thirty-fifth year he entered a period of profound religious doubt. In *Twelfth Night*, Shakespeare interrogated the other crucial event which occurred at the inception of Christianity – the evangelization of the gentiles by St Paul. Like *Julius Caesar*, *Twelfth Night* contains a number of calendrical markers. These depend heavily upon the Epistles of Paul to the Corinthians. Chronologically, and in other ways, *Twelfth Night* is the successor play to *Julius Caesar*. The Corinth to which St Paul wrote was a colony Caesar founded for his veterans in 44 BC. No doubt Caesar was worshipped there as *Divus Julius*. Shakespeare certainly could have deduced that when Paul evangelized in Corinth the myths of Julius Caesar and Jesus Christ went head-to-head. In *As You Like It*, Shakespeare revisits Eden – the immortal garden where there are no clocks – a place where *men* have all the time in the world to hunt and sing and philosophize. Shakespeare discovers that the arrival of women with their internal menstrual clocks (and notions of romantic love) are Eden's confusion. Compared to these translucent plays we find *Hamlet* exceedingly complex. This play is Shakespeare's interrogation of that other defining moment in the life of Christianity: Martin Luther's Reformation. Against Reformation history Shakespeare reads a variety of passages from the Old and New Testament. When, for example, Hamlet dismisses his mother with 'frailty, thy name is woman', but rails on endlessly about his father being a Hyperion, a Hercules, a Jove, a Mars, a Mercury, and the locus 'Where every God did seeme to set his seale' (3.4.61), modern readers may see nothing but anachronistic sex discrimination. But Elizabethans who knew their Bible might have recognized a glance at how the troubles started in Genesis 6 when the sons of God came in unto the daughters of men.[1] In *Hamlet* a Protestant prince from Wittenberg sets out to justify revenge only to discover another kind of 'justification' in a world of inexorable predestination. In the introductory essays which follow I begin to examine Shakespeare's calendrical designs in *Twelfth Night* and *Hamlet*.

Note

1 'And it came to pass, when men began to multiply on the face of the earth, and daughters were born unto them, That the sons of God saw the daughters of men that they were fair; and they took them wives of all which they chose. And the LORD said, My spirit shall not always strive with man, for that he also is flesh: yet his days shall be an hundred and twenty years. There were giants in the earth in those days; and also after that, when the sons of God came in unto the daughters of men, and they bare children to them, the same became mighty men which were of old, men of renown. And God saw that the wickedness of man was great in the earth, and that every imagination of the thoughts of his heart was only evil continually. And it repented the LORD that he had made man on the earth, and it grieved him at his heart. And the LORD said, I will destroy man whom I have created from the face of the earth; both man, and beast, and the creeping thing, and the fowls of the air; for it repenteth me that I have made them. But Noah found grace in the eyes of the LORD' (Genesis 6:1–8).

17

Illyria's faulty calendar

In this chapter I will identify a series of calendrical markers in *Twelfth Night, Or What You Will*, and apply them to resolve certain cruces in the play. Principal among these cruces is the year of the play's composition – because the identity of the mysterious *Quinapalus* and the meaning of *the equinoctial of Queubus* are bound-up with the performance date for which *Twelfth Night* was written.

Lewis Theobald dated *Twelfth Night* to 1604. Eighteenth-century commentators including Steevens and Malone placed it last in the canon after *The Tempest*, and assigned a date of 1614. John Collier's discovery [1] of a reference in Manningham's 'diary' to a performance of *Twelfth Night* at Gray's Inn on Candlemas 2 February 1602 set a new *terminus ad quem*. Nineteenth-century scholars – Dyce, Halliwell-Phillipps and others – dated the play to 1599 or 1600. In the early twentieth century the identification of certain topical allusions led to the present scholarly consensus which assigns the principal composition of the play to mid-1601. Then in 1954 Leslie Hotson hypothesized that Viola first stumbled ashore to gasp 'What country, friends, is this' at Whitehall after supper on 6 January 1601. Hotson argued that Shakespeare purpose-wrote *Twelfth Night* for performance before Queen Elizabeth and a visitor with the evocative name of Virginio Orsino on the night of Epiphany – which Elizabethans erroneously called 'Twelfth Night' – or more properly 'Twelfth day at night' because it is the thirteenth night after Christmas Eve.[2] For two reasons Hotson's ingenious hypothesis 'has not won general acceptance' (Warren and Wells, 1994, 4). First, word of Orsino's impending visit reached London on Christmas Day 1600, and it seems implausible that Shakespeare could have written and rehearsed a new play in twelve days. Second, scholars are innately hostile to any suggestion that one of Shakespeare's timeless masterpieces might have begun its career as occasional work-for-hire.[3]

I believe that many of Shakespeare's plays were occasional. I believe that Shakespeare was writing new plays for performance on dates-certain as early as *The Comedy of Errors*, and at least as late as *Macbeth*. And why should he not have done so? The first English plays were – almost without exception – written for performance on occasions such as Corpus Christi, Candlemas and Midsummer. Yes, the new professional Elizabethan acting companies kept long seasons at fixed venues – and demanded a continuous flow of new plays. But Laroque has argued that Shakespeare set scenes in his plays on major holy days to endue the action with temporal symbolism (1993, 203). Setting a scene on a holy day, and writing a play for performance on a holy day, is various service to the same rubric.

In 1582 Pope Gregory XIII promulgated the reformed calendar which enjoys his name. Concurrently he caused the first New Testament in English to be published. These twin publications were not benign contributions to human knowledge. They were major incursions in the theo-political crusade we call the Counter-Reformation – a co-ordinated effort to re-establish the Roman Church's hegemony over holy writ and time. Gregory's Bull '*Inter gravissimas*' advanced the date ten days (not thirteen – an important innovation) by calling the day after Thursday 4 October Friday 15 October. Catholic countries were bound to adopt the Gregorian reform. Leading Protestant mathematicians Kepler, Brahe, Savile and Digges endorsed it, too. Governments scrambled to respond, throwing local calendars into pandemonium. In France the day after Sunday 9 December was called Monday 20 December. In the Catholic areas of Switzerland, Germany and the Netherlands [4] the day after Friday 21 December 1582 was called Saturday 1 January 1583 (those folks did without Christmas that year). The Protestant Netherlands [5] thought they could turn 15 December into the Nativity of Jesus Christ by fiat. [6] Depending on which country you were in (and whether you had heard the news), today could have been 11 December or New Year's Day or the first day of winter or the feast of St Thomas or the feast of the Circumcision. There were places where 12 December did not exist. And places where the 12 December was Christmas – among them Shakespeare's England. I have suggested that the English calendar controversy provides a subtext for Shakespeare's *Julius Caesar*, and that references to the calendar and liturgy can resolve cruces in that play. *Twelfth Night, Or What You Will* is chocked with jumbled references to 'the twelfe day of December', May Day, Midsummer, nights when 'late' and 'early' bleed into each other, a doctor drunk at eight in the morning, a clock chiming out of nowhere when love's night turns noon, etc. I believe that the play's title *'Twelfth Night, Or What You Will'* is reflexive. It means: 'Twelfth Night – or whichever date your personal calendar says it is.' And the 'twelfth night' to which it refers is not Epiphany. It is 12 December – the day of which Toby sings – the true date of the anniversary of the birth of Jesus Christ.

Twelfth Night contains a reference to time which is as startling to audiences as it is specific – and which provides an *entrée* to the play's internal clock. In the climactic fifth act Antonio says, 'Today, my lord, *and* for three months before, / No int'rim, not a minute's vacancy, / Both day and night did we keep company.' Orsino replies, 'Fellow, thy words are madness. / Three months this youth hath tended upon me' (5.1.91– 6). The stage is filled with other characters. None steps forward to refute these assertions. So I think we must accept that three months have passed since Viola entered Orsino's service – and that Antonio and Sebastian have been together three months and one day. Now, we know that Antonio and Sebastian met on the day of the shipwreck. Sebastian recalls that 'some hour before you took me from the breach of the sea was my sister drowned' (2.1.15–16). So we can deduce that Viola entered Orsino's service on the day following the shipwreck. I believe we can also deduce both the date of the shipwreck and the date of performance for which *Twelfth Night* was written. But to do that, we have to consider a calendrical phenomenon which occurred in England in 1600.

As the seventeenth century dawned, pious Elizabethans who thumbed their almanacs or scanned their liturgical calendars discovered a promise of golden time. Their Easter had been five weeks wrong in 1598; in 1599 they had observed All Fools' Day when they should have been exalting the Resurrection; but 1600 was going to be different. Yes, Protestant and Catholic solar holy days would continue to fall ten days apart. But Easter and the other lunar holy days would fall on the *same day* throughout all of 1600.[7] Protestants would celebrate Easter on the Julian 23 March, Catholics on the Gregorian 2 April. Though these *dates* were ten days apart, they signified the same Sunday. What was true for Easter was true for other movable feasts. Each fell on the same day in both calendars – beginning with the first movable feast of the year, Septuagesima Sunday – which was 20 January in the English Julian calendar – the Feast of Sts Sebastian and Fabian.

On the English feast of Sebastian and Fabian 1600 the calendars of

Protestant and Catholic lunar holy days synched-up and ran in synch through the rest of the year. The rival calendars even agreed that 1600 was a Leap Year, the last time they would concur on that until 2000. In this sense 1600 was an extraordinary year. And Quinquagesima Sunday, 3 February 1600, was its most extraordinary day because, after years of calendrical turmoil, Quinquagesima 1600 finally lived up to its name: for both Protestants and Catholics it was unequivocally the fiftieth day before the anniversary of the Resurrection.[8]

I suggest that in the closing months of 1599 Shakespeare wrote *Twelfth Night* for performance on 3 February 1600.[9] I know that this early date is at variance with received scholarly opinion which dates the play to mid-1601 based on certain topical references. But these topical references do not really date the principal composition of *Twelfth Night*. They date only the copy for the Folio text – which I believe was a scribal copy of a Jacobean acting version. Its topical references – such as teaching fencing to the Sophy and becoming his pensioner (3.4.236 and 2.5.149) – imply a date no earlier than 1601. But it is equally logical to argue that these topicalities merely indicate how late the copy for the Folio may have been revised. Each of the topicalities which suggests a later date for *Twelfth Night* exhibits three qualities suggestive of later emendation: each is in prose; each comes at the end of a line, and often at the end of a speech; and the speech (and scene) make perfect sense without it. Regarding the copy for the Folio text as encumbered with later encrustations also explains such nuances as the reference to the Lady of Strachey marrying the yeoman of the wardrobe – which could not have been added before 1606 if it refers to events tangential to Shakespeare's company.

The text of *Twelfth Night* contains a number of calendrical markers for Quinquagesima 3 February and certain other dates. One of the most conspicuous markers is Feste's jig at the close of the play:

> When that I was and a little tiny boy,
> With hey, ho, the wind and the rain,
> A foolish thing was but a toy,
> For the rain it raineth every day.
> But when I came to man's estate, etc.

> (5.1.379–83).

In 1935 Richmond Noble recognized that Feste's jig was a parody of a famous passage in St Paul's First Epistle to the Corinthians (Noble, 1935,

212). Paul wrote: 'When I was a child, I spake as a child, I understood as a child, I thought as a child: but when I became a man, I put away childish things' etc. (1 Corinthians 13:11). This is the Epistle reading for Quinquagesima, 3 February in 1600 by the Julian calendar.[10] An English audience attending a performance of *Twelfth Night* on 3 February would have heard these verses in church that very morning.

George Steevens was first to detect a connection between Shakespeare's Illyria and St Paul's Corinth. In his notes to the edition of 1785, Steevens catches sight of Corinth when Sebastian greets Feste as a 'foolish Greek' (Johnson and Steevens, 1788, ix.76). Steevens asks, 'Can our author have alluded to St. Paul's epistle to the Romans, ch.i.v[erse]. 23 – "to the Greeks foolishness?"' In fact the citation should be 1 Corinthians 1:23, which the Geneva records as: 'But wee preach Christ crucified: unto the Jewes, even a stumbling blocke, and unto the Grecians, foolishnesse.'

Another of *Twelfth Night*'s calendrical markers appears as Feste is about to begin his first interview with Olivia. He offers a mock prayer:

> Wit, an 't be thy will, put me into good fooling! Those wits that think they have thee do very oft prove fools, and I that am sure I lack thee may pass for a wise man. For what says Quinapalus? 'Better a witty fool than a foolish wit.'
>
> (1.5.29–33)

The muddy Oxford footnote explains that 'Feste invents an authority (Quinapalus). Hotson thinks that the name may be pseudo-Italian, meaning "there on the stick" and referring to the figure of a jester … Terry Hands thinks it may be French.'

Now, thinking about Quinapalus, Quinquagesima and Paul, we might suspect that 'Quinapalus' may be what Lewis Carroll would come to call a 'portmanteau word' – that is 'a factitious word made up of the blended sounds of two distinct words and combining the meanings of both' (*OED* n.4.b). In this light one might read Feste's line as: 'What says Paul of a Quinquagesima? "Better a witty fool than a foolish wit."' I don't think it stretches credibility to suggest that a Christian audience might have caught a glimpse of Paul behind Feste's Quinapalus foolery, particularly if this audience heard the play on Quinquagesima. After all, *Twelfth Night* is Shakespeare's great play about fools, foolishness and foolery. 'Fool' and its variants occur here more frequently than in any other play in the canon. For his part, St Paul is the New Testament authority on things foolish. 'Fool' and its variants appear forty-one times in the New Testament – thirty-one of those in the writings of Paul, and most of these in his 'Call me fool' letters to the Corinthians. As Paul says in the opening chapter of 1 Corinthians, 'hath not God made the wisdome of this worlde foolishnes? ... For the foolishnes of God is wiser than men ... God hathe chosen the foolish things of the worlde to confounde the wise' etc.

But before we get too smug about this new reading of 'Quinapalus', let me suggest that there is another way of parsing this nonce-word which may have precedence. Rather than approaching 'Quinapalus' as a portmanteau, if we read it as an anagram we can see that QUINAPALUS *minus* PAUL *leaves* 'QUINAS. Is it possible that Shakespeare fashioned 'Quinapalus' from the names of Sts Paul and Thomas Aquinas? And, if he did, why would Shakespeare link Aquinas with a statement about witty fools and foolish wits? Well, Thomas Aquinas had more than a little to say about fools – particularly in *Summa Theologiae*. He wrote, 'folly is the way to arrive at wisdom, for it is written' – now Aquinas quotes Paul to the Corinthians 1 3:18, 'If any man among you seem to be wise in this world, let him become a fool that he may be wise.' Following Paul, Aquinas argues that folly is not necessarily the opposite of wisdom; on the contrary, folly for Christ's sake *is* wisdom. After citing Isidore and Gregory, Aquinas concludes with a citation from the apocryphal book of Ecclesiasticus 20:7: 'A babbler and a fool will regard no time.' In Elizabeth's church this chapter was the liturgical reading for the morning lesson on 5 November – a date which will assume a surprising prominence below.

Citing in this context an obscure passage from *Summa Theologiae* may appear hyperbole. But Feste began his encounter with Olivia with one prayer ('Wit, and't be thy will, put me into good fooling!') and concluded it with another: 'Now Mercury endue thee with leasing, for thou speak'st well of fools!' No one has ever been able to say with confidence why a Madonna speaking well of fools causes the Greek god Mercury to pop into Shakespeare's mind and Feste's vocabulary. But a few pages on in his *Summa*, Thomas Aquinas reflects: 'As he who casts a stone into the heap of Mercury, so is he who gives honour to a fool' (Proverbs 26:8).[11] Yet – any reasonable person must ask – why would Shakespeare rake St Paul's Epistles to the Corinthians for the subtext of a love-comedy set in Illyria? For one thing Paul brought the Gospel to Illyria. He says so in Romans 15:19. Paul preached there while shuttling to-and-fro from Corinth. The reading of St Paul's two letters to the Corinthians began each year with the evening lesson on 19 January, the vigil of Sebastian and Fabian. Paul wrote to the Corinthians twice, and visited them three times. He lavished attention upon them because the idolatrous crew was having difficulty adapting to Paul's egalitarian 'brethren and sistern' brand of Christianity. Let me enumerate some of the Corinthians' problems. There were divisions and factionalism between households (1 Corinthians 1:11) – and within households. Stewards were in danger of becoming unfaithful (4:1–2). Servants were seized with ambition (7:20) and bridling at their low station (7:21). There was fornication (5:1) – and raillery and drunkenness (10:21, 11:21). (Shakespeare knew that Corinth was synonymous with licentiousness; in *1 Henry IV* the tavern-boys recognize Hal as 'a Corinthian' (2.4.11).) Unmarried women were refusing to marry (8:28ff.). Corinthian men had become haughty; to use Paul's phrase, 'puffed up' (4:18) – that's Malvolio's condition – as Fabian observes, 'see how imagination blows him' (2.5.40–1). Some Corinthians were speaking in strange and undecipherable tongues (14) – as do Feste, Toby and Andrew. *Caritas* was in decline, and the collecting of alms had lapsed (16). One could go on. But I think it does not stretch credibility to suggest parallels between the problems Paul confronted in Corinth and those Shakespeare contrives for his Illyria. Paul also reprimanded Christians for bringing lawsuits against each other in pagan courts (6:1–6). Does this explain Shakespeare's sudden and otherwise inexplicable allusion to Malvolio's lawsuit against Viola's loyal captain? 'The Captain that did bring me first on shore ... upon some action is now in durance at Malvolio's suit' (5.1.258–60). Most important, the Corinthians had lost faith in the resurrection of the dead (1 Corinthians 15). Is Shakespeare glancing at this when he pointedly resurrects Sebastian on Viola's third day in service to Orsino? Valentine tells us that Viola has been in service three days when she is sent on the mission to Olivia. After their interview Olivia sends Malvolio with a ring in chase of Viola. Between Malvolio leaving the house in 1.5 and his encounter with Viola in 2.2, Shakespeare intrudes the arrival of Sebastian and Antonio in Illyria (2.1). This cutaway scene is such an awkward intrusion that directors often shift it elsewhere. But Shakespeare may have positioned it here to emphasize that Sebastian surfaces on Viola's third day with Orsino. Is not the promise of eternal life at stake in Feste's chastisement of Olivia:

> *Fest.* Good madonna, give me leave to prove you a fool ...

> Dexteriously, good madonna ...
> I must catechize you for it, madonna ...
> Good madonna, why mournest thou?
> *Olivia.* Good fool, for my brother's death.
> *Fest.* I think his soul is in hell, madonna.
> *Olivia.* I know his soul is in heaven, fool.
> *Fest.* The more fool, madonna, to mourn for your brother's
> soul, being in heaven.
>
> (1.5.53–67)

In this encounter with the Madonna Feste also parodies the Gospel of St Mark:

> bid the dishonest man mend himself: if he mend, he is no longer dishonest; if he cannot, let the botcher mend him. Anything that's mended is but patched. Virtue that transgresses is but patched with sin, and sin that amends is but patched with virtue.
>
> (1.5.41–4)

St Mark quoted Jesus as having something to say about patching sin with virtue: 'No man sews a piece of new cloth on an old garment: else the new piece take away from the old, and the rent be made worse' (Mark 2:21).[12] This is the reading for the morning lesson on 2 February. An audience at a performance of *Twelfth Night* on 3 February would have heard or read these words on the previous day. Not incidentally, in Act 5 Shakespeare jokes about the rigid linking of Scripture and dates. Feste declares that since 'a madman's epistles are no gospels, so it skills not much when they are delivered' (5.1.270–1) – a sidewise glance at the order requiring that particular Gospels must be delivered on particular days.[13]

Shakespeare's choice of the name 'Sebastian' invokes a number of neglected overtones – such as the Catholic and Protestant movable feasts for 1600 falling into synch on his feast day. St Sebastian was condemned to death by the Emperor Diocletian (an Illyrian), tied to a tree trunk (reminiscent of Jesus's crucifixion) and peppered with arrows. Like Jesus, Sebastian recovered (temporarily). Shakespeare drops two hints that he has St Sebastian in mind when he names Viola's brother. With his first breath Toby declares Olivia's protracted grief for her brother a 'plague' (1.3.1). Then, in Act 4, Olivia herself characterizes love as 'a plague' (4.1.285). Sebastian was the saint invoked to cure the plague.[14] But why would Viola imitate Sebastian? Remember, she says

> even such and so
> In favour was my brother, and he went
> Still in this fashion, colour, ornament,
> For him I imitate.

(3.4.331–4)

To imitate is to create a false copy – an icon, an idol. In their meeting in 3.1 Feste doesn't take to Viola – and commentators have speculated that he might see through her disguise. Rather, I think, Feste perceives that Viola *is in disguise* – which makes her a kind of idol. If you find this far-fetched, remember that Antonio confesses himself an idolater: 'And to his image, which methought did promise / Most venerable worth, did I devotion.' (3.4.313–14) [15] and he reproves Viola, 'But O, how vile an idol proves this god!' (3.4.357). Paul hated idols and idolaters. The Corinth to which he wrote undoubtedly worshipped Caesar as *Divus Julius*. This, I think, at last explains why Shakespeare named the little 'idol' of *Twelfth Night* 'Cesario'. It may also account for Andrew confessing, 'Methinks sometimes I have no more wit than a Christian . . . I am a great eater of beef, and I believe that does harm to my wit' (1.3.81–4). In 1 Corinthians 8 Paul warned believers against eating meats which had been sacrificed to idols – including, perhaps, statues of *Divus Julius*. [16]

Paradoxically, imitation is an important theme of 1 Corinthians as it is of *Twelfth Night*. In chapter 11 Paul calls upon believers to imitate him as he imitates Christ – which leads him to discourse on the relative status of women and men: 'Christ is the head of every man, and the man is the woman's head . . . For the man is not of the woman, but the woman of the man.' (1 Corinthians 11:3). The Geneva gloss adds, Paul 'proveth . . . the man is the matter whereof woman was first made' (Kkk2, i.e. 74). This allusion to the mode of creation of our first parents goes a long way to resolving another of the nagging cruces of *Twelfth Night*: how can twins of different sexes – fraternal twins like Sebastian and Viola – be identical in appearance? Elizabethans surely knew that fraternal twins were unlikely to resemble each other more than ordinary brothers and sisters. William Shakespeare knew this firsthand; his wife Anne was delivered of fraternal twins christened Hamnet and Susannah on Candlemas 2 February 1585. There was, of course, one set of 'twins' of opposite sexes who were identical, genetically and otherwise. Eve and Adam – that pair in the garden who got into trouble over 'an apple cleft in twain'. Thinking of Sebastian as Adam pulls our first image of him into focus. Viola's Captain says, 'I saw your brother / Most provident in peril, bind himself ... / To a strong mast that lived upon the sea' (1.2.11–14). Sebastian was carried away tied to a mast – a tree trunk – the traditional symbol which links the fall of the first Adam with the death and resurrection of the second. Viola's poetical Captain describes it: 'like Arion on the dolphin's back, / I saw him hold acquaintance with the waves' (1.2.15–16). The scholarly notes refer us to the story of Arion in Ovid's *Fasti*. Ovid associates Arion's plunge and redemption with 3 February. This, I think, is Shakespeare at his playful, mischievous best.

If the link between Sebastian and Christ as the first and second Adams seems too arcane for an Elizabethan audience, consider the usual reading at evening prayer on 3 February: 'For as in Adam all die, even so in Christ shall all be made alive ... The first man Adam was made a living soul; the last Adam was made a quickening spirit ... The first man is of the earth, earthly: the second man is the Lord from heaven' etc. (1 Corinthians 15: 22, 45, 47).[17] It might be useful here to take a closer look at Olivia's father's fool. His name, FESTE, may be an anagram. FESTE = F[*oole*]. ETÉS. This incorporates 'F.' in the sense in which Elizabethans used 'M.' for 'Master', 'Dr.' for 'Doctor' and 'Fr.' for 'Frater'. *Etés* is French for 'summers'. Queen Elizabeth's father's fool was named Will Summers.[18] Shakespeare may be glancing at this when Feste says, 'let summer beare it out' (1.5.20). The Lord Chamberlain's Men are known to have performed at court on 6 January and 3 February 1600 – that is, on both Twelfth Night and Quinquagesima. Though the identity of the plays is lost, Shakespeare's *Twelfth Night* might have been played on either date (or both). If Robert Armin joined the company at the New Year, he could have triumphed as Feste at these performances. This might explain why Armin wrote so fondly of Summers in his 'Nest of Ninnies' (1608).

In any case, Feste is a fool, and proud of it. So was Paul. To hear Sebastian tell it, Feste is Greek. St Paul spoke Greek. Feste is a beggar. So was Paul – and both were good at it. In 4.1 Sebastian encounters Feste, and this exchange ensues:

Sebastian. I prithee, foolish Greek, depart from me. There's money
       for thee. If you tarry longer I shall give worse payment.
Feste.   By my troth, thou hast an open hand.[19] These wise men that

> give fools money get themselves a good report, after
> fourteen years' purchase.
>
> (4.1.16–21)

No one has ever explained Feste's allusion to 'fourteen years'. But in Galatians 2 Paul recalls delivering to the saints the money he begged for them: 'Then fourteen years after I went up again to Jerusalem' (Galatians 2:1).[20] Here and in other places Shakespeare has infused Feste's diction with borrowings from St Paul's other letters. For example, in the prison scene between Malvolio and Feste-as-Sir-Topaz, the pair debate:

> *Malvolio.* I am not mad, Sir Topaz. I say to you the house is dark.
> *Sir Topaz.* Madman, thou errest. I say there is no darkness but
>   ignorance, in which thou art more puzzled than the
>   Egyptians in their fog.
>
> (4.2.41–4)

This is a parody of Paul writing to the puffed-up Ephesians who have 'their cogitation darkened ... through the ignorance that is in them, because of the hardnes of their heart' (Ephesians 4:18). It was, of course, the Pharaoh of Exodus who suffered from hardness of the heart. Sir Topaz's metaphor of 'Egyptians in their fog' is thought to be an allusion to the 'blacke darkenesse' which hung over Egypt three days in Exodus 10:21–3 (Donno, 1985, 127n). This is not safe. There is another 'fog' which vexed the Egyptians: 'And the angel of God, which went before the camp of Israel, removed and went behind them; and the pillar of the cloud went from before their face, and stood behind them: And it came between the camp of the Egyptians and the camp of Israel; and it was a cloud and darkness to them' (Exodus 14:19–20). This passage was the Old Testament reading at the evening lesson on 3 February.

If I am correct in postulating that a number of calendrical markers link the climactic action of *Twelfth Night* to 3 February, and if we believe Orsino and Antonio when they say that three months and a day have elapsed since the shipwreck, then Viola must have come ashore on 2 November. Looking back at her arrival, we hear Viola's Captain reminisce, 'For but a month ago I went from hence' (1.2.28). If this speech is delivered on 2 November, the Captain must have begun his voyage on 2 October. This is appropriate: 2 October is the feast of the Guardian Angels. Both Viola and Sebastian each have their 'guardian angel'.

What about 2 November 1599? It was a Friday – considered unlucky, being the weekday upon which Christ died. November was the Eliza-bethans' 'month of the dead' – the topaz is the birthstone for November – and 2 November was the defunct Catholic feast of All Souls. In a real sense this sorts well with a 'Protestant' Viola's reluctance to mourn. Olivia's protracted, excessive mourning for her brother may be one of several clues to her 'Catholicism'. Valentine calls her a cloistress, and Feste addresses her as 'Madonna'. She seems to have a nunnish dis-position – with her cell, her veil, her black frock, her celibacy, her priest and chantry (4.3.22–4). Like a nun, Olivia marries a man raised on a third day. And Olivia insists she 'cannot' love Orsino. Not that she 'does not' or 'will not'. Three times she says she 'cannot'. Are Orsino and Viola, perhaps, the 'Protestant' side of the equation, and Sebastian and Olivia the 'Catholic' branch?

If Viola comes ashore on 2 November and enters Orsino's service on the following day, her first visit to Olivia would fall on 5 November. As that visit ends, Olivia dispatches Malvolio in pursuit of Viola with a ring, saying, 'If that youth will come this way tomorrow'. Sure enough, on the morrow Viola returns and greets Olivia most memorably: 'Most excellent accomplished lady, the heavens rain odours on you!' (3.1.73). Andrew, overhearing, snorts: 'That youth's a rare courtier – "rain odours" – well.' [21] What amounts to a treble repetition of 'odours' sug-gests that Shakespeare does not want us to overlook Viola's peculiar salutation. This crux is so obscure that no commentator has attempted it. However, if the date is 6 November, parsing the crux is not difficult: 'Leonardus means the perfume of the people, from *leos*, people, and *nardus*, which is a sweet-smelling herb; and Leonard drew people to himself by the sweet odor of his good renown.' This is from the life of St Leonard in *The Golden Legend*. Sweet-smelling Leonard's feast day was 6 November.[22]

Twelfth Night is strewn with markers which connect its text with the Julian calendar for 1600. Let me enumerate a few of the more beguiling. When Feste tells Maria that 'he that is well hanged ... needs to fear no colours', she replies: 'A good lenten answer.' 3 February – Quinqua-gesima – was Shrove Sunday, the precursor of Lent. In the same scene Olivia tells Viola, ''Tis not that time of moon with me to make one in so skipping a dialogue' (1.5.192–3). That is, it is not Full Moon, the time of lunacy. An audience attending *Twelfth Night* on the evening of 3 February 1600 might well have noticed that that night was moonless.

When Andrew enters with his crazy epistle challenging Viola, Fabian cracks, 'More matter for a May morning' (3.4.140). In 1600, 1 May was Ascension Day – and the Epistle was Mark 16:14–20. These verses were particularly well known and well loved by Reformation Christians because they contain St Mark's (apparent) affirmation of Paul's colossal promise: 'He that believeth and is baptized shall be saved' (Mark 16:16). These verses also include Jesus's commission to his Apostles to cast out devils, speak with new tongues and heal the sick – actions which are about to take place in Shakespeare's Illyria. Incidentally, Jesus also assured his Apostles (including Andrew) that no harm would come to them while this was a-doing (Mark 16:17–18).

It is also possible to work out the meaning of certain gibberish in *Twelfth Night* by reference to the liturgical calendar. While at Ephesus, Paul had received word that the Corinthians had begun speaking in tongues. The Apostle was appalled: 'God,' he maintained, 'is not the author of confusion.' In the reading for the Vigil of Quinquagesima Paul writes:

> hee that speaketh a strange tongue, speaketh not unto men ... For if I pray in a strange tongue ... mine understanding is without fruit ... I had rather in the Church to speak five words with mine understanding ... than ten thousand words in a strange tongue, etc.
>
> (1 Corinthians 14, etc.)

In Shakespeare's time this passage had colossal importance, too. It was the Protestants' *apologia* for translating the Bible into the vernacular, and for conducting sacred services in the language of the people. The Catholic Rheims New Testament of 1582 rises to a spirited defence of the Latin Mass in its lengthy notes to 1 Corinthians 14.

Like the Corinth of Paul's letters, Shakespeare's Illyria is vexed with indecipherable 'tongues'. For example, in 2.3 Andrew says to Feste, 'In sooth, thou wast in very gracious fooling last night, when thou spok'st of Pigrogromitus, of the Vapians passing the equinoctial of Queubus. 'Twas very good, i'faith.' Time out of mind, this passage has baffled audiences and scholars alike. But Andrew's phrases 'gracious fooling' and 'in faith' point to the subtext. 'Pigrogromitus' could be a corruption of Regiomontanus, for which it is very nearly an anagram. This was the assumed name of the distinguished mathematician Johann Müller.[23] In 1475 Pope Sixtus IV brought Müller to Rome to reform the Julian calendar. But Müller died, and it fell to Pontifex Gregory to complete the work. If a scribe or compositor misread the letter m where Shakespeare had written an n,[24] 'Pigrogronitus' is an exact anagram of 'Pont. Grigorius'. Andrew's 'the Vapians' may be a corruption of the 'the Vatican' – or, I think, 'the Pavians', a nod to the mathematicians at the University at Pavia – sometimes called 'the Oxford of Italy' – who helped to develop Gregory's newfangled calendar. In Andrew's phrase 'passing the equinoctial of Queubus' I read: *ratifying the equinoctial rule of Eusebius*. As I noted earlier, Gregory did not re-establish the heathen calendar of pagan Julius Caesar – which was thirteen days in error. Gregory's ten-day correction synchronized the new calendar with the celestial clock at the time of the Council of Nicaea in AD 325. By then Caesar's calendar had already slipped three days. It was the Nicaean Council which laid down the (foolish) rule that the vernal equinoctial would always be 21 March. Eusebius of Caesarea (*c.* 260–340) was that council's most famous attendee. In his *Ecclesiastical History* he writes that 'it is necessary for the feast of the passover, that not only the sun should pass through the equinoctial segment, but the moon also. For there are two equinoctial segments, the vernal and the autumnal' etc. (Electronic Bible Society, ECF24.TXT,319–20). If our reading of Andrew's gibberish is sound, then Feste has been explaining the Gregorian calendar reform to Andrew and Toby. In fact, I believe that Feste has *converted* Toby to the Gregorian formulation. In Act 5, Sir Toby abruptly deplores drinking, makes an honest woman of Maria and tells Andrew truly what he thinks of him. When the wounded Toby calls for a surgeon, Feste replies: 'O he's drunk, sir Toby, an hour agone; his eyes were set at eight i' the morning.' Hearing this, Toby growls: 'Then he's a rogue, and a passy measures panyn; I hate a drunken rogue' (5.1.185–6). The doctor is not merely drunk; he is drunk at an untimely hour. I think that Toby's 'passy measures' refers to that system of measures of time which was *passé*: the Julian calendar. Scholars have suggested that the curious word spelled *panyn* is a compositor's error for 'pavan', the stately dance. But I think the scribe or compositor inserted an n where Shakespeare had written an m. The word should be *panym*, that is *panim*, or *heathen* – which may say something about the playwright's view of those who stubbornly follow Caesar's calendar.[25]

The Malvolio subplot fits into – and supports – the play's calendrical architecture. The evening of 3 February Julian was, by the Gregorian Catholic reckoning, 13 February, the eve of St Valentine. I suggest that this concurrence of dates was the cue for Maria's notorious letter. Recusants watching a performance of *Twelfth Night* on the eve of St Valentine would certainly grasp why such a letter might be written and intentionally dropped where an unsuspecting beloved might find it. The victim of the ruse is Paul's archetypal wise man: arrogant, haughty, puffed up. Malvolio already believes that his appearance and virtue suit him for greatness above his birth. This makes him susceptible to suggestion. He over-closely reads and erroneously interprets a letter. In fact Malvolio mis-interprets five letters: one is the epistle of Maria. The other four are M, O, A and I.[26] Malvolio's arrogance leads him to conclude that he is Olivia's (and Jove's) elect. In a play strewn with allusions to the letters of St Paul, a character who misreads five letters and interprets them as proof of his election implies, I think, a searing judgement of sects who believe that their brand of Christianity is the one true religion.

I have suggested that Shakespeare purpose-wrote *Twelfth Night* for a performance on 3 February 1600 by way of celebrating the reunion of the two rival calendars. To explain why Shakespeare chose 2 November as the date of the shipwreck which separated his twins, I have to explain how the two calendars parted ways on that date. Now, Gregory's calendar was issued on 24 February 1582 – Julius Caesar's old bissextile day, perhaps a nod from one *pontifex maximus* to another – so that occasion will not do. To identify the date on which the two branches of faith parted ways, I think we have to look back to the beginning of the Reformation.

Now, *we* know that Martin Luther nailed his Ninety-Five Theses to the doors of the Castle Church at Wittenberg on 31 October 1517. But, as I will demonstrate in the following chapter, because of the mistranslation of one word in an obscure book, Elizabethans erroneously believed that Luther's Reformation began on 2 November. That is how 2 November became for the Elizabethans the day on which the body of Christ – Christianity – parted in twain.

As pious English Christians perused their new almanacs for 1600, I suggest that many felt a profound sense of deliverance. In the coming year they would celebrate Easter – and its dependent moveable feasts – on those days which God intended when he sent his son to preach his calendar. The schism which Luther began on 2 November 1517 which had led in 1582 to a body of Christ divided by two calendars (and their English Julian the worser of them) would be healed – temporarily – on

3 February 1600 when the rival calendars were reunited, like Shakespeare's castaway twins from the sea.

Notes

1 In 1831.
2 This misnomer may explain the play's subtitle: *What You Will*.
3 Or been tweaked-up for performance on an occasion.
4 Brabant, Luxembourg, Belgium etc.
5 Rotterdam, Amsterdam etc.
6 Then cooler heads prevailed, and 1 January became the date of the switchover. In Denmark 1 January had been New Year's Day since 1559 – and the Gregorian reform was not adopted until March 1700.
7 This argument cannot be made for 1601 because Septuagesima falls on 8 February, and Quinquagesima on 22 February.
8 Neither of the prior Sundays lives up to its name. Septuagesima is the sixty-fourth day before Easter, Sexagesima the fifty-seventh.
9 Our predecessors recognized some affinity between this play and certain dates. We know that Shakespeare's company performed *Twelfth Night* at the Middle Temple on Candlemas, 2 February 1602 (Donno, 1985, 1), and that it was also played at court on 2 February 1623 (Herbert's Diary). Pepys, who deplored the play, saw it three times: on 11 September 1661, 6 January 1663 and 20 January 1669. These three dates are intriguing: 11 September was the autumnal equinox; 6 January 1663 was Twelfth Night; 20 January is the feast of Sebastian and Fabian.
10 The Old Testament lessons were Genesis 9, the story of God's covenant (with Noah and his sons), and Genesis 12: Sarai pretending she was Abraham's sister.
11 Mercury appears in none of the Englished bibles – only in the Vulgate: '*sicut qui mittit lapidem in acervum Mercurii ita qui tribuit insipienti honorem quomodo si spina nascatur in manu temulenti sic parabola in ore stultorum*' (Proverbs 26:8–9).
12 Also in the Gospel of Matthew 9:16.
13 'Look then to be well edified', Feste declares (5.1.213). 'Edification' is one of Paul's favourite buzz-words. It signifies the 'building up' of faith, and appears repeatedly throughout his letters. Timeliness is as important to Viola as it is to Feste. At 1.2.85 she is determined not to be delivered untimely. Later, she admires Feste's care of the time: 3.1.62.
14 The Gospel reading for the feast of Sebastian and Fabian was Luke 6:17–23 – in which Christ heals those possessed with evil spirits.
15 As he is arrested, he calls out in desperation to Viola: 'Will you deny me now?' (3.4.298). In fact, she does deny him – thrice.
16 This may have crossed Shakespeare's mind while he was writing *Julius*

Caesar. 'Now in the names of all the Gods at once, / Upon what meate doth this our *Caesar* feede, / That he is growne so great?' (247–9).

17 This passage also contains 'eat and drink for tomorrow we die'.

18 Or 'Sommers' (d. 1560). Sommers was a servant of Richard Fermor of Northamptonshire. He was brought by his master to the court at Greenwich 'on a holy day' about 1525. The king is reported to have installed him at once in the royal household as the court fool. 'According to tradition, Sommers was soon on very familiar terms with the king. He puzzled him with foolish riddles, and amused him by playing practical jokes on Cardinal Wolsey, who "could never abide him." Sommers seems to have mingled with his clownish witticisms some shrewd comments on current abuses.' Armin wrote about Sommers in 'Nest of Ninnies' (1608). On the evidence of eye-witnesses, Armin describes Sommers as lean and hollow-eyed, with stooping shoulders. 'In the "Pleasant Comedie called Summers last Will and Testament" by Thomas Nash, written in 1593 and published in 1600 [because of the success of *Twelfth Night?*], Sommers figures as a loquacious and shrewd-witted Chorus.' *DNB on CD-ROM.*

19 Sebastian's hand can both give and strike.

20 While evangelizing the Gentiles, Paul collected money for the 'saints'. He delivered it in AD 51.

21 Viola continues, 'My matter hath no voice, lady, but to your own most pregnant and vouchsafed ear.' Sir Andrew: '"Odours," "pregnant," and "vouchsafed": I'll get 'em all three ready.'

22 He was often invoked by pregnant women in distress.

23 Born in Königsberg 6 June 1436, best-known for his *Ephemerides* (1474).

24 The compositor reversed this error when he set 'panyn' for 'panym'.

25 Toby has a lot in common with Falstaff. Both were probably played by the same actor. Both start with no conception of time, and then find time. When Toby says, 'call me cut', I hear an echo of Fastaff: 'Then I'm an Ebrew Jew.' Toby's disdain for the doctor who is untimely drunk – a failing which Toby shared, night and morning through half the play – may indicate that Toby has been converted. This underscores an important parallel between Toby and Falstaff. Falstaff's first line – and the subject of his first verbal joust with Hal – is time: 'Now, Hal, what time of day is it, lad? *Prince Harry.* Thou art so fat-witted with drinking of old sack, and unbuttoning thee after supper, and sleeping upon benches after noon, that thou hast forgotten to demand that truly which thou wouldst truly know. What a devil hast thou to do with the time of the day?' (1.2.1–6). By the end of his life Falstaff has found time (and he has been saved). He dies when a man should – 'A parted between twelve and one, ev'n at the turning of the tide' (2.3.12–13) – and makes his exit babbling of green pastures. Did the actor who played Falstaff play Sir Toby? Probably.

26 This might explain Viola's two little prayers to 'time'. There has been a lively scholarly debate about whether M.O.A.I. constitutes an anagram of

the passage from the Book of Revelation of St John, 'I am the Alpha and Omega.' The Geneva text reads, 'I am the Alpha and Omega, the beginning and the ending, saith the Lord, Which is, and Which was, and Which is to come.' That is to say, 'God is time.'

18

Real time in *Hamlet*

In early February 1998 Professor Alan H. Nelson of the University of California at Berkeley called my attention to the *Gesta Grayorum*, and particularly to those passages concerning the 'trial' of the Prince of Purpoole, which seems to have taken place on 30 December 1594. This mock 'Commission of *Oyer* and *Terminer*' met to consider the confusion on '*Innocents-Day* at Night [28 December 1594]; at which time there was a great Presence of Lords, Ladies, and worshipful Personages, that did expect some notable Performance at that time' (Foakes, 1962, 116–17). Instead of a notable performance the audience was offered 'Dancing and Revelling with Gentlewomen; and after such Sports, a Comedy of Errors (like to *Plautus* his *Menechmus*) was played by the Players'. Two nights later the Gray's men conferred on the Prince of Purpoole 'Judgments thick and threefold'. In the recitation of his misdemeanours, they noted that the pretended prince had

> caused the Stage to be built, and Scaffolds to be reared to the top of the House, to increase Expectation ... Also that he caused Throngs and Tumults, Crowds and Outrages, to disturb our whole Proceedings. And Lastly, that he had foisted a Company of base and common Fellows, to make up our Disorders with a Play of Errors and Confusions, etc.

In a recent publication Professor Nelson had expressed the view that the elaborate preparations for the performance of a play thought to have been Shakespeare's would support the inference that *The Comedy of Errors* was purpose-written for its performance at Gray's Inn (Nelson, 1997, 66). He asked me if I could detect textual evidence to support this view. In fact, *Errors* contains both temporal and textual markers which connect the play with a date in late December and, possibly, the feast of the Holy Innocents on 28 December. The temporal marker appears in the opening scene of the play. We learn that Egeon is doomed

217

to die at sunset: 'Yet this my comfort: when your words are done, / My woes end likewise with the evening sun' (1.1.26–7). In Act 5, we learn that the sun will set that day in Ephesus *c.* 5 p.m. As the Duke and Egeon and the executioners approach, the Second Merchant says:

> By this, I think, the dial point's at five.
> Anon, I'm sure, the Duke himself in person
> Comes this way to the melancholy vale,
> The place of death and sorry execution,
> Behind the ditches of the abbey here.
>
> (5.1.119–23)

A sunset *c.* 5 p.m. in London would have been observed on 19 October 1594. But sunset at Ephesus was 4.59 p.m. on 28 December 1594.[1] The location of Ephesus was certainly known to Elizabethans, and a mathematician could easily have calculated the time of sunset on that date. Furthermore, Hassel has identified a string of calendrical markers in the text of *Comedy of Errors* which are drawn from the liturgical readings for Innocents' Day:

> A glance at the liturgical tradition of Innocents' Day makes it even less likely that mere nostalgia or coincidence explains the dual performance of the play on that religious festival [in 1594 and 1604]. The repetition of *nativitie* in the final lines of the play seems to suggest a general awareness of the Christmas season. More specifically, as soon as we read the 'proper' Lesson prescribed for Holy Innocents' Day in the *Book of Common Prayer*, we are struck by the relationship to the framing story of Egeon and Emilia, Shakespeare's unique addition to his sources. Jer 31:1–17, like the framework of *The Comedy of Errors*, is about the dispersal and reunion of families. In fact, from such other prescribed passages as Bar 4:21–30, Mt 2:13–18, Rv 14:1–5, and Is 60, we realize that this theme was a central motif of the liturgical festival . . . Jeremiah 31 is insistently parallel to the first and final scenes of *Errors*.[2]

While work remains to be done on *The Comedy of Errors*, the presence of both temporal and textual markers in this early play suggests that Shakespeare was working with these devices at an early stage in his career. By 1601 Shakespeare had became more skilful (and subtle) in creating and placing calendrical markers. He had also grown more confident of his audience's ability to identify, remember and synthesize fragmentary information. This is apparent as the first scene of *Hamlet* unfolds. Shakespeare provides a series of minute markers to the date upon which the action takes place. Barnardo tells us ''Tis now struck twelve.' It is after midnight, and deeply dark. Though we can see Barnardo and Francisco, they cannot see each other. They identify each other by sound of voice.

> Bar. Who's there?
> Fra. Nay, answer me. Stand and unfold yourself.
> Bar. Long live the King!
> Fra. Barnardo?
> Bar. He.
>
>   (1.1.1–5) [3]

When Horatio and Marcellus enter, Francisco again identifies the arrivals not by sight but by voice:

> Fra. I think I hear them. Stand ho! Who is there?
> Hor. Friends to this ground.
> Mar. And liegemen to the Dane.
>
>   (1.1.13–15)

As Francisco makes his exit, Horatio and Marcellus still cannot see Barnardo. Marcellus must ask 'who hath relieved you?' and Francisco must explain 'Barnardo hath my place' (1.1.18–19). Marcellus calls, 'Holla, Barnardo!' (1.1.20). Even now Barnardo cannot see the arrivals and replies, 'Say, what, is Horatio there?' (1.1.21). Such emphasis on overwhelming darkness suggests a moonless night. It is also cold. Francisco has told us ''Tis bitter cold' (1.1.8). When Hamlet comes to the parapet in 1.4, he will tell us 'The air bites shrewdly, it is very cold' (1.4.1). Successive frosty nights suggest a wintry season, perhaps the months September to March. But we can be more precise about the season from clues Shakespeare provides. Marcellus reflects:

> Some say that ever 'gainst that season comes
> Wherein our saviour's birth is celebrated
> The bird of dawning singeth all night long;
> And then, they say, no spirit can walk abroad,
> The nights are wholesome; then no planets strike,
> No fairy takes, nor witch hath power to charm,
> So hallowed and so gracious is the time.
>
>   (1.1.163–9)

A ghost cannot be encountered during the season of Advent. So the dates on which Old Hamlet's ghost walks must fall during the cold days prior to 27 November, or those after Christmas (Leduc and Baudot, n.d., 47).[4] Barnardo also refers to a celestial object:

> Last night of all,
> When yon same star that's westward from the pole
> Had made his course t' illume that part of heaven
> Where now it burns, Marcellus and myself,
> The bell then beating one –

(1.1.38–42)

The very offhandedness of Barnardo's reference – 'yon same star that's westward from the pole' – suggests that the star is conspicuous enough to be identified by Horatio and, perhaps, by members of the audience who were versed in astronomy or astrology.[5] There are a variety of reasons to conclude that the star to which Barnardo refers is Deneb, a second-magnitude star in the constellation Cygnus the Swan. Modern readers may be unfamiliar with this constellation. But English Christians knew it as the 'Northern Cross' from the time of the Venerable Bede, and held it in awe. Because the Cross stands erect over Europe at 9 p.m. on the night before Christmas, the constellation was regarded as a divine portent of the crucifixion. In the night sky above London, the Northern Cross stands erect, and Deneb lies precisely 'westward from the pole', about 1 a.m. during the period 30 October to 10 November (Figure 20). No one who views the sky from the northern hemisphere in this season can fail to be struck by the prominence of this constellation.

The Northern Cross signifies the death and resurrection of Christ. But it also has a more ancient association with a myth of crossing and recrossing the bourne which separates the living and dead. Under its pagan designation, Cygnus, the constellation was dedicated to Orpheus – perhaps because of its close proximity to Lyra, the harp or *cythera*. The lyre was the instrument Orpheus used to enchant the creatures of the underworld in his quest for Euridice.[6] A third, nearby and related constellation is Draco, the Great Northern Serpent. Orpheus's beloved Euridice died from the poisonous bite of a snake, as did Old Hamlet: 'The serpent that did sting thy father's life / Now wears his crown' (1.5.38–9). Together the three constellations present an eternal *tableau vivant* of the archetypal myth of contact between the living and one who died from a serpent's sting.

As the Swan, Cygnus also has a mythological connection with a tale of adulterous love. Zeus, king of the gods, desired Leda, wife of

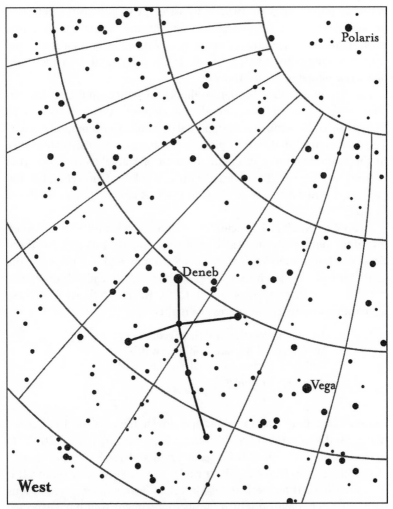

Figure 20. The western sky above London at 1 a.m. on the night of 2 November 1601. 'Distant Suns' software © Virtual Reality Laboratories (1991–2).

Tyndareus. In order to couple with her, Zeus transformed himself into a swan. One issue of this union was Helen, wife of Menelaus, who was abducted by Paris and became his adulterate concubine. The plot of *Hamlet* arises from the adultery of Gertrude with Claudius (1.5.42). The other issue of Zeus and Leda were the twins Castor and Pollux. *Hamlet* is thickly populated with 'twins'.[7] In astrology Cygnus is the patron of persons born with an 'adaptable, intellectual, contemplative, and dreamy nature. It generates disorderly and unstable relationships' and 'causes talents to mature late' (Sesti, 1991, 324), qualities which read like a horoscope of Prince Hamlet.

The hypothesis that Barnardo alludes to Deneb, and that the encounters between sentinels and ghost take place during the period 30 October to 10 November, are supported by a definitive temporal marker. This is the name Shakespeare gives to Horatio's companion: Marcellus. In the Catholic church calendar the feast of Marcellus the Centurion falls on 30 October. This Marcellus was a soldier who refused to engage in violence after his conversion to Christianity. He was martyred in AD 298.[8]

To Shakespeare's calendrical clues – 1 a.m., a cold and perhaps moonless night, not in Advent, Deneb westward from the pole, the Northern Cross erect, a namesake of Marcellus – we may add one more. As the action unfolds, we learn that the ghost has already walked twice: 'this dreaded sight twice seen of us' (1.1.28). Horatio tells us that these appearances occurred on successive nights:

> Two nights together had these gentlemen,
> Marcellus and Barnardo, on their watch
> In the dead waste and middle of the night
> Been thus encounter'd.
>
> (1.2.196–9)

Horatio also tells us that the ghost appeared again on a third successive night: 'And I with them the third night kept the watch' (1.2.208). On the fourth night the ghost will appear again and discourse with Hamlet (1.4.38ff.). So Old Hamlet's Ghost walks on four successive nights. It is no coincidence that the feast of Marcellus begins a sequence of four successive holy days on which Elizabethans might well have expected unquiet souls to prowl the earth (Table 9).[9]

Table 9

Date	Holy day
30 October	Marcellus the Centurion (feast)
31 October	All Hallows' Eve
1 November	All Saints' Day
2 November	All Souls' Day

Real time in *Hamlet*

These dates fall within the 30 October to 10 November window, and are compatible with Deneb westward from the Pole. Each of the holy days which follow the Feast of Marcellus is associated with the bond between the living and the dead. The vigil of All Hallows' Eve derived from the Celtic festival of Sambain; on that night spirits of the dead were thought to revisit their former earthly homes. 1 November was All Saints' Day. This observance dates from the seventh century and celebrates all dead saints known and unknown.[10] The All Souls' Day observances included prayers for the souls of baptized Christians who were believed to be in purgatory because they died without benefit of Extreme Unction.[11] Old Hamlet's Ghost appears to refer to purgatory:

> I am thy father's spirit,
> Doom'd for a certain term to walk the night,
> And for the day confin'd to fast in fires,
> Till the foul crimes done in my days of nature
> Are burnt and purg'd away.
>
> (1.5.9–13)

He declares that the cause of his punishment is that he died unshriven:

> Cut off even in the blossoms of my sin,
> Unhousel'd, disappointed, unanel'd,
> No reck'ning made, but sent to my account
> With all my imperfections on my head.
>
> (1.5.75–9)

The 'inky cloak' which Hamlet wears in 1.2 is appropriate All Souls' Day attire for a son mourning a father who died without benefit of Extreme Unction.

Dating the principal composition of Hamlet

The identification of the four ghost-walking nights of 30 October to 2 November holds intriguing implications for dating the principal composition of *Hamlet*. Scholars differ over whether the play should be referred to 1600 or 1601. All editors have noted the entry in the Stationers' Register of 26 July 1602 which refers to the play as having been 'latelie acted' by the Lord Chamberlain's Men. There are passages commonly cited which appear to date the play's composition to 1601.[12] On the other hand, Gabriel Harvey's praise of *Hamlet* in his copy of

Speght's Chaucer (1598) appears in association with a reference to the Earl of Essex being alive (he was executed in February 1601). But calendrical indicators may support the arguments for 1601 as the year of principal composition (or substantial revision) of the text.

The four-day sequence of holy days 30 October to 2 November did not unfold sequentially in every year. When All Souls' Day falls on a Sunday, the sequence is suspended. Thus, in 1600, the alternative year suggested for the principal composition of *Hamlet*, 2 November was a Sunday, and the observance of All Souls' Day was postponed to Monday 3 November. That is, the church calendar in 1600 ran as in Table 10.

Table 10

Weekday	Date	Holy day
Thursday	30 October	Marcellus
Friday	31 October	All Hallows' Eve
Saturday	1 November	All Saints' Day
Sunday	2 November	
Monday	3 November	All Souls' Day

In 1601 the four feast days succeeded one another in uninterrupted sequence as in Table 11.

Table 11

Weekday	Holy day
Friday	Marcellus
Saturday	All Hallows' Eve
Sunday	All Saints' Day
Monday	All Souls' Day

This perhaps lends weight to the argument that the principal composition of *Hamlet* took place in 1601, and that Shakespeare anticipated that the play's first performance would take place in that year.[13]

Hamlet *and the Purgatory debate*

Relating *Hamlet* to this sequence of holy days tends to call attention to the play's engagement with theological issues. The controversy surrounding the existence of Purgatory was certainly not new in 1601. It had been energetically argued since at least the time of Erasmus. Dismissing Purgatory was a principal endeavour of Martin Luther and the

Reformers. In *Hamlet* Shakespeare takes pains to stress the Danish setting of the play (Sjögren, 1968). Denmark had been a Lutheran country
since the accession of Christian III after the civil war of 1534–6.[14]
Shakespeare's Hamlet and Horatio were fellow-students in Wittenberg.[15] There are four references to Wittenberg in *Hamlet*, which are
unique in the Shakespeare canon. Luther nailed his Ninety-Five Theses,
which principally concern indulgences and Purgatory, to the door of
the Castle Church in Wittenberg on All Hallows' Eve, 31 October 1517.
The years 1517 and 1601 share a common calendar. In both 1517
and 1601 the four sombre feasts fell on these same four weekdays
(Table 12).

Table 12

Year	Weekday	Date	Holy day
1517, 1601	Friday	30 October	Marcellus
	Saturday	31 October	All Hallows' Eve
	Sunday	1 November	All Saints' Day
	Monday	2 November	All Souls' Day

This concordance of weekdays and holy days is *extremely* rare. Any
individual year may follow one of seventy different patterns of weekdays
and solar and lunar holy days. A concordance with 1517 occurred only
once in Shakespeare's working lifetime: in 1601. The suggestion that
Shakespeare took note of the recurrence of this 'pattern year' is not as
far-fetched as it may appear. Scholars have long wondered that Shakespeare's *King John* contains no mention of Magna Charta. That famous
document was signed in 1215, a year with Dominical Letter D and
Easter falling on 19 April. This pattern calendar of the Magna Charta
year 1215 recurred only once during Shakespeare's working lifetime –
in 1590, the year the playwright is believed to have written *King John*.
Again this may be coincidence. But the chance of coincidence is one in
seventy. Did Shakespeare turn (or return) to the writing of *Hamlet* in
1601 because its calendar of holy days was the same as 1517? Before
addressing this question, we should assess whether Shakespeare could
have known that 1517 and 1601 shared a common calendar. While
this may seem arcane to us, the information was readily accessible to
Elizabethans.

Neither 1517 nor 1601 is divisible by 4. Therefore, neither was a
leap year. Both were common years of 365 days. The church calendar

for any year can be described by cataloguing the dates and weekdays of the solar and lunar holy days. The solar holy days recur on the same dates each year, e.g. Christmas on 25 December. Therefore, the week-days on which the solar holy days fall in any common year may be determined by finding the 'Dominical Letter', the date of the first Sunday in January. Tables of Dominical Letters were provided by the popular almanacs. The Dominical letter for 1517 and 1601 is D. That is, the first Sunday in both years fell on 4 January, and the solar-based holy days on the same weekday in both years.

To determine the calendar of lunar holy days for a year, it is necessary to identify the date of Easter Sunday from which other lunar holy days are reckoned. To facilitate the dating of Easter, in AD 525 the monk Dionysius Exiguus published a table of 'golden' numbers which identify the moon's position in its nineteen-year cycle. To find a year's golden number, add 1 to the year and divide by 19. The remainder is the golden number. For 1517 and 1601 the computations are:

$$1517 + 1 = 1518 \div 19 = 79 \text{ and } 17 \qquad \text{Golden number} = 17$$

$$1601 + 1 = 1602 \div 19 = 84 \text{ and } 6 \qquad \text{Golden number} = 6$$

With Dominical Letter 'D' and golden numbers 17 and 6 in hand, an Elizabethan would next consult the Easter tables in the popular al-manacs. Here one would find that Easter Day fell on Sunday 12 April in both 1517 and 1601. Consequently, the calendars for 1517 and 1601 were identical. Based on Shakespeare's four allusions to Witten-berg (1.2.113, 119, 164, 168), scholars since Edmond Malone have suspected an explicit connection between Hamlet and Luther. But even if Shakespeare knew that 1517 and 1601 had identical calendars, is there any textual evidence that Shakespeare had Martin Luther in mind when he drew attention to the four ghostly days 30 October to 2 November 1601?

Luther at Elsinore

Martin Luther nailed up his Ninety-Five Theses on 31 October 1517, the day *before* All Saints' Day. Our analysis of the four ghost-walking days suggests that Hamlet encounters his father's ghost on 2 November, the day *after* All Saints' Day. To reconcile this apparent anomaly, we need to know what information Shakespeare might have had about the life of Martin Luther. In fact there were several *vitae* of Luther in print in Shakespeare's England. The earliest Luther *vita* in English appears in *Sleidanes Commentaries* by Johannes Phillipson, published in London in 1560 (STC 19848). Phillipson gives no date for the posting on the Castle Church, but records that Luther sent 'certen questions which he had lately set up at Wittenberg' to the Archbishop of Mainz on 1 November (B.iv). Another life of Luther appeared in Foxe's *Acts and Monuments* (1563). Intriguingly, Foxe gets the date of Luther's posting wrong. He writes that Luther

> published certaine propostions concerninge indulgences, which are in the fyrst Tome of his worckes, and set them openly on the temple that joyneth to the castel of Wittenberg, the morrow *after* the feast of al sainctes, the yere 1517
>
> (Foxe, 1563, 403, emphasis mine)

Foxe erroneously states that Luther nailed up his Theses on 2 November, the day *after* All Saints' Day. In his preamble to his life of Luther, Foxe acknowledges his source:

> The laborious travayles, and the whole processe, and the constant pre-achinges of this worthy man Luther, because they are sufficiently and at large in the history of Johannes Sleidane, and shall not neade to stande thereupon, but onely to runne over some briefe touchying, of his life and acttes, as they are briefly collected by Philippe Melanthon.
>
> (Foxe, 1563, 402)

Philip Melancthon (1497–1560) was Luther's close associate, sometime amanuensis, and successor as leader of Lutheranism. But Foxe did not draw his *vita* of Luther from Melancthon's Latin. The obscure book which Foxe followed is a translation from Melancthon's life of Luther, by one Henry Bennet of Calais, entitled:

> A famous and godly history, contaynyng the Lyves and Actes of three renowned reformers of the Christian Church, Martine Luther, John Coe-lampadius, and Huldericke Zuinglius. The declaracion of Martin Luthers faythe before the Emperoure Charles the fyft, and the illuste Estates of the Empyre of Germanye, wyth an Oration of hys death, all set forth in Latin by Phillip Melancthon, Wolfangus Faber, Capito. Simon Grincus and Oswald Miconus, Newly Englished by Henry Bennet Callesian.
>
> (STC 1881) [16]

On folio C. iir Bennet writers that Luther

published certain proposicions of Indulgences, whych are in the fyrst Tome of hys woorkes, and fixed them openlye on the Temple that joyneth to the Castell of Wittenberg, the morrowe *after* the feast of all Saynctes, the yeare. 1517.

(emphasis mine)

Bennet gives the wrong date for Luther nailing up his Ninety-Five Theses. Bennet writes that Luther nailed his Theses to the door of the Castle Church of Wittenberg on 2 November, the day *after* All Saints. Bennet's source, Melancthon, had written

edidit Propositiones de Indulgentiis, quae in primo Tomo monumentorum eius extant, & has publice Templo, quod Arci Vuitebergensi contiguum est, affixit pridie *festi omnium Sanctorum, Anno 1517.*

(fol. B. iir, emphasis mine)

Melancthon wrote the correct date, 31 October, the day *before* All Saints. Bennet mistranslated *pridie* as *after*. Foxe parroted Bennet's error.

To suggest that Shakespeare set Hamlet's encounter with the Ghost on 2 November because his source(s) provided an erroneous date for the posting of Luther's Ninety-Five Theses implies an intimate negotiation between Shakespeare's knowledge of Luther and his creation of Prince Hamlet. This hypothesis is not as far-fetched as it may appear. Commentators have already identified numerous parallels between Luther's conversion and Hamlet's (Waddington, 1989; Hassel, 1994; Hoff, 1988; Amott, 1973, 69–74). Young Martin Luther suffered a long period of guilt and depression (*anfechtung*), and eventually found conversion through humble surrender to God and his preordained providence.[17] Hamlet undergoes a similar course of spiritual development, from despairing his 'too sullied flesh' to faith in 'a special providence in the fall of a sparrow'. After returning to Denmark from his adventures at sea, Hamlet declares to Horatio that he was led by a 'divinity that shapes our ends' to discover the perfidious commission of Rosencrantz and Guildenstern. Hamlet writes to Claudius that he has returned to Denmark 'naked' (4.7.50). In this word which so puzzles the king and Laertes, Lutherans of the Elizabethan era and our own recognize the keyword Luther employs to describe his conversion through humble surrender to God: *nackt.*[18]

Elizabethans of all religions would also have recognized another and perhaps more obvious parallel between Hamlet and Luther. In Shakespeare's play Hamlet confronts a king who has married his dead brother's wife. It was widely remembered that Martin Luther had an exchange of rancorous pamphlets with a king who had married his dead brother's wife, Henry VIII.

Three disputed holy days

In his preface to *Hamlet* Harley Granville-Barker wrote that in performance the five-act play divides itself into three 'movements' (1931–71, i.73). The first movement, which comprises two days, begins as the play opens. It ends after Hamlet's encounter with the ghost and his decision to put on an antic disposition (1.5). According to Shakespeare's temporal markers, these scenes unfold in the period 1–2 November.

Hamlet's second movement begins with Polonius's drill of Reynaldo (2.1). From their conversation we cannot determine how long Laertes has been in Paris. But when Ophelia enters we recognize that significant time has elapsed since Polonius prohibited his daughter from sharing Hamlet's company:

> *Pol.* What, have you given him any hard words of late?
> *Oph.* No, my good lord, but as you did command
> I did repel his letters, and denied
> His access to me.
>
> (2.1.108–11)[19]

The anxious Polonius determines immediately to report Hamlet's condition to Claudius and Gertrude: 'Go we to the king' (2.1.118). On this same day Cornelius and Voltemand return from their embassy to Norway. Rosencrantz and Guildenstern also arrive, summoned to the court (perhaps from as far away as Wittenberg) on account of Hamlet's antic behaviour. The action proceeds seamlessly through Claudius's and Gertrude's interview with Rosencrantz and Guildenstern, the ambassadors' report, Polonius's reading of Hamlet's Valentine to Ophelia, Polonius's conversation with Hamlet ('You're a fishmonger, etc.'), the Prince's confrontation with Ophelia, his welcome to Rosencrantz and Guildenstern, and the arrival of the Players. All this takes place on a single day. As the players exit, Hamlet says, 'We'll hear a play tomorrow' (2.2.524). On the following night 'The Mousetrap' is performed, Hamlet confronts Gertrude in her closet and slays Polonius. Hamlet is dispatched to

England before dawn on the third day, and passes the army of Fortinbras (4.4). This movement comprises three days.

The third and final movement of the play begins at 4.5 with Gertrude's interview with mad Ophelia. Again through the agency of Ophelia we learn that significant time has elapsed since the death of Polonius; when Claudius observes Ophelia he demands, 'How long hath she been thus?' (4.5.65). A moment later Laertes enters, having journeyed to Elsinore from France seeking revenge. Letters from Hamlet are delivered to Horatio and to Claudius. Claudius and Laertes fall to plotting Hamlet's murder, and Gertrude brings news of Ophelia's death. All this action unfolds continuously on a single day. We know that Ophelia's funeral is held on the following day because Claudius reassures Laertes with a reference to their plotting against Hamlet: 'Strengthen your patience in our last night's speech. / We'll put the matter to the present push' (5.1.284–5). Claudius and Laertes immediately set the murder plot in motion, and the action runs seamlessly through to the end of the play. By this analysis each of Granville-Barker's three movements comprises two or three days. I will suggest that calendrical markers in the text of *Hamlet* centre these movements on three holy days which were sacred to Catholics but discarded or reshaped by Reformation Protestants: All Souls, Candlemas and Corpus Christi.

All Souls' Day. In the play's first movement we have noted that calendrical and astronomical markers coupled with reports of a ghost walking on four successive nights draw attention to the interval 30 October to 2 November. All Souls' Day, 2 November, was devoted to masses for those who had died without benefit of Extreme Unction. Since Reformation theology denied the existence of Purgatory as having no Scriptural basis, the Reformers discarded the holy day of All Souls.

Candlemas. If the ghost-walking scenes of the play's first movement are identified with 30 October to 2 November, then the play's second movement – which includes the 'Mousetrap', the closet scene with Gertrude, the murder of Polonius, the final appearance of Old Hamlet's ghost and Claudius's decision to banish Hamlet to England – occur on 2 February, Candlemas. We can deduce this as follows. Before the 'Mousetrap' Hamlet and Ophelia banter about how long Old Hamlet has been dead. Hamlet says 'my father died within 's two hours', and Ophelia responds, 'Nay, 'tis twice two months, my lord' (3.2.118–19). Ophelia, who is the reliable reporter in this exchange, declares Old Hamlet dead four months on the night of the 'Mousetrap'. By our reckoning Horatio, Barnardo and Franscico encountered the ghost on 1 November. They determine to report what they have seen to Hamlet, and their scene closes as Marcellus says: 'Let's do't, I pray, and I this morning know / Where we shall find him most conveniently' (1.1.156–7). Therefore the scene at the court of Claudius (1.2) must take place on the following day, 2 November. Claudius opens this scene: 'Though yet of Hamlet our dear brother's death / The memory be green' (1.2.1–2). Old Hamlet's death is recent. But how recent? Hamlet will shortly tell us that Claudius and Gertrude were married within a month of Old Hamlet's death:

> But two months dead – nay not so much, not two –
>
> ...
>
> A little month ...
>
> ...
>
>   ... within a month,
> Ere yet the salt of most unrighteous tears
> Had left the flushing in her galled eyes,
> She married. O most wicked speed.
>
>   (1.2.138–55)

Shakespeare's Hamlet is confused about how long his father has been dead because he has recently journeyed from Wittenberg, where the calendar is Julian, to a place where the calendar is Gregorian.

Just as Hamlet condemns the brevity of Gertrude's period of mourning ('a beast that wants discourse of reason / Would have mourned longer'), Claudius remonstrates against the protraction of Hamlet's grief:

> 'Tis sweet and commendable in your nature, Hamlet,
> To give these mourning duties to your father;
> But you must know your father lost a father;
> That father lost, lost his; and the survivor bound
> In filial obligation for some term
> To do obsequious sorrow. But to perserver
> In obstinate condolement is a course
> Of impious stubbornness, 'tis unmanly grief,
> It shows a will most incorrect to heaven,
> A heart unfortified, a mind impatient,
> An understanding simple and unschooled.
>
>   (1.2.87–97)

Claudius's allusion to a 'term' of 'filial obligation' is a reference to the

'Trental', or 'month's mind'. By the late Middle Ages the 'term' for which a survivor was 'bound In filial obligation' to do obsequies had been conventionally fixed at thirty days. 'Corporate intercession for the dead, being one of the most central aspects of late medieval religion, was highly regulated, highly formalized' (Duffy, 1992, 368).[20] Extended obsequies were proscribed, and Claudius chides Hamlet in strong language. Hamlet's mourning beyond the Trental is 'impious ... unmanly ... incorrect to heaven'. When Claudius adds 'unfortified' and 'impatient' he comes close to pronouncing Hamlet's behaviour heretical. Throughout *Hamlet* the dead are disposed of with perilous expediency. Old Hamlet's widow remarries before his Trental expires. Polonius is interred 'hugger-mugger' (4.5.80). Ophelia is shovelled-under on the day following her questionable death. Claudius's commission had ordered Hamlet be put to death with 'no leisure bated, / No, not to stay the grinding of the axe' (5.2.24–5). Rosencrantz and Guildenstern are 'put to sudden death, / Not shriving-time allowed' (5.2.46–7). Like Old Hamlet, *all* who die in the play go to their graves unshriven, 'unhousel'd, disappointed, unanel'd'. This hasty pace suggests that Old Hamlet's Trental has only just ended when Claudius and Gertrude importune the Prince to give over mourning. Since a Trental commenced on the day after an individual's death, Old Hamlet has been dead thirty-one days on 2 November. By this logic he died on 2 October.[21] By Ophelia's reckoning Old Hamlet has been dead four months on the night of the Mousetrap. Four months after 2 October is 2 February, the date of Candlemas. The dialogue surrounding 'The Mousetrap' is rife with markers which link that night to St Luke's account of the Presentation and Purification of the Blessed Virgin Mary (Luke 2:22–39), the Gospel reading for Candlemas. 'Lights' are called for. A mother is purified. A small animal ('A rat, a rat') is sacrificed. Most important, a spirit appears whose 'form and cause conjoined, preaching to stones, / Would make them capable' – an allusion to Christ's admonishment of the Pharisees on Palm Sunday that 'the stones would immediately cry out' (Luke 19:40). Luther rejected intercession by the saints and Blessed Virgin Mary. The Reformers reshaped Candlemas to emphasize the presentation of the infant Jesus in the temple.[22]

Corpus Christi. Hamlet's insistence that his father has been dead 'two hours' is significant for identifying the holy day associated with the third and climactic movement of the play. When Hamlet speaks these words we are approximately two hours into the performance of the play.[23] I have suggested above that the steeple bells of St Mary Overy and St Bennet could have been heard within the Globe, and that Shakespeare exploited this phenomenon in *Julius Caesar*. If *Hamlet* began *c.* 2 p.m. as Thomas Platter tells us *Julius Caesar* did, the bells would have chimed four times before Hamlet remarks that his father has been dead 'two hours'. This coupled with Ophelia's allusion to 'twice two months' conveys that in the dramatic universe of *Hamlet* two hours equals four months. This dialogue is very near the mid-point of the play. If the balance of the play runs another two hours, it spans the four-month interval from 2 February to 2 June. In 1602 the Vigil of Corpus Christi was 2 June.

This is only one of Shakespeare's temporal markers for Corpus Christi. On the first of the two days which close the play, Ophelia performs her mad scene with songs and herbs, Laertes arrives at the door of Elsinore at the head of a mob, and Ophelia's death is announced. On the second day, Ophelia is buried, Claudius and Laertes contrive an elaborate murder plot, and Hamlet's swordplay with Laertes and its bloody outcome conclude the action. Corpus Christi celebrated the 'real presence' of Christ in the Eucharist. From 4.5 to the end of the play, Shakespeare contrives a series of parodies of the principal rituals of the feast. As in *Julius Caesar*, there are two 'processions', one of the temporality and another of the spirituality. The former is the mob led by Laertes. The latter is the priest leading the corpse of Ophelia. On the following day a 'play' is staged – the rigged fencing match with all its props and stage directions. More explicitly, the final catastrophe in *Hamlet* centres on 'the Altare sacrament'. Placing the onixe/union in the lethal chalice, Shakespeare parodies the wine of eternal life (4.7.135). In this context the defeat of the elaborate Claudius–Laertes murder plot by Hamlet's faith in providence is an unmistakable triumph of predestination over the schemes and plans of unrighteous men.

These three holy days – All Souls, Candlemas and Corpus Christi – had vivid connections with the Reformation. They were among the most sacred of all holy days in the Catholic calendar. But each had been discarded or reformed by Luther and the Protestants. Just as the four ghost-walking days fell in sequence 30 October to 2 November in the years 1517 and 1601, Candlemas fell on 2 February and Corpus Christi on 2/3 June in both 1518 and 1602.[24] By this reckoning, the visit of 'The Dead Man', Lamord ('two months since', 4.7.80), fell on 2 April, which in 1602 was the anniversary of the death of Christ, Good Friday (Table 13).[25]

Table 13

Date	Holy day
2 November 1601	All Souls' Day
2 February 1602	Candlemas
2 April 1602	Good Friday
2 June 1602	Vigil of Corpus Christi

Testing the calendrical design of Hamlet

We have all been taught that Shakespeare, whose mind moved upon a high and noble plane, was careless about the dates and times in his plays. This book has argued the contrary: Shakespeare's use of dates is specific and precise; coupled with Scriptural allusions, these dates can be clues to the subtext and meaning of a speech or scene, and may even be useful in dating the principal composition (or revision) of a play. As in *Julius Caesar*, *Twelfth Night* and *Comedy of Errors*, there appear to be calendrical markers in *Hamlet* which cannot be explained away as coincidental. But can we test whether this analysis of calendrical design in *Hamlet* is valid? I believe there is a way to test these findings by dating the event which is the *sine qua non* of the drama in *Hamlet*: the marriage of Old Hamlet and Gertrude. Is the date of this marriage recoverable from internal evidence in the play? And, if it is, has it any relevance to Luther and the Reformation?

On the surface of it, Shakespeare's text is silent about the date of the Old Hamlet–Gertrude marriage. However, in 'The Mousetrap' Shakespeare provides *imagunculae* of Old Hamlet and Gertrude, and alludes to the date of the wedding of these puppets, the Player King and Queen:

> Full thirty times hath Phoebus' cart gone round
> Neptune's salt wash and Tellus' orbed ground,
> And thirty dozen moons with borrowed sheen
> About the world have times twelve thirties been
> Since love our hearts and Hymen did our hands
> Unite commutual in most sacred bands.
>
> (3.2.150–5)

The repetitive cadence of this speech – 'thirty times ... thirty dozen moons ... twelve thirties' – makes it curiously memorable.[26] Its arithmetic tells us that these *imagunculae* of Old Hamlet and Gertrude have been married one solar month of thirty days plus thirty synodic years on the day of the murder.[27] The many obvious parallels between the Player-King-and-Queen and Old Hamlet–Gertrude might have tempted Elizabethan auditors to compute the length of this marriage as follows.

'Full thirty times hath Phoebus' cart gone round' describes thirty solar days. 'Phoebus' is the Sun, which was thought to circle the Earth once each day.

'And thirty dozen moons with borrowed sheen / About the world have twelve times thirties been' describes 360 synodic months. The synodic period of the moon equals 29 days, 12 hours, and 44 minutes.

360 × 29.5 days = 10620 days

To account for the 44 minutes, add:

360 × 44 minutes = 15840 minutes
15840 minutes ÷ 60 per hour = 264 hours
264 hours ÷ 24 per day = 11 days

Which yields:

10620 days + 11 days = 10631 days

To this we must add Phoebus's thirty solar days:

10631 days + 30 days = 10661 days = 29 years 69 days

According to the Player King's speech, on the day of his murder 10661 days – or 29 years and 69 days – have elapsed since his wedding. If this is the duration of the Old Hamlet–Gertrude marriage, we can answer a question which has haunted scholars for centuries and is, perhaps, the greatest mystery in Shakespeare: why did young Hamlet not succeed to the throne immediately on his father's death?[28]

On the vigil of Corpus Christi, 2 June, Hamlet returns to the precincts of Elsinore and engages a Clown in badinage:

> *Ham.* How long hast thou been a gravemaker?
> *Clow.* Of all the days i' th' year I came to 't that day that our last
> King Hamlet o'ercame Fortinbras.
> *Ham.* How long is that since?
> *Clow.* Cannot you tell that? Every fool can tell that. It was the
> very day that young Hamlet was born ... I have been
> sexton here, man and boy, thirty years.
>
> (5.1.138–57)[29]

According to the Clown, Hamlet is thirty (solar) years old on the day of this encounter. Hamlet has already remarked 'How absolute the knave is!' (5.1.130), and Dowden insists 'we must accept dates so carefully determined' (1899, 195). Dover Wilson declares that the passage 'fixes the age of Hamlet in so pointed a fashion that ... Shakespeare clearly attached importance to it' (1934, 236). Shakespeare's device becomes transparent if Old Hamlet and Gertrude had been married 29 years plus 69 days when he died on 2 October of the prior year. The interval from Old Hamlet's death on 2 October to young Hamlet's encounter with the Clown on 2 June is eight months (243 days). Consequently, Old Hamlet and Gertrude would have been married 29 years plus 312 days when Hamlet encounters the Clown. But if Hamlet is 30 years old, he must have been born at least 29 years plus 365 days before his encounter with the Clown. Therefore, Hamlet must have been born at least 53 days *before* the Old Hamlet–Gertrude wedding. Now we understand why Shakespeare created a grave-digging Clown who is 'absolute'. Hamlet is illegitimate – which explains why he did not succeed to the throne on his father's death.[30]

The 'dram of eale' and Hamlet's illegitimacy

I suggest that Hamlet refers to his illicit conception and pre-marital birth as he stands with Horatio and Marcellus awaiting the appearance of the Ghost in Act 1. At 1.4.7 the quiet night is disturbed by the trumpets and ordnance of the king's rouse. Horatio asks, 'Is it a custom?' and Hamlet responds:

> Ay marry is't,
> But to my mind, though I am native here
> And to the manner born, it is a custom
> More honoured in the breach than the observance.
> (1.4.13–16)

Harold Jenkins's note on 'to the manner born' is useful: 'Not merely familiar with the custom *from birth*, but committed to it *by birth*. It is part of his *heritage*' (1987, 208, 15n, emphasis mine). In Q1 and the Folio Hamlet's speech ends here and 'observance' is the Ghost's cue to enter. But in Q2 (quoted here in old spelling) Hamlet continues with a speech which picks up the twinned themes of heritage and heredity:

> So oft it chaunces in particuler men,

That for some vicious mole of nature in them
As in their birth wherein they are not guilty,
(Since nature cannot choose his origin)
By the ore-grow'th of some complextion
Oft breaking downe the pales and forts of reason,
Or by some habit, that too much ore-leavens
The form of plausive manners, that these men
Carrying I say the stamp of one defect
Being Natures livery, or Fortunes starre,
His vertues els be they as pure as grace,
As infinite as man may undergoe,
Shall in the generall censure take corruption
From that particuler fault: the dram of eale
Doth all the noble substance of a doubt
To his own scandale.

(1.4.23–38)

Hamlet begins by enumerating three ways in which a man's virtue may be corrupted: by birth; by an imbalance of 'humours'; by bad habits. Hamlet finds the accident of birth most intriguing since the man is 'not guilty'. A child 'cannot choose' its parentage or the circumstances of its nativity. Despite his innocence, Hamlet believes that a 'vicious mole of nature' so pollutes this child with 'the stamp of one defect ... being Nature's livery' that, were all the offspring's other virtues 'pure as grace', notwithstanding he 'shall in the general censure [the Last Judgement] take corruption [not be saved on account of] that particular fault'. We wonder: with what form of obloquy could a newborn be endued to have forfeited its right to salvation? What stain could mark the soul of an infant which cannot be expunged by the water of the baptismal font? There is such a stain. It is one of a kind, and it can be found in Deuteronomy 23:2.

The Old Testament Book of Deuteronomy was closely read in Tudor England. Deuteronomy 25:5 was the law of the Levirate, which demanded that a brother should marry his dead brother's wife. Conversely, Deuteronomy 24:1 required a husband to divorce a wife in whom he found 'uncleanesse'. Before examining Deuteronomy 23:2, it will be useful to establish the identity of Shakespeare's 'vicious mole'. When Shakespeare framed this epithet, 'vicious' had not achieved its savage modern sense. Rather, 'vicious' was the adjectival form of 'vice'. When applied to habit and behaviour, 'vicious' carried the sense of 'contrary to moral principles; depraved, immoral, bad' (*OED* a.I.1). Applied to persons, the word meant 'addicted to vice or immorality; of depraved habits; profligate, wicked' (2.a). The little word 'mole' had two principal meanings: a 'spot or blemish on the human skin ... a fault' (mole n1 2. *spec*), or the familiar small mammal (n2 1.a). But in the latter sense it might be applied to persons 'whose (physical or mental) vision is deemed defective' (2.b). We know who the 'mole' is in *Hamlet*. It is 'Old Mole', the ghost of Hamlet's father. Viewed from this perspective Hamlet's train of ideas is not difficult to follow: mole, fault, corruption, defect, stamp. Shakespeare routinely employs 'stamp' when equating counterfeiting with the begetting of illegitimate children, as in *Measure for Measure*:

> Ha, fie, these filthy vices! It were as good
> To pardon him that hath from nature stolen
> A man already made, as to remit
> Their saucy sweetness that do coin God's image
> In stamps that are forbid.
>
> (2.4.42–6)

There is an uncanny series of echoes of *Hamlet* in Posthumus's rant:

> We are bastards all,
> And that most venerable man which I
> Did call my father was I know not where
> When I was stamped. Some coiner with his tools
> Made me a counterfeit; yet my mother seemed
> The Dian of that time: so doth my wife
> The nonpareil of this. O vengeance, vengeance!
>
> (2.5.2–8)

In his 'dram of eale' speech Hamlet is speaking of the offspring who bears the Old Mole's stamp – *himself*. He declares that this stamp is a defect-corruption-fault as unshirkable as livery, as indelible as Fortune's star.[31] It's a taint which even baptism cannot wash away. Now the relevance of Deuteronomy 23:2 is clear: 'A bastard shall not enter into the congregation of the Lord, even to his tenth generation shall he not enter into the congregation of the Lord' – not even if his vertues else are as pure as grace. Hamlet wraps up his musing about his illegitimacy with 'the most famous crux in Shakespeare':

> the dram of eale
> Doth all the noble substance of a doubt
> To his own scandale.

$$(1.4.36-8)$$

'Scandale' was closely associated with sexual incontinence; the *OED* cites, 'O God, that one borne noble should be so base, / His generous [ingendering] blood to scandall all his race' (*Nobody & Somebody*, E2b 1592).

As to the meaning of the mysterious 'dram of eale', if Hamlet's speech is a reverie upon his bastardy, we can finally parse this crux. Hamlet is responding to Horatio's question about the king's rouse. The cue for Hamlet's speech is a scene of excessive drinking of alcoholic spirits, and his diction is drawn from associated jargon. 'Dram' is a word Shakespeare uses as a measure of avoirdupois weight (an eighth of an ounce) and a measure of fluid (an eighth of a fluid ounce).[32] He also quibbles with the word in an *ethical* sense: dram = scruple = compunction.[33] At the close of Hamlet's speech Shakespeare is using the word 'dram' in the sense of a fluid measure *and* quibbling on an unspoken word: 'bastard'.[34] In addition to *bastard*'s familiar meaning of 'born out of wedlock, illegitimate', the homonym 'bastarde' described a 'sweet kind of Spanish wine, resembling muscadel in flavour; sometimes any kind of sweetened wine' (*OED* bastard n. 4).[35] Shakespeare uses the word in this sense in *1 Henry IV*: 'Score a pint of bastarde in the Half-moon' (2.4.30).[36] These *bastarde* sweetened or fortified wines – in Shakespeare's time the list included sherries, ports, muscatels and numerous other defunct variants – differ from 'pure' vintages by what the French call *dosage*.[37] That is, the natural wine is adulterated by the addition of a dollop of foreign substance. In the vinification of Falstaff's favourite, sack (modern: sherry), there are two intrusions into the fermentation and ageing process. The first is *flor* – a mould which is peculiar to the Xeres region of Spain which gives the wine its nutlike flavour. Second, sherries are aged (and dated) by the *solera* method. Small quantities of older sherries are added to young wines. The introduction of a few drams of older wine alters the new wine's character by a remarkable degree – a phenomenon well known to sherry vintners and drinkers in Shakespeare's time. In an oenological sense then, the *dosage* procedure adulterates the natural wine by the intrusion of a small quantity of foreign fluid. Wine adulterated in this way forfeits its varietal appellation. It loses its claim to a 'name', and is left a nameless 'bastard(e)'.[38]

As to the etymology of the mysterious 'eale', the word may be a variant derived from 'ealdren', an obsolete dialectical form of 'elder'. 'Elder' has two principal meanings, both relevant to a Danish prince's reflection on bastardy. The name of the familiar elder tree (*Sambucus nigra*) derives from the Old English word 'ellfrn', itself derived from an unknown Old Norse word but related to the Danish 'hyld' or 'hyldetrf' (*OED* elder n.1). The English vernacular name for the elder tree is 'Danewort', from the tradition that the plant sprang up in places where Danes slaughtered Englishmen or *vice versa*.[39] The elder is typically a low tree or shrub, and its young branches are remarkable for their abundance of pith.[40] In the context of Hamlet's speech about excessive drinking, two attributes of the elder are significant. It produces the elderberry, from which a 'wine' has been fermented in England since ancient times. Owing to the low sugar content of elderberries, the juice was 'bastardized' with a quantity of sugar or honey as an aid to fermentation. Second, the unfermented juice of the elderberry was employed in English folk medicine as a diuretic from at least medieval times.[41] So the elderberry is unique in that its juice can be associated not only with the consumption of fluid but with effluence.[42]

The other meaning of 'elder' which is relevant to Hamlet's reverie is the comparative of 'old', i.e. 'one who has lived longer'. The epithets 'bastard eigne' and 'bastard elder' were employed interchangeably in Elizabethan legal documents to describe 'the bastard son of a man who afterwards marries the mother' by whom he begets succeeding issue (*OED* bastard n.1.a).[43] Although Hamlet was legitimized by the marriage of Old Hamlet and Gertrude, Hamlet would become a 'bastard eigne' were a sibling to be born in wedlock to Claudius and Gertrude. A law book of 1536 outlines the prevailing English practice:

> A man hath a sonne of a woman before marriage, that is called a bastarde, and unlawful. And after he marrieth the mother of the bastarde, and they have another sonne, the seconde sonne is called *Mulier*, that is to say lawfull, and shall be heire to his father; but that other cannot bee heire to any man, because it was not knowen for certaine in the judgement of the law who was his father, and for that cause is said to bee no mans sonne or the sonne of the people, and so without father, according to these old beliefs.
>
> (Rastell 131–2)

Were the Claudius–Gertrude marriage to produce legitimate issue, that child would take precedence in the succession. Hamlet would be disenfranchised from the crown.[44] This is as good a reason as any for the prince to importune his mother not to mouse it back to the bloat-king's bed. 'Eale' may be a lost tipplers' colloquialism, or an Elizabethan nonce-word for an alcoholic drink derived from 'ealdern'. If so, the tiny and inscrutable 'eale' is pregnant with a remarkable concordance of ideas appropriate to Hamlet and his doubtful circumstances: wine, bastarde, bastard, Danes, diuretics, effluence, illegitimate conception, a first-born son whose stigma of bastardy was incompletely cured by the subsequent marriage of his parents, and a bastard eigne's vulnerable entitlements.

Hamlet's illegitimacy, and Luther's

Hamlet's illegitimacy provides an intriguing link between Shakespeare's prince and the father of the Reformation. Controversy still surrounds the date of Martin Luther's birth. His leading Catholic opponent, Johannes Cochlaeus (b. Johannes Dobeneck, 1479–1552), wrote that Luther was a bastard conceived when his mother copulated with the Devil in a bath-house (Friedensburg, 1892, v.1.541, 14–18).[45] In fact Luther's mother swore that she could remember the date of Martin's birth *but not the year*.[46] In his *vita* of Luther Melancthon writes:

> I have some tyme enquired of her Margarethe Luther at what time her sonne was borne: she answered, that she remembred the houre and the day of his nativity but of ye yeare she was ignoraunt. She affirmed he was borne the x [tenth] day of November at night, about a leven of the clocke. And ye cause why he was called Martin, was for that the morow after he received Baptisme, was S. Martins day. But his brother James, an honest and upryght man, said: the whole famely held opinion, he was borne the yere after the Nativity, 1483.
>
> (Bennet, 1561, B.ii.r–v)

The date of Luther's parents' marriage is unknown. What is known is that the couple moved house twice in the years 1482–4, first from Eisenach to Eisleben, and thence to Mansfield. A young couple occupying three residences in as many years is remarkable for that era. These movings of house – and the necessity for Luther's mother to conceal the year of his birth – would be understandable if Martin had been conceived out of wedlock. The 'official' year of Luther's birth is given as 1483 or 1484. But an earlier birthdate, say 1482, would resolve 'definite difficulties in the chronology of Luther's youth, such as his four-year period of schooling in Eisenach, for which it is difficult i.e. impossible to account' if a birthdate in 1483 or 1484 is accepted (Brecht, 1993, 1). Luther's father, George, began his career as a miner. This explains Hamlet's epithet for his own father's ghost: 'Well said, old mole. Canst work i'th' earth so fast? / A worthy pioner' (1.5.170–1). In Shakespeare's parlance, the term 'pioner' or 'pioneer' signified a miner.

Notes

1 Twilight lingered until 6.34 p.m.

2 Hassel, 1979, 38–41.

3 Text and lineation after Jenkins.

4 Advent marks the beginning of the ecclesiastical year, and engrosses the four Sundays prior to Christmas. Advent can begin no earlier than 27 November and no later than 3 December. However, in medieval France Advent began on the Feast of St Martin (11 November), and encompassed forty days and six Sundays.

5 The possibility that Bernardo's 'star' is a planet is discussed below.

6 *Alpha Lyrae* – Vega – (fifth brightest star in all the sky) is visible from London and northern Europe year-round. However, at 1 a.m. during the period 30 October to 10 November, Vega was visible from London only a few degrees above the northern horizon, which does not sort with the description 'westward from the pole'.

7 The play's 'twinned' males include: Old Hamlet with Old Fortinbras; Young Hamlet with Young Fortinbras; the 'impotent' Old Norway with the childless Claudius; Hamlet and 'my brother' Laertes (5.2.189); Cornelius with Voltemand; Rosencrantz with Guildernstern.

8 Marcellus is not the only namesake of an early Christian convert found in *Hamlet*. In 1.2 Shakespeare introduces a character named Cornelius. In Acts 10 St Luke tells the story of the conversion of a Roman centurion named Cornelius. Shakespeare pairs his Cornelius with another character named Voltemand, i. e. the 'turned' or 'changed' man.

9 An unspoken pun may be encoded here. Shakespeare's sentinel, Marcellus, holds the vigil on the Catholic church's vigil of Marcellus. Each holy day began on the previous evening with Vespers. The 'vigil' of Marcellus began at dusk on 29 October, of All Hallows on 30 October, of All Saints on 31 October, and of All Souls on 1 November. This may explain the uncertainty about the time of the Ghost's appearance to Hamlet on the fourth night, i.e. whether Horatio is correct that 'It lacks of twelve' or Marcellus is correct

that 'No, it is struck' (1.4.4–5). Hamlet has said he would arrive on the platform "twixt eleven and twelve' (1.2.254). Given his eagerness to see the Ghost, it is hard to believe he would arrive behind his time. In order to make its fourth appearance on All Souls' Day, the Ghost would have to appear before midnight.

10 November was the Elizabethans' month of the dead. In *The Shepheardes Calendar* Spenser's November eclogue characterizes the month as this 'sullen season'. Dennis Kay writes, 'November, the eleventh month, is traditionally associated with the commemoration of the dead. Further, the connection of the number eleven with mourning goes back to Sparta in the time of Lykourgos, when eleven days became established as the period of mourning ... In accordance with these ideas, presumably, Colin's elegy [in Spenser] consists of eleven stanzas of lament ... a meaning apparently accepted by Thenot, whose final words are "Up Colin up, enough thou mourned hast ..."' (Kay, 1990, 30, 36–7) (Spelling modernized).

11 This holy day was established in the time of Isidore of Seville (d. 636).

12 Rosencrantz's allusion to 'the late innovation' (2.2.331) is considered by some to refer to the abortive Essex *putsch*, and the reference to 'eyrie of children, little eyases' (2.2.337) to the Children of the Chapel who began to act at the Blackfriars in late 1600. They may be occasional emendations.

13 2 November 1601 was a moonless night, both in London and at Elsinore. The planets Mars, Neptune, Venus and Jupiter were *east* not west of Polaris. In any case, Barnardo speaks of a time when 'no planet strikes', suggesting that he knows the difference between a star and a planet.

14 The question of Denmark's 'elective' monarchy is considered below.

15 As were Rosencrantz and Guildenstern, whose namesakes were found among the Wittenberg student body in the decade 1586–95.

16 Printed by John (Sampson) Awdelie or Awdley (d. 1575; Plomer, 1903, 23). In the same year, Awdely printed George North's *The Description of Swedland, Gotland, and Finland, etc.* (STC 18662). In the prior year Awdley had printed two editions of *The Epistles and Gospels in Englishe* (STC 2980.2 .4).

17 Of the historical biographies: Heiko A. Oberman, *Luther* (New York: Doubleday, 1989). Of the psychological: Erik H. Erikson, *Young Man Luther* (New York: Norton, 1982). Of the theological: David C. Steinmetz, *Luther in Context* (Bloomington: Indiana University Press, 1986).

18 There are numerous parallels between Horatio and Melancthon. Both were Renaissance men with antique names (Melancthon = 'black earth' in Greek). Both were at Wittenberg. Luther was critical of Melancthon's philosophical approach to religion, just as Hamlet stresses the limits of Horatio's 'philosophy'. Hamlet asks Horatio to write his 'history'. Melancthon says he writes his life of Luther because 'hys [Luther's] fatal day hath prevented the publicacion of such an history' Luther had promised to write of himself. Hamlet knows a lot about flutes ('recorders'), and Luther was an excellent

flautist. Horatio's name comprises both 'ora = pray' and 'ratio = reason'. Melancthon was principally known for his logical confession of the Lutheran faith in *Loci Communes*, which ran through several editions beginning in 1521. Melancthon's father was an armourer, which may explain why Horatio (inexplicably) recognizes Old Hamlet's armour.

19 This is not the first time Ophelia has reported Hamlet's advances to Polonius. After her father's warning to her on the day of Laertes' departure (1.3), Ophelia has reported Hamlet's 'solicitings, / As they fell out by time, by means, and place' (2.2.125–6). Again, this suggests the passage of a substantial period of time.

20 For a fuller discussion of the Trental, month's mind and Purgatory, see Duffy, 1992, 338–76.

21 The Feast of the Guardian Angels – perhaps remembered in Hamlet's 'Angels and ministers of grace defend us!' (1.4.20).

22 Hamlet's sea voyage and his encounter with the pirates takes place on 3 February, feast of the patron saint of Denmark, St Anskar. Several of Anskar's adventures are curiously reminiscent of Hamlet's.

23 I am indebted to M. A. McGrail for this observation.

24 Candlemas had a particularly poignant connotation for Shakespeare. His late son, Hamnet, had been christened on Candlemas 2 February 1585.

25 Henry VIII's brother, Arthur, died on 2 April 1502. The hundredth anniversary of his death, 2 April 1602, may be remembered in Lamord's visit to Elsinore. The decisive event in English religious history 1500–1600 was the death of Arthur, which led to the wedding of Henry VIII to his widow, Catherine of Aragon.

26 Hamlet asks the Player King, 'You could, for a need, study a speech of some dozen or sixteen lines which I would set down and insert in't [the play], could you not?' (2.2.528–30). Hamlet would be painfully aware of the date of his parents' marriage. It may be that this speech is his interjection. Its vocabulary certainly sorts well with Hamlet's penchant for classical allusions.

27 Shakespeare may have tuned his auditors' ears to catch this calendar play through the 'two hours ... twice two months' byplay between Hamlet and Ophelia immediately preceding the playlet.

28 The received reason why Hamlet did not succeed his late father is that Denmark was an elective monarchy, and the electors had the power to bypass a lineal heir for another claimant. This is not sustainable. Until the eleventh century, the kingship of Denmark was settled by violence. In 1047 Sweyn Estridson was elected king, and his dynasty reigned until 1319. However, when King Erik Glipping was murdered in 1286, his twelve-year-old son was forced to sign a charter by the so-called 'hof' comprising bishops and magnates. A stricter charter was signed by Christopher II in 1319. The males of this royal line died out in 1375. By then the 'hof' had become a permanent institution, the Rigsråd, which proceeded to elect kings for

some seventy years with indifferent success. In 1448 the Oldenberg dynasty began with Christian I. This line ruled until 1523, when the unpopular Christian II abdicated in favor of his uncle Fredrick I, who invited the first Lutheran preachers into Catholic Denmark. When Fredrick died in 1533, the election became (momentarily) important. The obvious choice for king was Fredrick's great nephew, Christian. However, the Catholic bishops and nobles who dominated the Rigsråd feared that Christian would turn the country Lutheran. In 1534 they tried to invoke the old charter and elect a younger brother, Hans, a reliable Catholic. Denmark was plunged into a brief civil war which ended when Copenhagen surrendered to Christian's forces in 1536. He was proclaimed King Christian III, and the Rigsråd sanctioned a Danish Lutheran church the same year. Christian's son Frederick succeeded in 1559, and reigned until 1588. During that period the electoral powers of the Rigsråd were reduced to a rubber stamp. Christian IV succeeded in 1588 and reigned until 1648.

29 Dover Wilson (1934, 202) recognizes the connection between the Player King's speech and the Clown's. 'The repeated insistence upon "thirty" years of married life [*sic*] agrees with Hamlet's age given at 1.5.143–57.'

30 Henry VIII had at least one son who could not succeed to his throne because he was illegitimate: Henry Fitzroy, born in 1519 to Elizabeth Blount, lady-in-waiting to Catherine of Aragon. Fitzroy was created Earl of Nottingham and Duke of Richmond in 1533, and married to Mary Howard, daughter of the Duke of Norfolk. He died at St James's Palace in 1536 under suspicious circumstances. Shakespeare was personally associated with another man thought to be an illegitimate son of Henry VIII, Henry Carey (1524?–1596), son of Anne Boleyn's sister, Mary. Carey was said to have borne a strong resemblance to Henry VIII. He was Queen Elizabeth's favourite cousin, and she created him Baron Hunsdon in 1559. Hunsdon founded a company of players before 1565, and James Burbage claimed to be 'Lord Hunsdon's man' in 1584. A year later Hunsdon was named Lord Chamberlain. *Hamlet*, of course, was acted by the Chamberlain's Men, as the entry in the Stationers' Register for 26 July 1602 testifies.

31 'Fortune's star' might be a nickname for a birthmark or mole.

32 *Cymbeline* 1.4.135; *Winter's Tale* 2.1.138.

33 *2 Henry IV*, 1.2.130; *Twelfth Night* 3.4.79.

34 For other examples of Shakespeare's unspoken puns see Mahood, 1988.

35 The quibble on booze has an after-echo at 1.4.40 when Hamlet speculates whether the ghost is a '*spirit* of health'.

36 There are numerous references to *bastarde* wines in medieval and Renaissance literature, e. g. 'The fellows of Merton ... purchase some bastard in 1399.' Rogers, J. E. T. (1866) *A History of Agriculture and Prices in England*, etc. Oxford: Clarendon Press, 1.xxv. 619.

37 'Bastards ... seeme to me to be so called because they are oftentimes adulterated and falsified with honey.' Estienne and Liebault, 1616.

38 Hamlet's 'dram of eale' may be a metaphor for semen. 'Semen' may have
   been considered too rude a word for the stage in Shakespeare's time. Three
   detectable references are scrupulously oblique: (1) when Cleopatra refers
   to her eunuch, Mardian, as being 'unseminared' at 1.5.11; (2) when Emelia
   upbraids Iago at 1.4.149–52 for allowing his wit to be turned 'the seamy
   side without' to suspect her of infidelity with Othello; (3) when Hamlet
   refers to the 'rank sweat of an enseamed bed' at 3.4.92. There's also a
   concordance in *King John*: 'let wives with child . . . let seamen fear no wreck'
   (3.1.15–18).

39 *OED* citations: 1538 Turner *Libellus*; an annoymous *Herbal* of 1568, and
   1578 Lyte *Dodoens*, iii.xlv.380: *This herbe is called . . . in Englishe Walwort,
   Danewort, and Bloodwort*: 'While suggested in part by the abundance of the
   plant at certain spots historically or traditionally associated with slaughter,
   there was also an element of fanciful etymology in explaining the Latin
   name *Ebulus* from *ebullire* to bubble forth, with reference to the flowing of
   blood.' This may also be associated with the plant's diuretic qualities.

40 The qualities of elder wood were well known to Shakespeare, who refers
   to its soft, removable pith in *Henry V*: 'that's a perilous shot out of an
   elder-gun' (4.1.198). Elder pith could be hollowed out to leave a tube
   suitable for the making of a toy gun. We may detect a glance at this quality
   of the elder tree in Hamlet's 'indeede it takes / From our atchievements,
   though perform'd at height / The pith and marrow of our attribute'
   (1.4.20–2). In *Love's Labour's Lost*, Shakespeare remembers the tradition
   that 'Judas was hang'd on an elder' (5.2.606). We may detect a glance at
   this quality of the elder tree in Hamlet's speech.

41 *OED* citation: 1398 Trevisa Barth. *De R.*, xvii. cxliv. (1495) 700, *The Ellern
   tree hath vertue Duretica*.

42 That Shakespeare was familiar with the diuretic qualities of elderberries
   may be deduced from a previously overlooked concordance in *The Merry
   Wives of Windsor*: '*Host.* What says my Aesculapius, my Galen, my heart
   of elder, ha? Is he dead, bully stale, Is he dead? *Caius.* By gar, he is de coward
   jack priest of de vorld. He is not show his face. *Host.* Thou art a Castalion
   King Urinal Hector of Greece, my boy' (2.3.26–32). Shakespeare begins by
   quibbling the soft *heart of elder* against the traditionally resolute 'heart of
   oak'. But the quibble quickly switches focus to the ecclesiastical sense of
   'elder' with the introduction of 'priest', a word derived from 'presbyter',
   which was the literal translation into ecclesiastical Latin from the Greek
   presbyteros, meaning church elders (*OED* elder 3.4a). Finally, Shakespeare
   quibbles on the diuretic powers of the elderberry by the introduction of
   'Urinal' in close concordance with (*a*) the name of the Greek god of healing,
   Aesculapius, (*b*) the celebrated Graeco-Roman physician Galen, and (*c*) the
   word 'stale' (urine), as in 'Thou didst drink / The stale of horses, and the
   gilded puddle / Which beasts would cough at'. *Antony and Cleopatra* 1.4.61–
   3. Oliver parses the phrase as a reference to 'the urinal used by the hated

Philip II of Castile', but overlooks the Galen elder stale urinal quibbling (Oliver, 1990, 65n).

43 'Eigne' is a corrupt spelling of 'ayne', i.e. 'first-born, eldest'. *OED* citation: '1528 Perkins *Prof. Bk.* i.§49, A bastard eigne who is mulier in the spirituall law.'

44 Shakespeare glances at the possibility that offspring of a royal remarriage may disenfranchise an existing heir in *Two Gentlemen of Verona* (3.1). We know from *King John* and *Measure for Measure* that Shakespeare keenly understood the legitimacy laws of England.

45 The allegation was currency among Luther's detractors as late as the nineteenth century.

46 Melancthon feels obliged to defend Margarethe Luther's character: 'Hys Mother named Margaret, besydes that she had vertues worthy an honest Matrone, thys was syngular. Ther shined in her continency, feare of God, and invocacion, and al other vertuous persons constantly planted their eyes upon her, as on a patron president of al moral vertues' (Bennet, 1561, B.ii.r–v).

Appendix 1

Caesar's place of death

Although Plutarch records that Caesar was assassinated in Pompey's Theatre, Shakespeare shifts the murder scene to the 'Capitol'. This may derive from the playwright's further reading of St Luke's portrait of Zacharias. As if to underscore his intentional dislocation, Shakespeare's Cassius alludes three times to the historically correct site: 'And I doe know by this, they stay for me In *Pompeyes* Porch' (567–8); 'all this done, Repaire to *Pompeyes* Porch' (593–4); 'That done, repayre to *Pompeyes* Theatre' (599). Shakespeare's relocation of the scene could be related to the uncertain fate of the father of John Baptist. Luke records Christ's warning to certain Pharisees and lawyers: 'From the blood of Abel unto the blood of Zacharias, which was slaine betweene the altar and the Temple: verely I say unto you, it shalbe required of this generacion' (Luke 11:51). While the Geneva gloss (and most modern scholarly opinion) identifies the Zacharias of Luke 11 as a son of Jehoiada who was stoned to death on the order of King Joash *c.* 850 BC (2 Chronicles 24:22), this could hardly have seemed open and shut to anyone who knew his Bible as well as Shakespeare. A conscientious Bible reader would know that Matthew 23:25 identifies the victim as 'Zacharias son of Barachias', i.e. the prophet of the Book of Zacharias. References to other men named Zacharias (Zacharia, Zechariah) occur in 2 Kings, 1 and 2 Chronicles, Ezra, Nehemiah and Isaiah. Even today a body of scholars insist that the Zacharias of Luke 11:51 was the old priest who fathered John the Baptist (Fitzmyer, 1985, v29.951). If Shakespeare the playwright identified the slain Zacharias as the old priest of Luke 1:5–25, that may explain why he relocates the assassination from Pompey's Theatre to the Capitol.

Plutarch's site of the assassination was the first permanent theatre at Rome, erected in 55 BC by Pompey the Great. The structure referred to in Shakespeare's play as '*Pompeyes* Porch' was a *porticus* shelter which adjoined the theatre's *scaena* (Spevack, 1988, 72–3n). The structure stood in the Campus Martius, originally a park and recreation ground situated outside the city boundary (Howatson, 1989, 114). But Shakespeare places Caesar's assassination on the Capitoline Hill, the most sacred part of Rome. This was the site of the *altar* at which victorious generals made sacrifice during the celebration of a triumph – such as Caesar's triumph over the sons of Pompey which Shakespeare conflates with the Lupercal in Act 1. The Capitoline was also the site of the *temple* to Juppiter Optimus Maximus – Juppiter, best and greatest of the gods (Howatson, 1989, 114). By relocating the assassination of Caesar to the Capitol, Shakespeare causes his Caesar to be slain as he may have believed Luke's Zacharias was, 'between the altar and the Temple'.

Appendix 2

The other *Pontifex Maximus* of Rome

In Act IV of *Julius Caesar* Shakespeare may be glancing at the shallow-ness of the English priesthood under the Tudors by sketching a scathing portrait of the new high priest of Rome, Lepidus, through an extended 'duet' between Antony and Brutus. Shakespeare knew from his sources that the Lepidus who participates in the 'black proscriptions' had been elected *Pontifex Maximus* of Rome after Caesar's death. In order to prevent Octavius from inheriting the office, Antony had contrived the election of Lepidus to fill the vacancy. But in 4.1 Shakespeare rewrites his sources to imply that Antony and Octavius have taken Lepidus into the Triumvirate as a matter of political expediency: 'we lay these Honours on this man, / To ease our selves of divers sland'rous loads' (1874–5). Modern commentators are silent on the meaning of this speech. The Edwardian Arden editor supposed 'Lepidus was to bear the odium of the most unpopular acts of the triumvirate' (Macmillan, 1902, 118n). This cannot be correct. Shakespeare knew from Plutarch that Antony was the most unpopular of the three.[1]

By forming the Second Triumvirate with Lepidus, Antony and Octavius had co-opted the Roman state religion. The Lepidus who sat at the table during the 'black proscriptions' may have been wardrobed in the furnishings which Caesar wore as *Pontifex Maximus* in Act 1: priestly robe, mitre, *lituus* crook. Despite Lepidus's exalted clerical office, Shakespeare's Antony has only disdain for the man, and likens him to an 'Asse' (1876), and to his horse (1885):[2]

> He shall but beare them, as the Asse beares Gold,
> To groane and swet under the Businesse,
> Either led or driven, as we point the way:
> And having brought our Treasure, where we will,

250

> Then take we downe his Load, and turne him off
> (Like to the empty Asse) to shake his eares,
> And graze in Commons.
>
> (1876–82)

Octavius attempts to defend Lepidus's repute as a warrior. But Antony extends his asse–horse metaphor:

> You may do your will:
> But hee's a tried, and valiant Souldier.
> *Ant.* So is my Horse *Octavius*, and for that
> I do appoint him store of Provender.
> It is a Creature that I teach to fight,
> To winde, to stop, to run directly on:
> His corporall Motion, govern'd by my Spirit,
> And in some taste, is *Lepidus* but so:
>
> (1883–90)

In the following scene 4.2, Brutus delivers a horse-homily which has strong parallels to Antony's blason on Lepidus, and is strikingly reminiscent of it:

> Ever note *Lucillius*,
> When Love begins to sicken and decay
> It useth an enforced Ceremony.
> There are no trickes in plaine and simple Faith:
> But hollow men, like Horses hot at hand,
> Make gallant shew, and promise of their Mettle:
> *Low March within.*
> But when they should endure the bloody Spurre,
> They fall their Crests, and like deceitfull Jades
> Sinke in the Triall.
>
> (1930–9)

The recurring horse-imagery suggests a continuity of subtext. There is also an odd nexus of theological language in Brutus's homily: 'Love … Ceremony … Faith.' This has never been satisfactorily parsed, largely because commentators have not recognized Shakespeare's parallel blasons of the *inward* Lepidus and Cassius. But Shakespeare's diction becomes transparent when we recognize that, by characterizing *Pontifex Maximus* Lepidus as 'barren spirited' (1892), Antony is delivering a stinging commentary on the official state religion of Rome (and, perhaps, England). Fulfilling his part of this extended 'duet', Brutus laments

When Love begins to sicken and decay
It useth an enforced Ceremony.
There are no trickes in plaine and simple Faith.

(1931–3)

In context with 'Ceremony' and 'Faith', the word 'Love' is charged with overtones. 'Love', as every reader of Paul knows, is 'the fulfilling of the law' (Romans 13:10). 'Ceremony' was a common synonym for 'religious ritual'. A 'trick' is a 'crafty or fraudulent device ... an artifice to deceive ... an illusory or deceptive appearance' (*OED* n. 1). The principal Calvinist quarrel with the rituals of Catholicism could be summarized in these nine words: 'There are no trickes in plaine and simple Faith' (1933). English Protestants of 'plaine and simple Faith' rejected transubstantiation, that 'tricke' of ceremony by which the wine and wafer miraculously became the blood and body of Christ.

Notes

1 'Now the government of these Triumviri grewe odious and hatefull to the ROMANES, for divers respects: but they most blamed *Antonius*, bicause he being elder then *Caesar*, and of more power and force then *Lepidus*, gave him selfe againe to his former riot and excesse, when he left to deale in the affaires of the common wealth' (North, 1579, 979).
2 The twin metaphors of 'Asse' and 'Horse' were, perhaps, suggested to Shakespeare by the fact that Lepidus had been Julius Caesar's Master of the Horse in 45 BC.

Appendix 3

Brutus's reading of Cicero

There are several instances where Shakespeare's Brutus reveals himself to be the intellectual hostage of Cicero. Brutus's change-of-mind regarding the suicide of Cato in Act 5 is remarkably congruent with Cicero's view:

> But Cato departed from life with a feeling of joy in having found a reason for death; for the God who is master within us forbids our departure without his permission; but when God Himself has given a valid reason as He did in the past to Socrates, and in our day to Cato, and often to many others, then of a surety your true wise man will joyfully pass forthwith from the darkness here into the light beyond. All the same he will not break the bonds of his prison-house – the law forbid it – but as if in obedience to a magistrate or some lawful authority, he will pass out at the summons and release of God. For the whole life of the philosopher, as the same wise man says, is a preparation for death.
>
> (King, 1989, 86–7)

Another intriguing passage in the *Tusculan Disputations* examines 'glory'. In *Julius Caesar* the words 'glory' and 'glories' are generally associated with Caesar: first, by Antony looking down at Caesar's body: 'Are all thy Conquests, Glories, Triumphes, Spoiles, / Shrunke to this little Measure?' (1370–1); then by Brutus, who tells the plebeians that Caesar's glory is 'not extenuated, wherein he was worthy' (1567–8). Brutus urges Antony to 'Do grace to *Caesars* Corpes, and grace his Speech / Tending to *Caesars* Glories' (1591–2). As the play ends, another Caesar will exit 'To part the glories of this happy day' (2730). Only in Act 5 is 'glory' associated with anyone who is not a Caesar when Brutus declares, 'I shall have glory by this loosing day / More then *Octavius*, and *Marke Antony*, / By this vile Conquest shall attaine unto' (2681–3). Shakespeare did not find Brutus's hope for future 'glory' in Plutarch. Rather, Plutarch's Brutus spoke of his reputation:

I thinke my selfe happier than they that have overcome, considering that I leave a perpetuall fame of our corage and manhoode, the which our enemies the conquerors shall never attaine unto by force nor money, neither can let their posteritie to say, that they being naughtie and unjuft men, have slaine good men, to usurpe tyrannical power not pertaining to them.

(North, 1579, 1080)

It was perfectly in tune with Stoic ideals for a wise man to be satisfied to die with his good reputation intact. Cicero wrote: 'But assuredly death is encountered with most equanimity when the failing life can find solace in the reputation it has won' (King, 1989, 130). But in the same passage of *Tusculan Disputations*, Cicero hints at a rather unStoical appetite for *gloria*: 'For though consciousness will have gone, nevertheless the dead, unconscious though they be, are not without their own peculiar blessings of fame and glory. There is, it may be, nothing in glory that we should desire it, but none the less it follows virtue like a shadow.' Cassius also echoes a Ciceronian view when he declares that Romans have become 'Womanish' (524). Cicero wrote: 'sed nos umbris, deliciis, otio, languore, desidia animum infecimus, opinionibus maloque more de lentium mollivimus' (504–6); '*Quid est autem nequius aut turpius effeminato viro?*' (207); '*Quid est enim fletu muliebri viro turpius?*' (212). Cicero blamed Epicurus for Rome's 'womanish' sentiments: '*deinde ad hanc enervatam muliebremque sententiam satis docilem se Epicurus praebuit*' (160). All this falls so close to the Epicurean Cassius's 'O I could weepe / My spirit from mine eyes' (2078–9) as to be difficult to ignore.

Cicero may also be lurking behind the reason Brutus offers why he can bear with patience the news of the death of Portia. Brutus says, 'With meditating that she must dye once, / I have the patience to endure it now' (2187–8). Shakespeare found this reason not in Plutarch but in Cicero's *Tusculan Disputations*:

There it does not admit of doubt that everything which is thought evil is more grievous if it comes unexpectedly. And so, though this is not the one cause of the greatest distress, yet as foresight and anticipation have considerable effect in lessening pain, a human being should ponder all the vicissitudes that fall to man's lot.[1] And do not doubt that here is found the ideal of that wisdom which excels and is divine, namely in the thorough study and comprehension of human vicissitudes, in being astonished at nothing when it happens, and in thinking, before the event is come, that there is nothing which may not come to pass.

(King, 1989, 262–3)

This passage precisely anticipates Brutus's saying. The linguistic cue '*meditata*' is highly suggestive. Likewise, when Cicero reconsiders how unanticipated events bring a more violent shock, he employs a metaphor from the art of war, 'that which has not been previously foreseen brings a more violent shock: but surprise is not everything. Yet it is true that a sudden advance of the enemy causes a good deal more consternation than an advance which is expected' (King, 1989, 286). There is an echo of this in Brutus's decision which costs him the battle of Philippi, and his life: 'Let them set on at once: for I perceive / But cold demeanor in *Octavio*'s wing: / And sodaine push gives them the overthrow' (2474–6).

Finally, there is one startling moment in 4.2 which has never been satisfactorily explained by commentators: Brutus's disproportionate and unprepared fury at the intrusion of the Cynicke Poet. That this represents the pinnacle of Brutus's ferocity is clear from Cassius's observation: 'I did not thinke you could have bin so angry' (2130). Why does Brutus, the great reader and idolater of words, suddenly turn savage towards the Poet? The answer can be found in Cicero, who – though he frequently translated and quoted from Greek and Roman poets – expresses only contempt for poets in the *Tusculan Disputations*.[2]

But do you not see the harm which poets do? They represent brave men wailing, they enervate our souls, and besides this they do it with such charm that they are not merely read, but learnt by heart. Thus when the influence of the poets is combined with bad family discipline and a life passed in the shade of effeminate seclusion, the strength of manliness is completely sapped. Plato was right then in turning them out of his imaginary State, when he was trying to find the highest morality and the best conditions for the community.

(King, 1989, 174)

In particular, Cicero faults the poets for leading men towards false virtue (*TD* III.i.1–3), and for over-valuing love:

In fact the whole passion ordinarily termed love (and heaven help me if I can think of any other term to apply to it) is of such exceeding triviality that I see nothing that I think comparable with it ... But let us allow the

255

poets to make merry, whose stories let us see Jupiter himself implicated in this shame.

(King, 1989, 406–8)

Most particularly, Cicero disdains the poets for praising love between men:

Atque, ut muliebres amores omittam, quibus maiorem licentiam natura conces-sit, quis aut de Ganymedi raptu dubitat quid poetae velint aut non intelligit quid apud Euripidem et loquatur et cupiat Laius?

Again, not to speak of the love of women, to which nature has granted wider tolerance, who has either any doubt of the meaning of the poets in the tale of the rape of Ganymede, or fails to understand the purport of Laius' language and his desire in Euripides' play?

(King, 1989, 408)

Brutus's sudden rage, and his angry dismissal of the Cynicke, concord with Cicero's contempt for poets. Brutus's 'shews of love' to Cassius have brought the republic to ruin.

Note

1 '*Sint semper omnia hominis humana meditata*' (III.xiv.30).
2 Although Cicero quotes the Cynic Anacharsis in *Tusculan Disputations*: 'My clothing is a Scythian mantel, my shoes the thick skin of the soles of my feet, my bed is the earth, hunger my relish' etc. (King, 1989, 517). The letter which Cicero quotes is now believed to be a forgery.

Appendix 4

'Wit' or 'writ' in Antony's funeral oration?

There is some question regarding whether 'writ' or 'wit' was intended when Antony protests to the plebeians,

> For I have neyther writ nor words, nor worth,
> Action, nor Utterance, nor the power of Speech,
> To stirre mens Blood.
>
> (1758–60)

Although Johnson and Malone favoured 'writ', our scholarly contemporary editions adopt Kitteridge's emendation of 'writ' to 'wit'.[1] This is not correct. Brutus has told the plebeians: 'The Question of his [Caesar's] death, is inroll'd in the Capitoll: his Glory not extenuated, wherein he was worthy; nor his offences enforc'd, for which he suffered death' (1566–9). It was the practice of the Roman Senate that decrees, criminal charges and other legal documents should be written out and filed or 'inroll'd' in the library where they could be read and consulted by interested parties. In his oration the only reason Brutus cited for Caesar's murder was Caesar's 'ambition'. It goes without saying that Caesar could hardly have risen to his prominent and legally sanctioned positions as *Pontifex Maximus* and dictator if he lacked ambition. As to the actual criminal charges against Caesar, Brutus tells the plebeians that these have been written out, 'inroll'd in the Capitoll', and may be examined there. And Brutus tells this to the plebeians in such a way as to suggest that this ought to satisfy any friend of Caesar. Antony, contrasting himself to Brutus, laments he has no such authoritative 'writ' – no written legal document to bolster his view of Caesar and his assassins. Seen in this light, the Folio reading 'writ' ought to be restored.

Appendices

Note

1 For example: Humphreys, 1984, 214n, and Dorsch, 1983, 86n.

Appendix 5

Antony's wordplay on 'honourable men'

Although Plutarch's *Life of Antony* was Shakespeare's principal source for his character, there is evidence that the playwright was also familiar with Cicero's depiction of Antony in his *Philippics*.[1] Antony's memorable play on the words 'honorable men' has no basis in Plutarch, but Bloom and Jaffa imply that 'The "honourable men," of Antony's oration seems to come from Philippic II.xii.30–1, where Cicero says that this is the way Antony spoke of the conspirators' (Bloom and Jaffa, 1964, 110). Shakespeare certainly had sufficient knowledge of Latin to know that Antony's wordplay on 'honourable' would not have been possible for a Roman. The Latin *honorabilis* describes high condition and political position, not exemplary character (Miles, 1989, 276). The Latin word which engrosses our definition of 'honourable' is *pius*. This word, *pius*, is the focus of a passage in Philippic 13 in which Cicero reads aloud to the Senate an open letter in which Antony claims the ethical high ground in his conflict with Cicero. Antony declares he is determined not to tolerate insults, not to desert the republican cause, and will not allow his veterans to be humiliated. Antony then characterizes his friendship with Lepidus – '*nec Lepidi societatem violare, piissimi hominis*' – which sends Cicero into a paroxysm:

> tibi cum Lepido societas aut cum ullo, non dicam bono civi, sciut ille est, sed homine sano? id agis ut Lepidum aut impium aut insanum existimari velis ... tu porro ne pio quidem, sed piissimos quaeris et, quod verbum omnino nullum in lingua Latina est, id propter tuam divinam pietatem novum inducis.
>
> (Bailey, 1986, 13.43.18–25)

Bailey translates Cicero's invective:

You an ally of Lepidus or any other – I won't say good citizen, as he is, but sane man? You are out to have Lepidus thought either a traitor or a madman ... And then you look not merely for honorable men but for 'honorablest,' importing a new word which does not exist in the Latin language to gratify your marvelous sense of honor!

(Bailey, 1986, 353)

In a real sense Lepidus was *piissimus homo Romani*. After Caesar's assassination Lepidus succeeded him as *Pontifex Maximus*, an office he held until his death in 12 BC. While this nice distinction may have eluded Cicero's most distinguished contemporary translator, it would not have been obscure to an Elizabethan Latinist. The standard Latin–English 'dictionary' during Shakespeare's adolescence was Thomas Cooper's *Thesaurus Linguae Romanae & Britannicae* (London, 1565), which defined *pius* as '*Pius, Adiectiuum. Virg. Religious*: devoute: godly: mercifull: benigne: that beareth reverent love toward his countrei and parentes: Naturall to his kinsefolke' (Cooper, 1565, AAAaa5). The Latin vocabulary was only a fraction as large as our modern English vocabulary. Not only reverence for religion but also reverence toward country and parents were collocated in the Latin *pius*. Given that at the time of his assassination Caesar was *Pontifex Maximus* and *pater patriae* – and, perhaps, natural father to one of his murderers – one now detects a previously unplumbed irony in Antony's sobriquet 'honourable men'.

Cicero was no admirer of Antony's. He wrote:

tu vero qui te ab eodem Caesare ornatum negare non potes, quid esses, si tibi ille non tam multa tribuisset? ecquo te tua virtus provexisset, ecquo genus? in lustris, popinis, alea, vino tempus aetatis omne consumpsisses, ut faciebas, cum in gremiis mimarum mentum mentemque deponeres.

(Bailey, 1988, 338)[2]

Even after two thousand years the allusion to cunnilingus shocks us. Worse, the actors' calling was disdained by right-minded Romans as little better than prostitution. Shakespeare may well have been influenced by Cicero's portrait of Antony as he shaped his character of the man who spoke in Caesar's funeral.

Notes

1 'Cicero's *Epistolae* and *Philippics* ... all were standard grammar school texts'

Antony's wordplay

(R. E. Rose, 1964, 31). The old republican's Antony is one of the most excoriating, pestilential portraits one politician ever wreaked upon another.
2 'You, on the contrary, who cannot deny that you were favoured by the same Caesar, where would you be if he had not done so much for you? Would your worth or your intellect have advanced you? You would have spent your entire life in brothels, cookshops, gaming, drinking, as you used to do when you laid your mind and your mouth in the lap of actresses.'

Appendix 6

The priesthood of Julius Caesar

Shakespeare would have known that the historical Gaius Julius Caesar was a descendant of a prominent and priestly family. The Julii were numbered among 'the "Trojan" families of Rome, that is, to those who traced their descent from Aeneas or one of his companions. The [clan's] founder was Ascanius, son of Aeneas, who was also called Iulus' (Weinstock, 1971, 5). That Shakespeare was aware of Caesar's distinguished lineage is detectable in Cassius's slur:

> I (as *Aeneas*, our great Ancestor,
> Did from the Flames of Troy, upon his shoulder
> the old *Anchyses* beare) so, from the waves of Tyber
> Did I the tyred *Caesar*.
>
> (210–13)

Cassius ironically usurps the role of Caesar's forebear, Aeneas.

Cassius also offers a comparison of Caesar's and Brutus's names in the 'seduction' scene (241–9). This, too, is ironical. Shakespeare and fellow Elizabethan Latin readers would have understood that the name 'Julius' implies sacred antecedents, which the *gens* 'Brutus' does not. Julius is a 'a diminutive form of Iovis [Jove] and therefore the name of a "young" Iuppiter [Juppiter], his son' (Weinstock, 1971, 9). 'The Julii also claimed descent from Venus, and had a close association with Apollo, the god of medicine and protector of those born by the "Caesarian" operation' (Weinstock, 1971, 12). Elizabethans believed that Gaius Julius adopted the *cognomen* Caesar because he was born by Cesarean section. In fact the appellation probably derived from the birth of Caesar's forebear Sextus Julius Caesar, proconsul in 208 BC (Weinstock, 1971, 13). The claim of the Julii to divine antecedents did not sound as bizarre to Roman ears as it does to ours. It was commonplace in the ancient world that great men could be descendants of gods.

Alexander was said to have descended from Zeus, who copulated with his mother in the form of a serpent (North, 1579, 793).[1] Seleucus I was thought to be descended from Apollo, Caesar's putative ancestor Aeneas from Venus, and Romulus from Mars. Scipio Africanus Maior was rumoured to be descended from Juppiter (Weinstock, 1971, 19).

Plutarch records at length Caesar's campaign to win the elective office of *Pontifex Maximus* of Rome in 64 BC. It was an all-or-nothing gamble. 'When the day of the election came, his [Caesar's] mother bringing him to the dore of his house, *Caesar* weeping, kissed her, and sayd: Mother, this day thou shalt see thy sonne chiefe Bishoppe of Rome, or banished from Rome' (North, 1579, 766). North everywhere translates *pontifex maximus* as 'chiefe Bishop[pe] of Rome'. Both titles are additions of the Pope, a detail which could hardly have failed to register on Elizabethan readers including Shakespeare. Caesar's Julian calendar reform of 45 BC was only one aspect of a top-to-bottom overhaul of Roman religion which Caesar began in 49 BC. Dio writes that when the Civil War with Pompey began, many among the Roman aristocracy – including many priests and augurs (Cicero being one) – fled Rome to join Pompey, or to hold themselves neutral. When Caesar entered Rome, the praetor Marcus Aemilius Lepidus nominated Caesar dictator. In this capacity Caesar named new secular officials, and 'appointed priests in place of those who had perished' or fled (Cary, 1916, vi.64–5). With these appointments Caesar began a reform of the Roman state religion. Though it may strike the modern reader as odd to hear Caesar styled as a religious reformer, his intentions are a matter of history and would have been known by Elizabethan readers of Cicero. Though Caesar's reform charter (the *lex Julia de sacerdotiis*) is lost, it was quoted by Cicero in a letter to Brutus (Bailey, 1988, 755). Like Henry, Edward and Elizabeth Tudor, Caesar aimed at becoming head of both state and state religion. When he achieved this goal after the battle of Munda, he returned to Rome and put in place his most significant and lasting religious reform, the Julian calendar (North, 1579, 791; Holland, 1606, 17).

In 44 BC Caesar ensured that his heir would inherit both his political and religious power. Caesar pressed the Senate to pass a law which declared that 'Caesar's son, should he beget or even adopt one, should be appointed high priest' (Cary, 1916, 317). Since Caesar had already determined on Octavius as his heir by written will, this edict secured for Octavius both the most powerful secular and sacred offices. Octavius became *Pontifex Maximus* on the death of Lepidus in 12 BC. After that date Roman emperors reigned as both head of state and head of state religion, a bizarre and primitive custom perpetuated by certain monarchs in Shakespeare's day and our own.

Note

1 Also Holland, 1600, 598.

Appendix 7

'Wrong in a just cause'

There is a crux in Caesar's rejection of the conspirators' plea which has never been satisfactorily parsed: 'Know, *Caesar* doth not wrong, nor without cause / Will he be satisfied' (1247–55). Writing '*De Shakespeare nostrati*' in the posthumously published *Timber: or, Discoveries; Made upon Men and Matter*, Ben Jonson recalled:

> I *remember*, the Players have often mentioned it as an honour to *Shakespeare*, that in his writing, (whatsoever he penn'd) hee never blotted out line. My answer hath beene, would he had blotted a thousand ... Many times hee fell into those things, could not escape laughter: As when hee said in the person of *Caesar*, one speaking to him; *Caesar thou dost me wrong*. Hee replyed: *Caesar did never wrong, but with just cause* and such like: which were ridiculous.[1]

There is a good deal of Shakespeare's work that Jonson seems not to have understood, and these lines are an instance.[2] Even so, one needs to weigh carefully Jonson's recollection of Caesar's speech; playwrights' ears are keenly tuned to one another's lines. Nor should we doubt that the speech provoked ridicule. Doing wrong for just cause *appears* to be an oxymoron. But it is not. Edmond Malone, who believed that Caesar was being asked to repeal a banishment, observed that 'wrong' does not always mean 'harm' (Malone, 1821, xii.76). In a legal sense, 'wrong' meant to 'dispossess (a person) wrongfully' (*OED* v.2). According to Malone, Caesar's lines can be understood to mean 'Caesar does not send men into exile unless they have deserved it'. It is that simple – and *not* that simple if 'Publius Cimber' is dead. In order to understand what Caesar means when he declares he does wrong only with just cause, we must recover something Cicero said which has previously been thought irretrievable.

In 1.2, Casca describes for the benefit of Cassius and Brutus the circumstances of Antony's off-stage offer of a crown to Caesar. As Casca completes his tale of Antony's three offers – Caesar's refusal, his swoon and the reaction of the multitude – Cassius enquires:

> *Cassi.* Did *Cicero* say any thing?
> *Cask.* I, he spoke Greeke.
> *Cassi.* To what effect?
> *Cask.* Nay, and I tell you that, Ile ne're looke you
> i'th'face againe. But those that understood him, smil'd
> at one another, and shooke their heads: but for mine
> owne part, it was Greeke to me.
>
> (382–8)

Casca's circumspection is tantalizing. He implies that if he repeats Cicero's words he may not be able to face his friends again. Then he describes *cognoscenti* sharing stealthy grins and headshakes. Clearly, the implication of Shakespeare's passage is that Casca understood what Cicero said but dared not repeat a remark so unflattering to Caesar. The mystery surrounding what Cicero said is heightened by the likelihood that Shakespeare, and at least some members of his first audiences, knew that Casca spoke fluent Greek. Plutarch's dramatic report of Caesar's assassination begins:

> *Caska* behinde him [Caesar] strake him in the necke with his sword, how-beit the wounde was not great nor mortall, bicause it seemed, the feare of such a develishe attempt did amaze him [Caska], and take his strength from him, that he killed him not at the first blowe. But *Caesar* turning straight unto him, caught hold of his sword, and he held it hard: and they both cried out, *Caesar* in Latin: O vile traitor *Caska*, what doest thou? And *Caska* in Greeke to his brother, brother, helpe me.
>
> (North, 1579, 794)

Although it has long been thought that what Cicero said was unre-coverable, it is possible that some of Shakespeare's auditors would have detected in Casca's clues an allusion to a Renaissance commonplace for grasping ambition, employed even by Queen Elizabeth in correspond-ence. In *De Officiis* Cicero wrote that Caesar

> used to have continually upon his lips the Greek verses from the *Phoenissae*, which I will reproduce as well as I can— awkwardly, it may be, but still so that the meaning can be understood:

'Wrong in a just cause'

> ... if wrong may e'er be right, for a throne's sake
> We wrong most right: – be God in all else feared!
>
> (Miller, 1990, 356–7)

Cicero's jibe caught the notice of Suetonius, who reproduced it in his *Historie of Caius Julius Caesar Dictator*:

> in his 3. book of duties [Cicero] writeth, that Caesar had alwaies in his mouth, these verses of Euripides ... which Cicero himselfe translated thus.

> '*Nam si violandum est ius, impery^{um} gratia Violandum est, alijs rebus pietatem colas.*'

> > For if thou must do wrong by breach,
> > Of lawes, of right and equitie,
> > Tis best thereby a Crowne to reach,
> > In all things els keepe pietie
> >
> > (Holland, 1606, 14)

Holland's Elizabethan translation of Euripides highlights its relevance to the Caesar of Shakespeare's play. As the *Pontifex Maximus* Caesar enters with his entourage on the holy feast day of the Lupercal, he flaunts his piety: 'Set on, and leave no Ceremony out' (100). Moments later Caesar is the object of his sycophant Antony's three offers of a crown. In the Renaissance, Euripides' verses were a commonplace for importunate royal ambition:

> 'But to continue our matter,' writes La Primaudaye, 'if right (say ambitious men) may be violated, it is to be violated for a kingdome.' The employment of the same caustic argument is also noted by Charron in his anatomy of the passion of ambition, '*Si violendum est jus, regandi (sic) causa violendum est, in caeteris pietatem colas.*' If a man may at any time violate Justice, it must be to gaine a kingdome; in the rest observe justice and piete.
>
> (W. A. Armstrong, 1946, 178)

Queen Elizabeth herself was known to have played upon the trope: 'This Latin tag seems to have had a popular currency; Queen Elizabeth writes to Sir Henry Sidney, Governor of Ireland, "*Si violandum jus regnandi causa*"' (Chamberlin, 1923, 152).[3] Elizabeth's cause was just because she was the reigning monarch. But in what sense was Caesar's cause just?

A number of Renaissance political thinkers including Machiavelli believed that Caesar was entitled to his principality over Rome as a reward for his feats of arms:

The errors made in the cause of liberty are, among others, these: giving offence to citizens who should be rewarded ... [This] may occasion great evils and the coming of tyranny is thereby often accelerated, as happened in Rome when Caesar took by force what ingratitude had denied to him.

(Crick, 1970, 183)

Machiavelli's syllogism is simple: Caesar deserved the principate; it was denied him by ingratitude; he took it. Machiavelli's Discourses proceed from the view that ingratitude, envy and emulation are the pre-eminent destabilizing political force: 'Although owing to the envy inherent in man's nature' (Crick, 1970, 97). The corrosive effect of envy and emulation are the leitmotif of the Discourses, from its preface to its longest section 'On Conspiracies'. Both 'emulation' and 'envy' have their place in Shakespeare's *Julius Caesar*. Artemidorus 'laments, that Vertue cannot live / Out of the teeth of Emulation' (1140–1). Brutus does not wish Caesar's murder to appear 'Like Wrath in death, and Envy afterwards' (797). It is to envy that Antony refers the murder of Caesar in his famous encomium over the dead body of Brutus: 'This was the Noblest Roman of them all: / All the Conspirators save onely hee, / Did that they did, in envy of great *Caesar*' (2717–9). On this evidence, Shakespeare's 'Caesar does not wrong without just cause' ought to be restored, and – ironically – Jonson thanked for remembering it.[4]

Notes

1 In Chambers, 1951, ii.210. See Velz, 1969, 109–18. Jonson's phrase 'hee said ... Hee replyed' might lend further credence to the notion that Shakespeare played the part of Caesar.

2 J. D. Wilson makes a powerful and effective case for the veracity of Jonson's recollection in 1969, 39–42. 'Certainly Jonson quite failed to understand Shakespeare; his praise of him in the First Folio proves that. Misunderstanding, however, does not quite account for all. There was rancour in the cup.'

3 The Queen modifies Cicero's language to suggest that wrong is right only to defend a lawful crown.

4 These observations first appeared in *Notes & Queries* (New Series, vol. 44, March 1997) 56–8.

Appendix 8

Dating the two battles at Philippi

From his sources Shakespeare would have known that the weather at Philippi had turned cold and the autumn rains had begun at the time of the two battles, which were fought twenty-one days apart in 42 BC (North, 1579, 1077). But upon what date did Shakespeare believe the battles of Philippi were fought? Since the publication of the *Praenestine Fasti* in 1955, scholars have known that the second battle of Philippi occurred on 23 October (Ehrenberg and Jones, 1955, 54).[1] Using the Roman system of inclusive reckoning, the first battle must have taken place on 3 October. But if Shakespeare were relying on Suetonius, he might have believed that the battles took place in November.[2] Writing of the birth of Tiberius, Suetonius recorded *'natus est Romae in Palatio XVI Kal. Dec. M. Aemilio Lepido iterum L. Munatio Planco consulibus* per bellum Philippens'* (Rolfe, 1913, 298).[3] That is, Tiberius was born at Rome on 16 November 'during the Philippic war'.

Notes

1 '[*imp. Caesa*]*r Augustus vicit Philippis posteriore proelio Bruto occiso.*'
2 Holland translates the passage in Suetonius's life of the emperor Tiberius: 'borne hee was at *Rome* in the *Mount Palatium*, the sixteenth day before the Calendes of December [16 November], when M. Aemilius Lepidus was Consull the second time together with Munatius Plancus, even after the warre at Philippi' (Holland, 1606, 90). But this is a mistranslation.
3 *Tiberius* (5). I am indebted to Professor C. B. R. Pelling for advice about the *Praenestine Fasti*.

Appendix 9

Luther's exchange of pamphlets with Henry VIII

In 1520 Luther published *Of the Babylonian Captivity of the Church*, a polemic against the pope and Roman rite, which denied five of the seven sacraments. Luther argued that the Scriptures provide for two sacraments only: baptism, and the Lord's Supper (communion). Luther dismissed the other five sacraments (marriage, confirmation, ordination, penance and extreme unction) as man-made 'custom'. In response, and with an eye to currying favor with the pope, Henry VIII published his *Assertio septem sacramentorum adversus M. Lutherum* (1521, STC 13078), defending the sanctity of all seven Catholic sacraments. In 1522 Luther replied to Henry with a vitriolic pamphlet published in both Latin and German, *Contra Henricum Regem Angliae*. Luther vilified Henry as a 'Thomist', repeatedly deplored 'custom', and affirmed that only Scripture could designate sacraments. This broadside of Luther's is so scurrilous that it went unpublished in English until 1928, and does not appear in the English edition of Luther's *Werke*. (See Buchanan, 1928.) Among the many linguistic details in Luther's riposte which find correlatives in *Hamlet*, 'custom' is one of the most intriguing. Melancthon Bennet Foxe emphasized Luther's disdain for 'custom' as superstition, folly and fashion:

> Nevertheles it is certain, ther were seedes of supersticion in the tyme of the Fathers and auncient Doctors, & therefore S. Austen ordeyned some thyng of vowes, although he wrote not therof so straungely as other: for both ye best some tymes shal be spotted wyth the blemysh of the follyes that reygne in theyr age. For as naturally we love our Country, so fondly we favour the present fashions, wherin we be trained & educated. And very wel alludeth Euripides to thys. 'What cusomtes we in tender youth

by Natures love receave: The same we love & lyke alwayes, and lothe our
lust to leave.'

(Melancthon, 1548, fol. C.viiiv–D.i.r.)

The word 'custom' appears more frequently in *Hamlet* than in any other
Shakespeare play (Spevack, 1969, 259). Looking at each appearance
of the word, one sees that 'custom' appears in conjunction with references to holy days, or parodies of religious rituals, e.g. when Hamlet
seeks to 'purify' Gertrude. Though Luther's *Contra Henricum* was not
published in English until our century, it was available to Shakespeare
in Latin. When Henry VIII and Luther exchanged salvos in 1525, Henry
published a book containing both letters, *Literarum, quibus invictissimus
princeps, Henricus octavus, respondit, ad quandam epistolam M. Lutheri* etc.
(1526, STC 13084). The same was published two years later in English:
Answere unto a Certaine Letter of Martyn Luther, etc. (London, 1528).

Appendix 10

Principal holy days in the Julian and Gregorian calendars, 3 June–5 September 1599

	Julian	Protestant	Catholic	Gregorian
TH	31 May		C. CHRISTI	10 Jun
F	1 Jun		BARNABAS	11 Jun
SA	2 Jun			12 Jun
SU	3 Jun		ANTONY	13 Jun
M	4 Jun			14 Jun
T	5 Jun			15 Jun
W	6 Jun			16 Jun
TH	7 Jun	C. CHRISTI		17 Jun
F	8 Jun		Marcus/Marcill.	18 Jun
SA	9 Jun			19 Jun
SU	10 Jun			20 Jun
M	11 Jun	BARNABAS		21 Jun
T	12 Jun	(SOLSTICE)	ALBAN	22 Jun
W	13 Jun	ANTONY	VIGIL JOHN BAPTIST	23 Jun
TH	14 Jun		BIRTH JOHN BAPTIST	24 Jun
F	15 Jun			25 Jun
SA	16 Jun		JOHN & PAUL	26 Jun
SU	17 Jun			27 Jun
M	18 Jun	Marcus/Marcill.	VIGIL PETER & PAUL	28 Jun
T	19 Jun		PETER & PAUL	29 Jun
W	20 Jun			30 Jun
TH	21 Jun			1 Jul
FR	22 Jun		VISITATION	2 Jul
SA	23 Jun	VIGIL JOHN BAPTIST		3 Jul
SU	24 Jun	BIRTH JOHN BAPTIST		4 Jul

Principal holy days

	Julian	Protestant	Catholic	Gregorian
M	25 Jun			5 Jul
T	26 Jun	JOHN & PAUL		6 Jul
W	27 Jun		THOMAS BECKET	7 Jul
TH	28 Jun	VIGIL PETER & PAUL		8 Jul
F	29 Jun	PETER & PAUL		9 Jul
SA	30 Jun			10 Jul
SU	1 Jul			11 Jul
M	2 Jul	VISITATION		12 Jul
T	3 Jul			13 Jul
W	4 Jul			14 Jul
TH	5 Jul		SWITHUN	15 Jul
F	6 Jul			16 Jul
SA	7 Jul	THOMAS BECKET		17 Jul
SU	8 Jul			18 Jul
M	9 Jul			19 Jul
T	10 Jul			20 Jul
W	11 Jul			21 Jul
TH	12 Jul		MAGDALENE	22 Jul
F	13 Jul		MAGI	23 Jul
SA	14 Jul			24 Jul
SU	15 Jul	SWITHUN	JAMES	25 Jul
M	16 Jul		ST ANN	26 Jul
T	17 Jul			27 Jul
W	18 Jul			28 Jul
TH	19 Jul			29 Jul
F	20 Jul			30 Jul
SA	21 Jul			31 Jul
SU	22 Jul	MAGDALENE		1 Aug
M	23 Jul	MAGI		2 Aug
T	24 Jul			3 Aug
W	25 Jul	JAMES		4 Aug
TH	26 Jul	ST ANN		5 Aug
F	27 Jul			6 Aug
SA	28 Jul			7 Aug
SU	29 Jul		DOMINIC	8 Aug
M	30 Jul			9 Aug
T	31 Jul		LAWRENCE	10 Aug
W	1 Aug			11 Aug
TH	2 Aug			12 Aug

Appendices

	Julian	Protestant	Catholic	Gregorian
F	3 Aug			13 Aug
SA	4 Aug			14 Aug
SU	5 Aug		ASSUMPTION BVM	15 Aug
M	6 Aug			16 Aug
T	7 Aug			17 Aug
W	8 Aug	DOMINIC		18 Aug
TH	9 Aug			19 Aug
F	10 Aug	LAWRENCE	BERNARD	20 Aug
SA	11 Aug			21 Aug
SU	12 Aug			22 Aug
M	13 Aug			23 Aug
T	14 Aug		BARTHOLOMEW	24 Aug
W	15 Aug	ASSUMPTION BVM		25 Aug
TH	16 Aug			26 Aug
F	17 Aug			27 Aug
SA	18 Aug		AUGUSTINE	28 Aug
SU	19 Aug		DEATH JOHN BAPTIST	29 Aug
M	20 Aug	BERNARD		30 Aug
T	21 Aug			31 Aug
W	22 Aug			1 Sep
TH	23 Aug			2 Sep
F	24 Aug	BARTHOLOMEW		3 Sep
SA	25 Aug			4 Sep
SU	26 Aug			5 Sep
M	27 Aug			6 Sep
T	28 Aug	AUGUSTINE		7 Sep
W	29 Aug	DEATH JOHN BAPTIST	NATIVITY BVM	8 Sep
TH	30 Aug			9 Sep
F	31 Aug			10 Sep
SA	1 Sep			11 Sep
SU	2 Sep			12 Sep
M	3 Sep			13 Sep
T	4 Sep		HOLY CROSS	14 Sep
W	5 Sep			15 Sep

Appendix 11

From the Book of Common Prayer (1560), folio 4v

The order how the Psalter is appointed to be read

The Psalter shall be read thorow once every Moneth. And because that some moneths bee longer than some other be, it is thought good to make them even by this means. To every moneth shal be appointed (as concerning this purpose) just thirtie dayes.

And because January and March have one day above the sayd number, and February which is placed between them both, have only xxviii days: February shall borrow of either of the Moneths of January and March one day: and so the Psalter which shall bee read in February, must begin at the last day of January, and end the first day of March.

And whereas May, July, August, October and December have xxxi days apiece: it is ordered that the Psalmes shall be read the last day of the said Moneths, which were read the day before, that the Psalter may begin againe, the first day of the next Moneth ending.

Now to know what Psalmes shall be read every day: looke in the Kalendar the number that is appointed for the Psalmes, and then finde the same number in the Table placed at the end of the Kalender for that purpose: and upon that number shall you see what Psalme shall be said, at Morning and Evening prayer.

And where the Cxix Psalme is divided into xxii portions, and is over long to be read at one time: it is so ordered, that at one times shall not be read above foure or five of the said portions, as you shall perceive to be noted in the said Table.

And here is also to bee noted, that in the said Table, and in all other partes of the Service, where any Psalmes are appointed, the number is expressed after the great English Bible, which from the ix Psalme, unto the Cxlviii Psalme, following the division of the Hebrews, doeth vary in number from the common Latine Translation.

The order how the rest of the holy Scripture (beside the Psalms) is appointed to be read

The Old Testament is appointed for the first Lessons at Morning and Evening Prayer, and shall be read thorow every yeere once, except certain Bookes and Chapters which be least edifying, and might best bee spared, and therefore are left unread [including the Song of Solomon, thought too sensational].

The New Testament is appointed for the second Lessons at Morning and Evening Prayer, and shall bee read over orderly every yeere thrice, besides the Epistles and Gospels: except the Revelation, out of the which there be onely certaine Lessons appointed upon divers proper Feasts.

And to know what Lessons shal be read every day: Finde the day of the Moneth in the Kalender going before, and there yee shall perceive the Bookes and Chapters that shall bee read for the Lessons both at Morning and Evening prayer.

And here is to be noted, that whensoever there be any proper Psalmes or Lessons appointed for the Sundayes, or for any Feast mooveable or unmooveable: then the Psalmes and Lessons appointed in the Kalender, shall be omitted for that time.

Yee must note also that the Collect, Epistle, and Gospel appointed for the Sunday, shall serve all the weeke after, except there fall some feast that hath his proper.

When the yeeres of our Lord may be divided into foure even parts, which is every fourth yeere: then the Sunday letter leapeth, and that yeere the Psalmes and Lessons which serve for the xxiii day of February, shall be read againe the day following, except it be Sunday, which hath proper Lessons of the Old Testament appointed in the Table serving to that purpose.

Also, whersoever the beginning of any Lesson, Epistle, or Gospel is not expressed: there yee must begin at the beginning of the Chapter.

And, wheresoever it is not expressed how farre shall bee read: there you shall reade to the end of the Chapter.

Item, so often as the first Chapter of S. Matthew is read either for

Lesson or Gospel, yee shall begin the same at verse xviii, *Now the birth of Jesus Christ was, &c.* And the third Chapter of Saint Lukes Gospel shall be read unto the middle of verse xxiii. *Being as men supposed the sonne of Joseph, &c.*

Bibliography

Editions of The Tragedie of Julius Caesar

Capell, E. (n.d.) London: H. Hughs.
Dorsch, T. S. (1983) London: Methuen.
Furness, H. H. (1913) Philadelphia: Lippincott.
Hinman, C. (1968) New York: Norton Folio Facsimile.
Humphreys, A. (1984) Oxford: University Press.
Johnson, S. (1765) London: J. & R. Tonson.
Kittredge, G. L. (1936) Boston: Ginn.
Macmillan, M. (1902) London: Methuen.
Malone, E. (1821) London: F. C. and J. Rivington.
Pope, A. (1723) London: J. Tonson.
Rosen, W. and B. (1963) New York: Signet.
Rowe, N. (1714) London: J. Tonson.
Spevack, M. (1988) Cambridge: Cambridge University Press.
Theobald, L. (1733) London: A. Bettesworth et al.
Wilson, J. D. (1948) Cambridge: Cambridge University Press.
—— (1974) Cambridge: Cambridge University Press.
—— (n.d.) London: Faber & Gwyer Folio Facsimile.
Wright, W. A. (1878) Oxford: Clarendon Press.
—— (1894) London: Macmillan.

Editions of Twelfth Night

Donno, E. (1985) Cambridge: Cambridge University Press.
Johnson, S. (1765) London: J. & R. Tonson.
Johnson, S. and Steevens, G. (1788) London: Bell.
Malone, E. (1821) London: F. C. and J. Rivington.
Theobald, L. (1733) London: A. Bettesworth et al.
Warren, R. and Wells, S. (1994) Oxford: Oxford University Press.

Editions of The Tragedie of Hamlet

Dowden, E. (1899) London.

Bibliography

Edwards, P. (1985) Cambridge: Cambridge University Press.

Greg, W. W. (1965) *First Quarto*. Oxford: Clarendon Press.

—— (1964) *Second Quarto*. Oxford: Clarendon Press.

Hibbard, G. R. (1987) Oxford: Clarendon Press.

Jenkins, H. (1987) London: Arden-Methuen.

Johnson, S. (1765) London: J. & R. Tonson.

Johnson, S. and Steevens, G. (1788) London: Bell.

Malone, E. (1821) London: F. C. and J. Rivington.

Theobald, L. (1733) London: A. Bettesworth *et al.*

Wilson, J. D. (1934) Cambridge: Cambridge University Press.

Secondary sources

Adams, J. C. (1961) *The Globe Playhouse*. London: Constable.

Adams, J. Q. (1917) *Shakespeare Playhouses*. Boston: Houghton Mifflin.

Addington, M. H. (1993) 'Shakespeare and Cicero'. *N&Q* (August), 116–18.

Alvis, J. (1979) 'The Coherence of Shakespeare's Roman Plays'. *Modern Language Quarterly* (*MLQ* used hereafter), 40, 114–34.

Amott, D. (1973) 'Hamlet's Salvation and Luther's Justification by Faith'. Diss. Carleton University, Ottawa.

Anonymous. (1599) *A Terrible Deluge or Overflowing in Roome*. London: J. Wolfe.

—— (1710) *The Church of England Man's Companion, or a Rational Illustration of the Harmony, Excellency, and Usefulness of the Book of Common Prayer, etc.* Oxford: Printed at the Theatre for Anth. Peisley, And are to be Sold by J. Knapton *et al.* Booksellers in London.

—— (1899) 'Shakespeare's Legerdemain with Time in Julius Caesar'. *Poet Lore* 11 277.

—— (1966) *The Book of Catholic Worship*. Washington, D.C.: The Liturgical Conference.

Armstrong, W. A. (1946) 'The Elizabethan Conception of the Tyrant'. *Review of English Studies* (*RES* used hereafter), 22, 87, 174–9.

Bailey, D. R. S. (ed. and tr.) (1986) *Cicero: Philippics*. Chapel Hill: University of North Carolina Press.

—— (1988) (ed.) *Cicero's Letters to his Friends*. Atlanta: Scholars Press.

Baldcock, J. (1990) *The Elements of Christian Symbolism*. Longmead, Dorset: Element Books.

Baldwin, T. W. (1924) 'Shakespeare's Jester: The Dates of *Much Ado* and *As You Like It*'. *Modern Literary Notes* (*MLN* used hereafter), 39 (December).

—— (1944) *William Shakespeare's Small Latine and Less Greek*. Urbana: University of Illinois Press.

—— (1963) *On the Compositional Genetics of The Comedy of Errors*. Urbana: University of Illinois.

Bate, A. J. (1986) 'The Cobbler's Awl: *Julius Caesar*, I.i.21–24'. *Shakespeare Quarterly* (*SQ* used hereafter), 35, 461–2.

Bibliography

Beadle, R. and King, P. (1995) *York Mystery Plays*. Oxford: Oxford University Press.

Bellringer, W. A. (1970) '*Julius Caesar:* Room Enough'. *Critical Quarterly (CQ* used hereafter), 12, 31–48.

Bennet, H. (1561) *A Famous and Godly History, Contayning the Lyves & Actes of Three Renowned Reformers, etc.* Imprinted at London by John Alwdely, dwellying in lytle Brittaine Streete, by great Saint Bartelmewes.

Binz, G. (1989) 'Londoner Theatre und Schanspiele im Jahre 1599', *Anglia* 22 456–64.

Blatherwick, S. and Gurr, A. (with additional comments by J. Orrell), (1992) 'Shakespeare's Factory, *etc.*' *Antiquity* 66, 251, 315–33.

Bloom, H. and Jaffa, A. (1964) *Shakespeare's Politics*. Chicago: University of Chicago Press.

Bond, J. J. (1869) *Handy-Book of Rules and Tables for Verifying Dates with the Christian Era, etc.* London: Bell and Daldy.

Bowden, W. R. (1966) 'The Mind of Brutus'. *SQ* 17.

Brecht, H. (1993) *Martin Luther: His Road to Reformation*. Minneapolis: Fortress Press.

Buchanan, S. E. (1928) *Martin Luther's Reply to Henry VIII, etc.* New York 1928.

Burkhardt, S. (1968) *Shakespeare's Meanings*. Princeton: Princeton Unversity Press.

Burlingame, R. (1966) *Dictator Clock: 5000 Years of Telling Time*. New York: Macmillan.

Carter, T. (1905) *Shakespeare and the Holy Scripture*. London: Hodder & Stoughton.

Cary, E. (1987) *Dio's Roman History*, IV, books 61–5. Cambridge Mass.: Harvard University Press.

Chamberlin, F. (1923)) *The Sayings of Queen Elizabeth*. London: John Lane.

Chambers, E. K. (1923) *The Elizabethan Stage*. Oxford: Clarendon Press.

—— (1925) *The Medieval Stage*. Oxford: Oxford University Press.

—— (1951) *William Shakespeare*. Oxford: Clarendon Press.

Chang, J. S. M. J. (1965) 'Shakespeare and Stoic Ethics'. *Dissertation Abstracts International (DAI* used hereafter), 25, 5902.

—— (1970) '*Julius Caesar* in the Light of Renaissance Historiography'. *Journal of English and Germanic Philology (JEGP* used hereafter), 69, 63–71.

Charney, M. (1961) *Shakepeare's Roman Plays: The Function of Imagery in the Drama*. Cambridge: Harvard University Press.

Cheney, C. R. (ed.) (1991) *Handbook of Dates*. London: Royal Historical Society. 1991.

Collison, P. (1979) *Archbishop Grindal, The Struggle for a Reformed Church*. London: Jonathan Cape.

Cooper, T. (1565) *Thesaurus Linguae Romanae & Britannicae, etc.* London: Berthelei.

Coyne, G. D., S. J., and Hoskin, M. A. and Pedersen, O. (1983) 'The Papal Bull of 1582 Promulgating a Reform of the Calendar'. *Gregorian Reform of the Calendar Proceedings of the Vatican Conference to Commemorate Its 400th Anniversary, 1582–1982*. Specola Vaticana.

Cox, J. and Kasten, D. (eds) (1997) *A New History of English Drama*. New York, Columbia University Press.

Crick, B. (1970) *Niccolo Machiavelli: The Discourses*. London: Penguin.

Bibliography

Davies, H. (1970) *Worship and Theology in England.* Princeton: Princeton University Press.

de Gerenday, L. (1974) 'Play, Ritualization, and Ambivalence in *Julius Caesar*'. *Literature and Psychology*, 24, 24–33.

The Dictionary of National Biography on CD-ROM (1995) Oxford: Oxford University Press.

Dodens, R. (1578) *A Niewe Herball, or Historie of Plantes.* First set foorth in the Doutche tongue, and now tr. out of Fr. by H. Lyte. London: G. Dewes.

Dolman, J. (tr.) (1561) *Those Fyve Questions, which Marke Tullye Cicero, Disputed in his Manor of Tusculanum.* London: T. Marshe.

Donno, E. S. (ed.) (1992) *Twelfth Night.* Cambridge: Cambridge University Press.

Douce, F. (1807) *Illustrations of Shakespeare, and of Ancient Manners: with Dissertations, etc.* London.

Downing, F. G. (1992) *Cynics and Christian Origins.* Edinburgh: T. & T. Clark.

Duffy, E. (1992) *The Stripping of the Altars.* New Haven: Yale University Press.

Dutton, R. (1991) *Mastering the Revels.* Iowa City: University of Iowa Press.

Edwards, H. J. (1986) *Caesar: The Gallic War*, Cambridge, Mass.: Loeb Classical Library, Harvard University Press.

Ehrenberg, V. and Jones, A. H. M. (1955) *Documents Illustrating the Reigns of Augustus and Tiberius.* Oxford: Clarendon Press.

Estienne, C. and Liebault, J. (1616) Maison rustique *or the countrie farme* (tr.) R. Surflet, revised and enlarged . . . by G. Markham, London A. Islip for J. Bill.

Falconer, W. A. (1992) *Cicero: De Divinatione*, Cambridge, Mass.: Harvard University Press.

Farmer, D. H. (1992) *The Oxford Dictionary of Saints.* Oxford: Oxford University Press.

Farmer, W. (1587) *The Common Almanacke or Kalender, etc.* London. Bodleian: Ashm. 133 (10).

Fitzmyer, J. A. (tr.) (1985) *The Gospel According to Luke X–XXIV.* New York: Doubleday.

Fleay, F. G. (1886) *A Chronicle History . . . of Shakespeare.* London.

Foakes, R. A. (ed.) (1962) *The Comedy of Errors.* London: Methuen.

Foxe, J. (1563) *Actes and Monuments, etc.* London.

Frazer, Sir J. G. (1956) *The Golden Bough.* New York: Macmillan.

—— (1989) *The Fasti of Ovid.* Cambridge, Mass.: Loeb Classical Library, Harvard University Press.

Fulke, W. (1589) *The Text of the New Testament, etc.* London: Deputies of C. Barker.

Furness, H. H. Jr. (1888) *The New Variorum: The Merchant of Venice.* Philadelphia: Lippincott.

—— (1902) *The New Variorum: Twelfe Night, Or, What You Will.* Philadelphia: Lippincott.

Furnivall, F. J. (1882) *The Digby Mysteries.* London: The Shakespeare Society.

Gasquet, F. A. (1909) *The Eve of the Reformation.* London: Bell.

Glover, T. R. (tr.) (1984) *Tertullian: De Spectaculis*, Cambridge, Mass.: Harvard University Press.

Bibliography

Granville-Barker, H. (1946) *Prefaces to Shakespeare*. Princeton: Princeton University Press.

Gray, W. (n.d.) *Almanacke, etc. rectified for Dorchester*. Bodleian Ashm. 62 (5).

Green, W. M. (1944) 'Augustine on the Teaching of History'. *University of California Publications in Classical Philology*, 12, 315–32.

Greg, W. W. (1904) *Henslowe's Diary*. London: A. H. Bullen.

—— (ed.) (1940) *Hamlet: Second Quarto 1604–5*. London: Sidgwick & Jackson.

Gurr, A. (1987) *Playgoing in Shakespeare's London*. Cambridge: Cambridge University Press.

—— (ed.) (1992) *Henry V*. Cambridge: Cambridge University Press.

—— (1996) *The Shakespearean Playing Companies*. Oxford: Clarendon Press.

Halliwell-Phillipps, J. O. (1887) *Life of Shakespeare*. London: Longmans.

Harsnett, S. (1603) *Declaration of Egregious Popish Impostures*. London.

Harvey, J. (1583) *Leape Yeares. A Compendious Prognostication for the Yeere of our Lorde God MDLXXXIIII*. London: Richarde Watkins and James Roberetes. Bodleian Library, Ashm. 62 (70).

—— *Almanacke, etc. referred to London*. Bodleian Alm. f. 1589.1 (3).

Hassel, R. Chris, Jr (1979) *Renaissance Drama & the English Church Year*. Lincoln: University of Nebraska Press.

—— (1994) 'Hamlet's "Too too solid flesh"'. *Sixteenth Century Journal*, 25, 609–22.

Henley, W. E. (tr.) (1893) *The Tudor Translations: The Essays of Montaigne*, 2. London.

Hoff, L. K. (1988) *Hamlet's Choice – A Reformation Allegory*. Lewiston: Mellen.

Holinshed, R. (1587) *Chronicles*. London.

Holland, P. (tr.) (1600) *Titus Livius, The Romane Historie*. London: Adam Islip.

—— (tr.) (1606) *Suetonius' Life of the Twelve Caeasars*. London: Matthew Lownes.

Holmes, T. R. (ed.) (1914) *C. Iuli Caesaris Commentarii*. Oxford: Oxford University Press.

Holy Bible (1535) Coverdale, M. *Biblia: The Byble* ... London: Nicholson.

—— (1539) *The Most Sacred Bible*, whiche is the Holy Scripture, conteyning the Olde and New Testament, translated ... by Rycharde Taverner.

—— (1539) Taverner, N. *The Most Sacred Bible, etc.* prynted at London ... by John Byddell, for Thomas Barthlet.

—— (1541) *The Great Bible*, printed by Edwarde Whitchurch, with prologue by Thomas Cranmer, Archbishop of Cantorbury.

—— (1560) *The Newe Testament of Our Lord Jesus Christ*, Conferred diligently with the Greke, and best approved translacions in divers langauges. At Geneva, printed by Rouland Hall.

—— (1568) *The Bishops' Bible*.

—— (1582) *The New Testament of Jesus Christ, etc.* Printed at Rhemes by John Fogny.

—— (1599) *The New Testament, etc.*, trans. L. Tomson. London: Barker.

—— (1611) *The King James (Authorized) Version*.

Homan, S. (1975) 'Dion, Alexander, and Demetrius – Plutarch's Forgotten *Parallel Lives* as Mirrors for Shakespeare's *Julius Caesar*'. *Shakespeare Survey* (*ShS* used hereafter), 8, 195–210.

Bibliography

Hornblower, S. and Spawforth, A. (1996) *The Oxford Classical Dictionary*, third edition. Oxford: Oxford University Press.

Howatson, M. C. (1989) *Oxford Classical Literature*. Oxford: Oxford University Press.

Hunter, G. K. (1962) *John Lyly: The Humanist as Courtier*. London: Routledge & Kegan Paul.

Hutton, R. (1994) *The Rise and Fall of Merry England*. Oxford: Oxford University Press.

Jeremias, J. (1969) *Jerusalem in the Time of Jesus*. Philadelphia: Fortress Press.

Journals of the House of Lords, (1584/5) 16 March.

Kaufmann, R. J. and Ronan, C. J. (1970) 'Shakespeare's *Julius Caesar*: An Apollonian and Comparative Reading'. *Comparative Drama*, 4, 18–51.

Kaula, D. (1981) 'Let Us Be Sacrificers': Religious Motifs in *Julius Caesar*'. *ShS*, 14, 197–214.

Kay, D. (1990) *Melodious Tears*. Oxford: Oxford University Press.

—— (1992) *Shakespeare: His Life, Work, and Era*. New York: William Morrow.

Kelly, H. A. (1986) *Chaucer and the Cult of St. Valentine*. Leyden: Brill.

Kernan, A. (1995) *Shakespeare, the King's Playwright*. New Haven: Yale University Press.

King, J. E. (tr.) (1989) *Cicero: Tusculan Disputations*. Cambridge, Mass.: Harvard University Press.

—— (1989a) *De Divinatione*. Cambridge, Mass.: Harvard University Press.

King, P. M. (1998), 'Calendar and Text: Christ's Ministry in the York Plays and the Liturgy', *Medium Aevum*, 67, 30–59.

Laroque, F. (1993) *Shakespeare's Festive World*. Cambridge: Cambridge University Press.

Latham, A. (1975) *The Arden Shakespeare: As You Like It*. London: Routledge.

Leduc and Baudot. *The Liturgy of the Roman Missal*, London: Burns Oates & Washbourne (not dated, but prior to Vatican II).

Le Goff, J. (1980) *Time, Work & Culture in the Middle Ages*, trans. A. Goldhammer. Illinois: University of Chicago Press.

Lemon, R. (ed.) (1865) *Calendar of State Papers, Domestic Series, of the Reign of Elizabeth, 1581–1590, Preserved in Her Majesty's Public Record Office*. London: Longman.

Liebler, N. C. (1988) '"Thou Bleeding Piece of Earth": The Ritual Ground of *Julius Caesar*'. *ShS*, 14, 175–96.

Livingstone, E. A. (ed.) (1977) *The Concise Oxford Dictionary of the Christian Church*. Oxford: Oxford University Press.

Lloyd, M. (1962) 'Antony and the Game of Chance'. *JEGP*, 61, 548–54.

MacDonald, J. C. (1897) *Chronologies and Calendars*. London.

Mahood, M. M. (1988) *Shakespeare's Wordplay*. London: Routledge.

Malone, E. (1821) *The Plays and Poems of William Shakespeare*. London.

Marlorate, P. (1573) *Praelections upon the Sacred and Holy Revelation of S. John*. London.

Maxwell, J. C. (1956) '*Julius Caesar* and Elyot's "*Governour*"'. *Notes and Queries (N&Q* used hereafter), 201 (April), 147.

Melancthon, P. (1548) *Historia de Vita et Actis Martini Lutheri ... MDXLVIII.* [Microfilm: OmniSys Corporation, 211 Second Avenue, Waltham, MA Roll 130.]

Bibliography

Miles, G. B. (1989) 'How Roman are Shakespeare's "Romans"?'. *SQ*, 40 (Fall), 257–83.

Miller, W. (tr.) (1990) *Cicero: De Officiis*, Cambridge, Mass.: Harvard University Press.

Milward, P. (1973) *Shakespeare's Religious Background*. Bloomington, Indiana University Press.

Miola, R. S. (1983) *Shakespeare's Rome*. New York: Cambridge University Press.

—— (1985) *'Julius Caesar* and the Trannicide Debate'. *Rennaissance Quarterly* (*RQ* used hereafter), 38, 271–89.

—— (1987) 'Shakespeare and His Sources: Observations on the Critical History of *Julius Caesar'*. *ShS*, 40, 69–76.

Muir, G. H. (ed.) (1909) *Wilson's Arte of Rhetorique*. Oxford: Clarendon Press.

Muir, K. (1960) 'Shakespeare among the Common places'. *RES*, 10.

Nelson, A. H. (1974) *The Medieval English Stage*. Chicago: University of Chicago Press.

Noble, R. (1935) *Shakespeare's Biblical Knowledge and Use of the Book of Common Prayer as Exemplified in the Plays of the First Folio*. London: Society For Promoting Christian Knowledge. London: Macmillan.

Nolland, J. (1989) *Word Biblical Commentary: Luke 1–9:20*. Dallas: Word Books, 35A.

North, Sir T. (1579) *The Lives of the Noble Grecians & Romanes*. London: Thomas Vautroullier & John Wight.

Oliver, H. J. (1990) *The Merry Wives of Windsor*. London: Arden–Methuen.

Orrell, J. (1983) *The Quest for Shakespeare's Globe*. Cambridge: Cambridge University Press.

—— (1993) 'Building the Fortune'. *SQ*, 44, 2 (summer).

—— (1994) 'The Architecture of the Fortune Playhouse'. *ShS*, 47.

The Oxford English Dictionary on CD-ROM, (1992) second edition. Oxford: Oxford University Press.

Palmer, J. (1952) *Political Characters of Shakespeare*. London: Macmillan.

Paris, B. J. (1987) 'Brutus, Cassius, and Caesar: An Interdestructive Triangle', in *Psychoanalytical Approaches to Literature and Film*, ed. Maurice Charney and J. Reppen. Rutherford: Farleigh Dickinson University Press.

Patterson, A. (1984) *Censorship and Interpretation*. Madison: University of Wisconsin Press.

Peterson, D. L., (1965) '"Wisdom Consumed in Confidence": An Examination of Shakespeare's *Julius Caesar'*. *SQ*, 16, 19–28.

Phillipson, J. (1560) *Sleidanes Commentaries. A Famouse Cronicle of Our Time, etc.* London.

Plomer, H. R. (1903) *Wills of English Printers and Stationers*. London, East & Blades.

Pollard, A. W. and Redgrave, G. R. (1986) *A Short-Title Catalogue, etc.* London: Bibliographical Society.

Pont, R. (1599) *A New Treatise of the Right Reckoning Yeares and Ages of the World, etc.* Edinburgh: printed by Robert Walde-grave.

Poole, R. L. (1918) *Medieval Reckonings of Time*. London: Society for Promoting Christian Knowledge.

Purvis, J. S. (ed.) (1957) *The York Cycle of Mystery Plays*, London: SPCK.

Bibliography

Rabkin, N. (1964) 'Structure, Convention, and Meaning In *Julius Caesar*', *JEGP*, 63, 240–54

—— (1967) *Shakespeare and the Common Understanding*, Chicago: University of Chicago Press.

Rastell, J. (1536) *An Exposition of certaine Difficult ... Words and Terms of the Lawes of this Realme*. London.

Rees, J. (1955) '*Julius Caesar* – An Earlier Play, and Interpretation'. *Modern Language Review* (*MLR* used hereafter), 135–41.

Rolfe, J. C. (1985) *Sallust*, Cambridge Mass.: Harvard University Press 1985.

—— (1989) *Suetonius I*, Cambridge: Harvard University Press.

Rose, M. (1962) *The Wakefield Mystery Plays*, New York: Doubleday.

—— (1992) 'Conjuring Caesar: Ceremony, History, and Authority in 1599', in *True Rites and Maimed Rites*, ed. L. Woodbridge and E. Berry, p. 257. Urbana: University of Illinios Press.

Rose, R. E. II, (1964) *Julius Caesar and the Late Roman Republic in the Literature of the Late Sixteenth Century, with Especial Reference to Shakespeare's Julius Caesar*. Ann Arbor: UMI Dissertation Services.

Ryan, W. G. (tr.) (1993) *The Golden Legend*. Princeton: Princeton University Press.

Rymer, T. (1693) *A Short View of Tragedy, etc*. London.

Schanzer, E. (1955) 'The Problem of *Julius Caesar*'. *SQ*, 6, 297–308.

—— (1956) 'Thomas Platter's Observations on the Elizabethan Stage'. *N&Q* (November), 465–7.

Schoenbaum, S., (1975) *William Shakespeare: a Documentary Life*. New York: Oxford University Press.

—— (1977) *William Shakespeare: A Compact Documentary Life*. Oxford: Oxford University Press.

Sclater, W. (elder) (1619) *An Exposition with Notes upon the First Epistle to the Thessalonians*. London.

Sesti, G. M. (1991) *The Glorious Constellations*. New York: Abrams.

Shaheen, N., (1987) *Biblical References in Shakespeare's Tragedies*, Newark: University of Delaware Press.

—— (1993) *Biblical References in Shakespeare's Comedies*, Newark: University of Delaware Press.

Sherbo, A. (ed.) (1968) *The Yale Edition of the Works of Samuel Johnson*, New Haven: Yale University Press.

Siemon, J. R., (1985) *Shakespeare Iconoclasm*. Berkeley: University of California Press.

Simmons, J. L. (1973) *Shakespeare's Pagan World*. London: Harvester.

Sjögren, G. (1968) 'The Danish Background in Hamlet'. *ShS*, 4, 221–30.

Smith, W. D. (1953) 'The Duplicate Revelation of Portia's Death'. *SQ*, 4, 152–61.

Sohmer, S. (1996) 'Certain Speculations on *Hamlet*, the Calendar, and Martin Luther'. *Early Modern Literary Studies* (*EMLS* used hereafter), 2, 1 (April).

—— (1997) '12 June 1599 Julian: Opening Day at Shakespeare's Globe'. *EMLS*, 3, 1 (May).

Spencer, T. J. B. (1957) 'Shakespeare and the Elizabethan Romans'. *ShS*, 10, 27–38.

Bibliography

Spevack, M. (1969) *The Harvard Concordance to Shakespeare*. Hildesheim: Olms.

Spurgeon, C. F. E. (1968) *Shakespeare's Imagery, etc.* Cambridge: Cambridge University Press.

Stirling, B. (1959) 'Brutus and the Death Of Portia'. *SQ*, 10, 211–17.

Thomas, K. (1971) *Religion and the Decline of Magic*. London: Penguin.

Thomas, V. (ed.) (1992) *Julius Caesar*. New York: Harvester Wheatsheaf.

Velz, J. W. (1969) 'Clemency, Will, and Just Cause in *Julius Caesar*'. *ShS*, 22, 109–18.

Waddington, R. (1989) 'Lutheran Hamlet'. *English Literary Notes* (*ELN* used hereafter), 27, 2, 27–39.

Waith, E. M. (ed.) (1994) *The Oxford Shakespeare: Titus Andronicus*, Oxford: Clarendon Press.

Walker, L. J. (1983) *Niccolo Machiavelli: The Discourses*. New York: Penguin Classics.

Wallace, C. W. (1909) *The Times*, London, 2 and 4 October.

—— (1914) *The Times*, London 30 April and 1 May.

Weinstock, S. (1971) *Divus Julius*. Oxford: Clarendon Press.

Wells, S. and Taylor, G. (eds) (1987) *William Shakespeare: a Textual Companion*. Oxford: Clarendon Press.

White, H. (tr.) (1979) *Appian: The Civil Wars*. Cambridge, Mass.: Harvard University Press.

Wickham, G. (1981) *Early English Stages*. London: Routledge.

Wiles, D. (1993) *Shakespeare's Almanac*. Cambridge: Brewer.

Wills, G. (1995) *Witches and Jesuits: Shakespeare's* Macbeth. Oxford: Oxford University Press.

Willson, F. W. Jr (1990) '*Julius Caesar*. The Forum Scene as Historic Play-within'. *Shakespeare Yearbook* 1, (Spring) 14–27.

Wilson, J. D. (1957) 'Shakespeare's "Small Latin" – How Much?'. *ShS*, 10, 12–26.

—— (1969) 'Ben Johnson and *Julius Caesar*'. *ShS*, 11 36–43.

Wilson, R. (1987) '"Is This A Holiday?": Shakespeare's Roman Carnival'. *English Literary History*, 54, 31–44.

—— (1992) *Shakespeare's Julius Caesar*. London: Penguin.

—— (1993) *Will Power*. Hemel Hempstead: Harvester Wheatsheaf.

Winstedt, E. O. (tr.) (1956) *Cicero: Letters to Atticus*. Cambridge, Mass.: Harvard University Press.

Index

Note: Dates are in a separate numerical sequence at the beginning of the index. Names of plays are indexed under their titles. Books of the Bible are in alphabetical order under Bible. 'n' after a page number refers to a note on that page.

287

Index

Index

Index

Index

Index